Bruce Herschensohn

LOST TRUMPETS

A CONSERVATIVE'S MAP
TO AMERICA'S DESTINY

BRUCE HERSCHENSOHN

Introduction by
Larry P. Arnn

THE CLAREMONT INSTITUTE PRESS
Claremont, California

About The Claremont Institute

Founded in 1979, The Claremont Institute is a non-profit educational foundation that studies state and national public policy issues. The work of the Institute addresses the disastrous trend toward unproductive governmental regulation of business and industry, excessive taxation, and a disintegration of the moral character that once provided the backbone of our nation. To reverse this trend The Claremont Institute provides scholarship on the principles upon which America was founded: equality, liberty, and limited government.

The Institute is divided into four centers: the Golden State Center for Policy Studies which operates out of their Sacramento office, the Salvatori Center for the American Constitution, the Asian Studies Center, and the Center for Land Use and Environmental Studies. In 1989 The Claremont Institute published the ground-breaking book, *The Imperial Congress: Crisis in the Separation of Powers.*

Published by The Claremont Institute Press

Library of Congress Cataloging-in-Publication Data

Herschensohn, Bruce, 1932-
Lost trumpets – a conservative's map to America's destiny / Bruce Herschensohn;
p. cm.
Includes index.
        1. United States–Politics. 2. United States–Economic policy. 3. United States–Foreign policy.
I. Title.
© Copyright 1994 The Claremont Institute for the Study of Statesmanship and Political Philosophy. All rights reserved. Printed in the United States of America.

ISBN 0-930783-24-7

 THE CLAREMONT INSTITUTE
250 West First Street, Suite 330
Claremont, CA 91711
Tel. (909) 621-6825

Dedicated to Vi.

A lot of people have sisters.
All through our lives, Wes and I have had a Saint.

LIST OF CHAPTER TITLES

LIST OF MAJOR SUBJECTS

INTRODUCTION

By Larry P. Arnn
President, The Claremont Institute

Shortly after the beginning of this century, the so-called Progressive Movement began to make its way into the active politics of our country. It was an ambitious movement. It meant to replace America's Founding principles with new principles, and to make radical changes in our politics based on those principles.

The progressives wanted a government that could do much more. The old kind of government was too comfortable in its acceptance of the limits of human nature. The old kind of government did not see the wonderful possibilities for society. Society could be made more harmonious, more happy, more perfect in every way. It could achieve our *security* (a term that recurs in this book) much better than ever before. But society and its members had to be led. Human nature itself had to be altered and improved.

The work of government would not, under the progressives, be to protect our right under nature—our "natural rights." Rather it would be to work upon our nature. We would have to be molded to think less about ourselves and our families and more about the common things. Such work requires a big effort, carried on by sophisticated people. Government, under the progressives, had to be unified, which means centralized; and government, under the progressives, had to be run by highly qualified people, which means bureaucrats.

The Progressive vision has lost much of its charm today. We can now see that centralized, bureaucratic government is wasteful, ineffective, unjust, and intrusive. The actual harm that it does is much more important even that the untold fortunes it squanders. Who could imagine that the United States government would run a welfare system that inspires and supports illegitimacy as its chief effect? Who could imagine that the United states government would load heavy burdens on those who work—especially if they employ other people—while making comfortable those who are idle?

Although bureaucratic government has lost its charm, it has not by any means lost its power. Currently the President is attempting to move the nation's health care industry under the direct control of the government, even to the extent of government price setting. True to progressive principles, the First Lady justifies this on the ground that we must "change what it means to be a human being in the 21st century."

The Progressive Movement had a lethal undercurrent to it that is more apparent today than it was at the beginning. The progressives believed that the bureaucratic state, once established, could never be removed. People would become so heavily involved with the government—so deeply *interested* in its actions—that any fundamental reform would be impossible.

We find ourselves, therefore, in a dangerous situation. The community, as a whole, has an interest in changing this kind of oppressive and clumsy government back into the old kind that worked. But change is very hard, because very large numbers of us of all income levels are now dependent, at least to some extent, on the government in Washington. What are we to do?

The book that follows attempts to answer that question. Taken together with the character and actions of the author of the book, it gives an excellent model. The life and work of Bruce Herschensohn are built upon a few simple messages which amount finally to this: "You can be free, if you have the courage to be."

Bruce himself is an example of what is needed. As broadcaster, as civil servant, as film maker and as statesman, Bruce has always been willing to say the thing that is unpopular and difficult. To a fault, or nearly so, he speaks his mind and tells the truth when all others are trimming to the wind. He has won the loyalty and affection of millions because he stands up for the right, even when it costs him.

In this book, Bruce reminds us of an old truth that statesmen used to recite: "Those who promise security in exchange for liberty, intend to take away both." If we remember that truth, all will be well. Without it, all is lost.

PART ONE

WHERE THE ROAD STARTED

CHAPTER ONE

CONFLICT

People do not grow old gradually like the spilling of sand through an hourglass. Instead, people grow old in inconsistent leaps after long periods of stillness. Like watching a frog, there is no way to predict when the next jump will occur, or how much distance the jump will cover.

In the space between jumps, people fill their problem-cups each morning to the worry-level that has become a life habit — one worry after another after another after another, their collective degree of intensity prolonging or inviting the next jump of their hidden frog.

But most worries are the same worry in different clothes. Stripped naked, it reveals itself as the worry of Adam and Eve and of the United States and totalitarian states and of Republicans and Democrats and of conservatives and liberals and of every person who has ever lived and of every thinking entity. It is the worry that comes with the two conflicting instincts that start with birth and rarely end before death: the instinct to be secure under protection, and the instinct to be left alone at liberty.

The game starts at birth when independence is finally achieved, and in the moment after independence, the newborn cries for protection. Liberty is lonely. Security is stifling. So, as life goes on, most people wander in perpetual conflict between the two without defining their conflict, and therefore it never becomes resolved.

Decisions become perpetual balancing acts between being safe and being free; the balancing requiring the acquisition of one by surrendering just that amount of the other.

A young person leaving home gives up a measure of personal security for the same measure of personal liberty.

A person joining an organization with rules for its members gives up a measure of personal liberty for the same measure of personal security.

A person resigning from a job gives up a measure of personal security for the same measure of personal liberty.

The same conflict, the same choice comes dozens of times a day in the smallest and least thought-provoking decisions:

A person who drives rather than rides as a passenger becomes the administrator of the destination. Security gone. Liberty in exchange.

A person who expects to be taken to lunch must be prepared to eat at the restaurant selected by the host. Liberty gone. Security in exchange.

Even a person who turns off an alarm clock and goes back to sleep has made a decision between the two instincts. Security gone. Liberty in exchange.

It is possible for a person to surrender all personal liberties for personal securities or to surrender all personal securities for personal liberties by making nothing but small decisions, but making them in such quantity that there are no decisions left to make for the reversal of the course already established by the seemingly mundane. Through errors, the freedom-lover can become the servant and the security-seeker can become the master.

Neither are happy.

Both failed.

If an individual wants to be totally free, that individual cannot expect others to take care of him or her. If an individual wants others to take care of him or her, that individual can not expect to be totally free. There are those individuals who want to be taken care of only to a small extent, but those individuals must be prepared to give up exactly that amount of liberty in return. Because of that, all people must beware of those who offer even the hint of taking away another's liberty or security; whichever is cherished most, and to equally beware of those who offer even the hint of giving either liberty or security; whichever is cherished least.

That is not only true of people; it is true of nations, and so it is vital not only to beware of the person whose choices between liberty and security are not your own, but beware of the government whose choices between the two are not your own.

The prime role of government, of course, is to insure that its citizens are free from the risk of violence from foreign powers and domestic lawbreakers since the citizen, acting alone, is incapable of providing safety for the nation from foreign powers, and is incapable of guarding an entire community from violators. But when a government supplies the securities over the softer falls of daily life involving personal decisions of its citizens, it gains power over those it pretends to protect. Eventually such a government, demanding payment for its social services, suffocates its citizens by regulations, handouts, and taxes. Such a government will enslave those for whom it provides services. But there are always those who demand that government provides the most risk-free society possible. Government readily accommodates, because its accommodation guarantees its greater power over the people.

In both personal life and national life the script is the same. In striving for a balance between liberty and security, most people in their private lives and most nations in their public lives, live in chaos and perennial debate, and persons risk their peace of mind and nations risk their flags.

It's why mental institutions are filled and why governments are deposed.

It's why squabbles and wars between the few are joined by the many.

Other than matters beyond human control, it's what people and nations are all about.

The newborn nation, just like the newborn person, is born fighting for independence and freedom. Both attain their victories of birth in a cyclone of emotion; crying, kicking, and bloodied. But as soon as the acquisition of independence and freedom is assured, the newborn nation, just like the newborn human, clings to quick security. The person or the nation seeks chains because chains prevent wandering too far from an authority that can shield them from the unknowns of liberty.

Chains are easily found. They're on every road of life. Grabbing the first one in sight and locking its two ends to each ankle, the person or the nation hobbles until it falls and then it crawls to find the key to unlock the chain. It's found, but the finding is valueless because after unlocking the chain, the quest begins for another chain and there's always one there and another is picked up and clasped like the first, ankle to ankle. Then the walk begins again with the short steps as limited as the length of chain allows. Between the short steps, the person or the nation comes to a trumpet lying on the road: a trumpet that, if played, could signal liberty. It is so inviting that it cannot be passed by and so the person or the nation bends to pick it up, being careful that the chain doesn't make the person or the nation fall by the bending. After it's picked up, a few notes are played on the trumpet to tell others of the freedoms that are there for the asking, and before the full melody can be completed, a longer step is attempted and the person or the nation falls again, and to ease the fall the hands of the person or the nation are expanded and the trumpet is given to the ground.

And so both persons and nations spend their time on earth in conflict between trumpets and chains, playing only a few notes of liberty while ensuring the chains of security are fastened. The conflict goes on and on, and for most nations as for most people, personal security is the victor.

Personal securities are easier to accept with their guarantees of safety, rather than personal liberties that guarantee risk. And so liberty is chosen only by the confident and courageous who are very few. Even fewer are the confident and courageous with a sense of responsibility and duty and with the self-discipline not to misuse their liberty. They are the only ones who step over the chains and around the chains and even, at times, upon the chains, but never within their clasps. They are the only ones who play enough notes on the trumpets to make a melody.

This is the story of chains and trumpets and, most of all, it's the story of a melody called the United States of America.

CHAPTER TWO
DISCOVERY

There was a time, we are told, when most people believed that the world was flat, and most of those who lived by the Atlantic shore of the Eurasian and African continents watched the sun leave them each day, and they thought it went on a worthless trip beyond the sea to disappear and light nothing for at least eight hours.

Only the dreamer and the philosopher and the adventurer dared to question the exit of the sun beyond the ocean's rim. They sat by the shore staring and squinting in the hope of seeing more, and they cursed the limitations of their vision. But dreamers and philosophers and adventurers were not important to the more practical people who ignored the sea and ignored the sun and ignored the horizon. As years, and then decades, and then centuries passed, and as the practical people continued to ignore what they could not see, history ignored the practical people. And the dreamers and the philosophers and the adventurers were rewarded by those who went in quest of whatever the horizon would bring.

What it brought was more than the continuation of sunlight, and more than the continuation of the sea, and more than the beginning of another land. What it brought was the opportunity for liberty.

And in the last quarter of the Eighteenth Century, that liberty was proclaimed by both the painful giving of lives and the careful movement of pens.

Since then, seven generations of Americans have recognized the importance of maintaining and enhancing that liberty, with many in each of those generations willing to give their lives in the pursuit of leaving an immortal nation of liberty for those who would come after them on the American road.

And now, during the eighth generation, which is immersed in new offers of chains, each one expertly packaged by government with the sharp edges of the links hidden from view, the age-old instincts are playing their game to new heights, with dangers unknown in generations past.

The decisions of the eighth generation should be made only after recognizing the political conclusions reached when the nation was new and the journey had just begun, as the Founder's trumpets blared their first notes so loud that the echo can still be heard.

CHAPTER THREE
MOSES AND MADISON

In the mask of idealism, the weak have always chosen security for themselves over liberty for others. Their history of weakness is always the same; a history of yelling for peace while the real idealists were dying for liberty.

It was that way at the beginning of the United States. And after the liberty-seekers won, they created the most unlikely form of government, limiting their own power in favor of the power of the individual. They devised a progression of responsibility turned upside down from the governments of past centuries. They prescribed a government that would not be the master of the citizen, but the citizen would be the master of the government, with each individual being responsible for him or herself.

And if the individual should be unable to take care of him or herself, then the responsibility for that individual would go to his or her family.

And if the family should be unable to do that, or if there should be no family, then the responsibility for that individual would go to friends and neighbors.

And if the friends and neighbors should be unable to do that, then the responsibility would go to the church, the synagogue, or charities.

And if those institutions should be unable to do that, then the responsibility for that individual would go to the township.

And if the township should be unable to do that, then the responsibility for that individual would go to the city.

And if the city should be unable to do that, then the responsibility for that individual would go to the county.

And if the county should be unable to do that, then the responsibility for that individual would go to the separate state.

And if the separate state should be unable to do that, then and only then, after all the closer entities had failed, the responsibility for that individual would go to all the citizens of the nation chipping in for that one individual.

That was the planned progression of responsibility, with the federal government as the last resort for the individual.

The Founders of the United States of America did not claim to be the originators of such a progression of responsibility; the idea of such layered government without overlap was in the Bible. It was Jethro (Yethro), the father-in-law of Moses, who was the inventor.

Moses was leading three million people he had brought across the Sinai Desert, out of Egypt. The only leadership with which he was familiar was the leadership of the Pharaoh, who delegated nothing since he was a totalitarian, who wanted his citizens to be his possessions. Moses had no desire to be a totalitarian, but rather to be a sensitive leader who would hear his people's problems, and he would try to reach just determinations for them. One night his father in law, Jethro, said that enough was enough, and Jethro warned Moses that he would do himself grave injury if he continued to devote his time to solving the individual problems of three million people. He told Moses to appoint wise and experienced commanders of thousands, and then commanders of hundreds from those thousands, and then commanders of fifties from those hundreds, and commanders of tens from those fifties. Only the most difficult cases, unsolved by the layers of commanders, would be brought to Moses. With enthusiasm, Moses endorsed the solution of reduced power for himself and increased power closer to the individual.

That was the birth of layered government.

The establishment of an overseer (which in those days was Moses, and across the seas and across the centuries, would be Philadelphia and then Washington, D.C.), was to serve the barest of necessary functions, so as to prevent a tyranny.

It worked.

But over the years of the Twentieth Century the line of responsibility and procedure steadily reversed, with the federal government becoming more and more possessive — becoming not the last resort of the individual but, rather, the first call of the individual, therefore providing selective security for some at the expense of common liberty for all.

As the Twentieth Century was ending, the individual in trouble was handed a form to send to Washington D.C., corrupting the idea of Jethro and the government of Moses and the basis of the United States.

Washington, D.C. reached without reluctance for greater jurisdiction, taking the individual responsibility away from the layered governments so painstakingly created. It was able to do that because the people forgot, or never knew, how the United States was formed. And so the people applauded when an officer of the federal government or a nominee for such office advocated the idea of helping the individual. They did not know that the only way the federal government could have such power was to take away the power from those who were closer to the individual.

They forgot that the closer entity can see the individual in trouble, can see the individual's face, can hear the individual's voice, can feel the skin and inhale the smell of that individual. But those far away in the District of Columbia, at such great distance, could only see and hear and touch and smell file-cabinets and computers and paper upon which the individual is reduced to a nine-digit number. And for individuals to become numbers, giant bureaucracies had to be built and massive amounts of bureaucrats had to be hired.

And immense power had to be taken by the federal government.

Jethro would shudder.

And so would James Madison.

They would wonder at the huge buildings that currently house the federal bureaucracies, and wonder why taxpayers do not revolt against those bureaucrats who, paid by the taxpayers, busy themselves with functions that have nothing to do with the legitimate purposes of the federal government.

Layered government has become a memory, no longer a reality. From education to the environment, there is now not only a local jurisdiction but a city jurisdiction and a county jurisdiction and a state jurisdiction and a federal jurisdiction all in overlap. With each need of the public (some real and some imagined, and some invented by those who want larger bureaucracies), each layer of government receives the same mission as other layers, until the individual has an overwhelming burden of regulations and reports and certifications and taxations.

Once a bureaucracy has been established in Washington D.C. for purposes unspecified by the Constitution, it becomes a permanent fixture with an investment in failure. As long as it fails, the bureaucracy survives. As long as the bureaucrats don't succeed, they have a job. Success is their greatest threat. Where would they go with a mission that is done? Failure breeds additional funds appropriated by the Congress who view failures as being due to a lack of enough taxpayer's money, and so the Congress provides that money. Such provisions increase the power of the Congress as well as the bureaucracies, and diminish the economic liberties of the citizens through increased regulations and higher taxes.

Most of the Congress and most of the federal bureaucrats do not want the federal government to be the most limited layer of government. Unlike Moses or Madison they have no passion for lesser authority, but for greater power.

And they gain greater power by promising the citizens more and more securities that are none of the federal government's business. The horror is that too many of the people who become regulated and pay the taxes through their labor, have never read the 52 words of the Preamble of the United States Constitution that tells the citizen why we have a federal government.

CHAPTER FOUR

WHY WE HAVE A FEDERAL GOVERNMENT

The federal government, with its elected officers serving terms of two, four, and six years, mimics life and death. There is never a total change of elected officers all at once, but rather Washington, D.C.'s cast of characters arrive and leave at different intervals, until one day none of the old faces are there anymore. But all of them, by their method of entrance and exit at staggered times, have touched one another. The newest member of government, in the eighth generation of Americans, touches a hand that touched a hand that touched a hand that touched a hand that touched a hand that touched a hand that touched the hand of James Madison. The responsibility of such a bond is immense, with the kinship of purpose moving across time.

With such heritage, such access in touching the past, it would be logical to think that the new members of government would be able to recite, be imbued, be impassioned about those few duties for which they have been assigned by the founders of the nation.

And it would be logical to think that the new members of government would be able to abdicate, to dismiss, to reject the multitude of functions not given them to perform.

What were they assigned to do? For what purposes should they open the public purse and withdraw funds?

There is no need to guess or theorize or argue. The jurisdictions of the federal government are so clear and so few and so well-itemized within the Preamble of our Constitution that every citizen should have them memorized. There are only five reasons that we have a federal

government:
1. To establish justice.
2. To insure domestic tranquillity.
3. To provide for the common defense.
4. To promote the general welfare.
5. To secure the blessings of liberty to ourselves and our posterity.

That's it.
That's all.
And that is enough.

It is equally dangerous for the officers of the federal government to do more than that, as it would be for them to do less than that. But in contemporary times, the federal government has done both less and more — less of what they were assigned to do, and more of what they were not assigned to do. If those five duties had been taken seriously through recent decades, our federal budget would not only have been balanced with ease, but our nation would have had citizens with greater freedoms, and federal taxation would have been paltry. If such seriousness of purpose would have been observed, the federal government would never have started its competition with individuals, families, charities, the clergy, the townships, the cities, the counties, the states, and private enterprise.

But the federal government no longer has the appetite for its documented duties. They are not the "right" duties for those whose mouths froth to have jurisdiction over the taxpayers. The five prescribed constitutional duties have become the five prescribed constitutional nuisances.

Justice has not been and will not be established as criminals are treated as victims of society, and when paroles and probations substitute for penalties and punishments, and when a special prosecutor's office can be created at the expense of all, but answerable to none, and when the innocent are pauperized in legal fees unbilled to the one who brought false charges. Nor can justice be properly respected when the preservation of habitats of selected animals, fish, insects, and plants take precedence over the livelihood of the citizens. Justice has not been done when there are no sunset provisions to terminate and abolish departments, agencies, bureaus, and programs of the federal government where bureaucrats relish in the dismemberment of justice.

Domestic tranquillity is not insured when our great cities are allowed to live in a state of terrorism and anarchy, and children fear for their lives in classrooms and in hallways and in school restrooms, and parents are uncertain of the safe return of their children from the schoolyard, and sweep them indoors from the porch when night comes.

The common defense is not provided when the nation's effort for a strategic defense is abandoned, and funding for the nation's common defense is reduced to a percentage of the federal budget as low as it was before Pearl Harbor, and when we exhibit a greater will to crush the nation's military capabilities than to remain a deterrence to tyrannies.

The general welfare is not being promoted when selective welfare is being provided. Unlike the demand to "establish" or "insure" or "provide" or "secure" (the words used for the other four purposes of the federal government), the word for welfare within the Preamble is to "promote," and the reference is to the "general welfare," not certain segments selected by the federal government to be recipients.

The blessings of liberty are not being secured to ourselves and our posterity when the economic rewards of liberty are confiscated disproportionately from the successful, and when the fruits of labor are taken from our posterity, as our government continues to steal wages from the pockets and purses of future generations, so as to pay for services for the current generation to enjoy.

At the beginning of a new administration one new federal officer after another takes an oath to preserve, protect and defend the Constitution. It's tradition. But not much more than tradition, as evidenced when the appointees of the Clinton Administration followed the taking of the oath with speeches of their own, telling the assembled officials and friends and journalists what they wanted to achieve in office. So many oath-takers of that January revealed, by their speeches, that they had not read the Constitution they had just pledged to preserve, protect, and defend; or worse yet, they had read it and had chosen to violate, abridge, and erase it.

It was as though they drafted for themselves a new Preamble to the United States Constitution that set out duties with which they were more comfortable than the ones prescribed by the Founders of the nation, whose directives they inherited:

"We the people of the United States, in order to form a more perfect union, must build a better infrastructure, and establish a pristine environment, and we must seize property from its owners to guarantee the well-being of that environment.

"We insure that criminals are treated with understanding, putting the criminal back into society as quickly as rehabilitation and job-training can be performed.

"And since the common defense is a business of the past, we should now provide defense from disease, with a common national health care system.

"And we must reward those who have children without spouses beyond those who do have spouses, and reward those who have chosen not to work beyond those who find work, and we must provide as near to a risk-free society as government can oversee.

"And finally, our citizens should secure the blessings of services provided by government."

We could change the Constitution to read that way, and then preserving, protecting and defending the Constitution would be compatible with current governmental passions. But the nation would no longer be the United States of America.

The duties of the federal government, as written in the United States Constitution, are sacred; and our task, our mission, our destiny, is to make those duties, prescribed by our Founders, endure. It is the greatest quest in human history, because the success of that pursuit will determine the immortality of those Americans who came before us, and the scope of liberty for those Americans yet unborn.

CHAPTER FIVE

THE TOTALITY, THE ABSENCE, OR THE LIMITATION OF GOVERNMENT

One day, long ago, the leaders of the French National Assembly counted how many of their members supported stronger government jurisdiction over the people, and how many of their members were opposed to such government jurisdiction. The leaders then assigned each assemblyman a chair in the Assembly Chamber, with those who supported a more encompassing government being assigned seats on the left side of the room, and those who opposed such government jurisdiction being assigned seats on the right side of the room, with an aisle between the two.

And that's how the world started referring to the left wing and the right wing.

That would have been just fine if the meanings of the terms didn't change over the years, misdefining their reasons for being. By the end of the Twentieth Century it was common for people to *justifiably* assume that the left wing carried to its extreme would be communism, and it was common for people to *unjustifiably* assume that the right wing carried to its extreme would be nazism. Nazism (the National Socialist German Workers' Party), like communism, is the totality of government jurisdiction.

Those people who have lived under both of those Twentieth Century totalitarianisms have a common dialogue; that the evils of living under nazism and communism were so encompassing and so similar that their differences were indistinguishable. That indistinguishability was apparent because both communism and nazism belong on the same side of the political spectrum: totalitarianism, which is the ultimate of the left. Are the expansionist and dictatorial policies of Vladimir Zhirinovsky and his Liberal Democrat Party of Russia, communist or nazi? Both. The policies require the strongest of central governments.

What, then, would be the ultimate of the right wing, advocating less government jurisdiction? The ultimate would be anarchy. That extreme could easily be a replica of Beirut of the 1980s or Mogadishu of the 1990s, with no authority, with no laws, no structure of order, no government at all.

Those two extreme entities of totalitarianism and anarchy are the definitions of security versus liberty. One offers All-Government, while the other offers No-Government.

If the world was inhabited only by good people who never wanted to do anything but good, then anarchy would be perfect, with no need for a government. But since that isn't the way of all human beings, there has to be some kind of order, and the United States of America with its Constitution requiring a limited government, is as close as a nation has ever come to having liberty within a framework of order. Common sense calls for liberty with responsibility. A free nation devoid of responsibility, like a free person devoid of responsibility, becomes a menace to others, defeating the very purpose of liberty for all.

Even less accurate than the contemporary use of the terms, "right" and "left," are the terms "liberal" and "conservative." It could too easily be assumed that a liberal, like a libertarian, would treasure personal liberties over personal securities. It is exactly the opposite: a modern-day liberal tends to advocate guaranteed hospitalization benefits and increased unemployment benefits and government guaranteed child-care and no-smoking laws and helmet laws for motorcyclists and anti-gun laws and seat-belt laws and 55 mile per hour laws and a host of regulations and social programs provided by the federal government. Those laws add to the security of the individual, but take away the same amount of liberty from the individual, and take more from the wage-earner by demanding that the wage-earner finance all those government jurisdictions.

A modern-day conservative tends to advocate that each person should reap both the rewards and the losses of each person's own endeavors.

For clarity, a conservative should be called a constitutionalist, because modern-day conservatism advocates the limited government established by the Founders of the nation, and a liberal should be called a governmentalist, because modern-day liberalism advocates the government's authority over issues of personal risk and personal security. Libertarians have exactly the name that defines them. The difference between a constitutionalist and a libertarian is that a constitutionalist believes in the Founders decree of a limited government, while many libertarians believe in a more limited government than authored by the writers of the Constitution.

The issue of national defense appears, on the surface, to be an inconsistency, in that a conservative (or constitutionalist) tends to support a stronger defense, imposing an economic burden on the taxpayers, while the liberal (or governmentalist) wants no more of it and, in fact, generally less of it, with the libertarian also wanting less of it.

Make sense?

It does.

The Constitution demands that the federal government "provides for the common defense." The conservative wants the taxpayer to keep more of his or her own money, but not when it comes to funding the few constitutional duties called for, including defense. (See Chapter 30.) Unlike the host of non-prescribed governmental quests, defense is a federal matter since the individual, the charities, the localities, the separate states cannot have their own missiles, their own submarines, their own air forces without having fifty individual nations rather than fifty united states. Without national security (in contrast to personal security) all personal liberties can be lost.

Although the libertarian and liberal advocate reduced defenses, they advocate such reductions for totally different reasons from the other, in keeping with their individual philosophies.

The libertarian, wanting a reduced government, views defense as an arm of a stronger government, and wants the money saved from a reduced defense to remain in the pockets and purses of the taxpayer.

The liberal, wanting less national defense, does not advocate that the funds saved be given back to the taxpayers to spend as they choose, but rather that those unexpended funds be used for increased government social programs. The liberal leadership's arguments against the U.S. military have a history that exhibit the liberals deeper philosophy. During the cold war between the United States and the Soviet Union, the liberal leadership perceived communism as being tolerable and co-existent rather than a world evil that should be contained. That tolerance and co-existence came from the liberals preference of economic security over economic liberty, so a foreign government that also preferred economic security over economic liberty did not seem evil.

Through the years, the rusty terminology of the right-wing and the left-wing, and conservative and liberal, have been bent into shapes they no longer define. Constitutionalists vs. governmentalists with libertarians offering a third choice, are the political realities of the Eighth Generation. That is not to say that there isn't a fourth choice and a fifth choice and even more choices, but all the choices are versions of security versus liberty, with different beliefs of what should be made secure and what should be free.

The United States Constitution uses a rare combination of both security and liberty in a single sentence within the Preamble, mandating that the federal government "secure the blessings of liberty." It does not call for the federal government to secure the blessings of hospitalization and unemployment benefits and social programs and regulated life or anything but liberty. All other securities are left to the individual to decide what is worthy and not worthy for that individual.

What the Constitution is all about and what the entire American journey is all about is what everything is all about: trumpets and chains.

PART TWO

TOLL BOOTHS TO DISMANTLE

(ECONOMIC POLICY)

CHAPTER SIX

THE POWER OF PROVIDING

Capitalism is the economic dimension of liberty.
Socialism is the economic dimension of security.

Under capitalism, taxation is limited, since liberty of the individual demands that government functions are few. Under socialism, taxation is expanded, since security for the individual demands that government functions are many.

Recognizing these facts have caused recent U.S. Congresses to be very careful in the naming of their congressional acts:

There has not been one piece of federal legislation entitled a "Tax Increase Bill" or an "Increased Government Powers Bill" or a "Socialism Bill." Such pieces of legislation, so titled would, of course, be doomed to failure, their authors banished to swift retirement from elective office. The great talent, among no others, of recent Congresses has been the talent of lexicography. Surely the taxpayer will find it more difficult to reject the same bills if titled a "Tax Equity Bill" and a "Jobs Bill" and a "Fiscal Responsibility Bill" and a "Deficit Reduction Bill" and a "User's Fee Bill" and even a "Revenue Enhancement Bill." The taxpayer will be embarrassed to reject such congressional ability to put things right. It is generally believed that even if the bill does include a cost of some kind, payable by someone, the good will outweigh the cost.

What is ignored, what is disguised, is that the taking of earnings from the citizen is the removal of time from a citizen's clock and calendar of life. If the cost of taxation is thought of as money alone, the totality of taxation is misunderstood.

Capitalism, as a system, demands that the individual stay in control of his or her own funds as a means for the individual to be in control of his or her own time, and therefore, to be in control of the individual's own destiny — to do what the individual wants to do with his or her own life.

Socialism demands that the government take the lead role in the determinations of importance, and it establishes the collective as a higher authority than the individual.

Capitalism requires the responsibility of the individual for that individual's well-being, comfort, and ambitions.

Socialism requires the responsibility of government for that individual's well-being, comfort, and ambitions. To assume that responsibility, the government must have administration of much of the citizen's funds, therefore assuming administration of much of the citizen's time, and the administration of much of the citizen's destiny. It has to happen in that sequence because when a government is responsible for the citizen, the citizen becomes responsible to the government.

If a free people want to have a central government at all, then those free people can and should expect to be taxed to pay for the necessary costs of the government. The risk comes when that government starts writing checks for the people, because the money the government uses isn't the money of the members of the government, it's money from the public purse; and what such payment does is reverse the purpose of government, with the government becoming the employer of the people rather than the employee of the people. Government slowly becomes the provider rather than the provided, and as provider it becomes the order-giver and director and regulator of the people, rather than the government remaining the entity that is given orders and given direction and given regulation by the people.

The more endeavors of a federal government, the less endeavors of the individual. The more funds that government extracts to implement those endeavors, the more able government is to make demands of the citizens, because government then holds rewards and punishments in its hands for dispersal.

Recognizing all of this, the Founders of the United States fought a revolution to be free from unjustified taxation from abroad. But it makes little difference if money-transfers are demanded by those across the Atlantic or by those across the Potomac. Those funds have been earned by work that took time away from those who did the earning. Clocks and calendars are far too precious to allow their theft to be greeted with acceptance or indifference.

President Thomas Jefferson entered and left office without an Office of Management and Budget, without a Council of Economic Advisors, and without a single regulatory agency or officer. Without such encumbrances, he said within his Inaugural Address, "a wise and frugal government which shall restrain men from injuring one another, shall leave them otherwise free to regulate their own pursuits of industry and improvement, and shall not take from the mouth of labor the bread it has earned." The people, of course, agreed. That was in the year 1801.

But now there is an Office of Management and Budget, and a Council of Economic Advisors, and regulatory powers and agencies unimagined by those who declared independence from such barriers to liberty.

In making the choice of an economic system, it should be taken into prime consideration that human beings have received the gift of birth, and each birth entitles the person to time separately, not collectively. Individual minds entitle each person to search for goals separately, not collectively.

If we, as humans, live with someone else in control of our time on earth, then we have reason to ask, "why were we born at all?"

In return for the most sacred of gifts — life — each individual must remain the master of his or her own minutes, hours, days, and years. That mastery of life's moments is what separates us from animals in a herd led by shepherds with sticks.

CHAPTER SEVEN

WINNING VOTES
BY PROMISING
TO STEAL

There was an inscription on the back of the Rolex watch that read, "Happy Birthday, Emily. I love you, Don."

But the man in the New York alley who was showing me the watch was not Don. Nor, of course, was he Emily. There was little doubt but that he was a thief, wanting to sell stolen merchandise.

The only difference between him and a Senator I once knew was that the man in the alley needed a shave.

The Senator had come home to his state from D.C. over the Thanksgiving holiday and announced that he was able to put into the Transportation Bill the funds needed for a mass transit system in the biggest city of his state. "It is something to be thankful for," he announced to the crowd at the town meeting. "I procured the federal funds and this city will have a mass transit system, second to none, without raising city taxes one cent!"

He wasn't ashamed of it. He was proud of it.

The crowd at the meeting didn't boo and hiss his announcement. They applauded and cheered it.

Didn't they know it was stolen merchandise? It was stolen from the earnings of a coal-miner in West Virginia, and a secretary in Iowa, and a waitress in Connecticut, and a dock-worker in Mississippi, none of whom would ever ride, or even see, the mass transit system in that far-away city of the state represented by the Senator.

What if there was a referendum on the California ballot asking the voters if they would like to pay for a bridge across a creek in Massachusetts? Would it even receive enough support to warrant its placement on the ballot? No possibility. Yet those kind of expenditures are made on a daily basis by the states without knowing it, because of the term, "federal funds," which the citizens are led to believe exist.

"Federal funds!" that Senator boasted. But there are no such things as federal funds — only funds earned by the taxpayers of the nation and sent to Washington, D.C. for the purpose of paying for those things that are federal in nature. The Senator pulled a fast one and brought home dollars taken from everyone in the nation for a local project. That is not unusual, it is the norm; the use of alleged federal funds suggests that the federal government has money of its own. It doesn't. It's broke. It's in terrible debt.

Such congressional favors to the localities increase the federal budget and the federal deficit and the federal debt to figures that come back to punish the very people they were told would be helped.

But the federal government willingly, cheerfully, and eagerly uses taxpayers funds from all over the nation for a local project because its payment allows the federal bureaucracies to hire and contract and write regulations and issue licenses and plan routes and have jurisdiction over the doings of a locality. The unfortunate city sending money to D.C. has lost its power over the project that it could have afforded and would have controlled for its own citizens. And more important, the project could have been built by the city residents without the stolen wages of others.

Allowing the U.S. Congress to give a gift to the state or community is not only accepting stolen goods, such acceptance of the gift allows the federal government to collect ransom at a later time. All the federal government has to do is wait until the project is partially completed and then make a demand on the locality, threatening to cut off payments for the local project already started unless the demand is met. "If you don't enact a 55 miles per hour speed limit on every state highway and city road, then all your funds will be cut off." And the local citizens look at the half-done construction clogging up the city, and they pay the ransom.

When it came time for re-election, the Senator reminded his audiences what he was able to do, and how comparatively ineffective his opposing candidate would be in obtaining "federal funds." His opposition tried to assure the voters that he could do the same — maybe even better, maybe he could even procure more "federal funds." He didn't know, nor did the people know that the representatives of states and districts at the federal level are supposed to be elected to represent them in the making of national and international policy, not local funding, which is the business of closer governments. They would, however, vote for the person who could *get* the funds from *other* states. They would never vote to *give* the funds to *another* state. In short, they would vote to be the recipient of theft but not the victim of theft.

The Senator who brought home the Thanksgiving gift was re-elected in a landslide. Like the man in the alley exhibiting the stolen Rolex, the Senator should not have been rewarded; he should have been imprisoned.

CHAPTER EIGHT

9,306 PIECES OF PAPER THAT IN THIS CASE WOULD HAVE BEEN BEST LEFT AS TREES

Before dawn small formations of people started gathering, and by the time the sun rose the formations had turned into long lines. All across the nation there were rows of people outside of financial institutions, waiting for the doors to open.

It was not the third decade of the century with people waiting to take their money out. It was a half-century later with people waiting to put their money in.

During the first days of 1981's October, the federal government was allowing the sale of what was called "All Saver's Accounts." In the first four days of availability, some 15 billion dollars were put into those accounts. They did not give a higher rate of interest than other savings plans. In fact they gave a lower rate of interest than most of the accounts offered by the same financial institutions. But there was one great attraction that made them golden. The attraction was that the interest earned on such accounts would be tax-free up to an investment of $1000 per person.

They waited patiently to move up in line, illustrating visually what had previously been invisible: the folly of the nations tax-code that could cause such time to be spent.

So much time. Time spent not only in working for the government, not only in figuring out how to pay taxes as ordered without paying more than required, not only in the time spent on the Internal Revenue Service's 1040 forms, and 1099's and W-2's and Schedule A's and B's and C's, but the time spent by those who save and file receipts on an every day basis, those who log every mile driven, every cent spent, weighing deductions and exemptions and credits, considering tax advantages and liabilities with every move because to regard or disregard them could mean the difference between solvency and bankruptcy.

There are not only deductions, exemptions, credits, and shelters but a glossary of terms that turn a tax form into a language of its own: Page 72: "If you had preproductive period expenses in 1991 and you checked the 'No' box on Line G of Schedule F because you decided to capitalize these expenses, you MUST enter the total of these expenses in parentheses on line 35f and write '263A' in the space to the left of the total."

Get it?

If no one in the nation had to be chained to such incomprehensibility, then this nation and almost everyone in it would be granted calenders of time for additional productivity and invention and creation and discovery and just plain liberty. It would add to the freedom of life of practically every person in the nation. The time that has already been wasted over pads of papers and adding machines, calculators, and computers can never be returned. It's gone.

As an average, the American taxpayer employed by private enterprise, has been working more time to pay federal, state, and local taxes, than to provide shelter, food, and clothes for the average American family.

James Payne, the Director of Lytton Research and Analysis estimated that the time spent in 1990 on tax-related activities was some five and one-half billion hours.

He further estimated that for every dollar the federal government raises in taxes, an additional 65 cents is spent by people on tax-related expenses to comply with Internal Revenue Service (IRS) rules, or a bill of some 618 billion dollars, more than twice the amount ever spent on defense in any single year of our history. Arthur P. Hall of the Tax Foundation reported in the *Wall Street Journal*, "for every $100 in taxes paid by America's small business, $390 was paid by these businesses to comply with the taxes."

Strange that those in the Congress who scream and yell against spending on providing the common defense, are mute when it comes to such greater expense spent on tax-related activity that provides the nation with common misery.

The taxation process is the most costly government program of all.

Computing taxes has become so complex that taxpayers commonly hire an accountant to figure out how best to declare income to the government. The charge for the hired accountant becomes a tax on a tax. In 1991, *Money Magazine* conducted a test of 49 top tax preparers, giving them an income that should have cost a taxpayer $18,724 in federal taxes. Only five preparers came within 10% of that sum. They ranged from presenting bills of $6,807 through $73,247. A Government Accounting Office study found that IRS computer notices contained errors 48% of the time, and 44% of penalties assessed by the IRS examiners were wrong.

When the income tax began back in 1913 by the ratification of the Sixteenth Amendment, there was a one sentence justification for it; to finance the necessary costs of the federal government. The tax code was printed on a single piece of paper.

Today that code takes 9,306 pages of complexity. It is 9,306 pages of complexity because it no longer has the purpose of financing the necessary costs of government but instead it has become its key system of rewards and punishments — rewards if you do what the government wants done with your money, and punishments if you do something with your money that the government doesn't want done with your money. Those 9,306 pages give the Congress, the bureaucracies, and the Internal Revenue Service immense power.

Since there is only a limited amount of power available in the nation, power being finite, such power can only be enlarged by government at the expense of those they govern.

Tyranny's greatest ally is a citizenry that is overwhelmed with complexity. The strongest enemy of tyranny is a knowledgeable citizenry that understands the processes of its government.

Democracy borders on failure when its rules become so complicated that those who have to obey the rules can't understand them. It *does* fail when the citizens accept such incomprehensibility.

At this point there is only one thing to do with the intentional complexity of those 9,306 pages of the tax code:

Throw them in the waste-basket.

To finance the necessary costs of government give the taxpayer a postcard that can be filled out at 11:00 P.M. on April 15 that would be so understandable that it could be completed and mailed before midnight. (Even better than April 15, Tax Payment Day should be October 31, just days prior to general elections.)

Such simplicity would come from government stopping its giving of rewards and punishments. And that would mean having a single flat rate of taxation for all wage-earners except the poor who would pay nothing. And abolish all the supplementary taxes accumulated over the years.

Abolish the capital gains tax that has been designed to punish the wise investor.

Abolish taxes on interest from savings accounts that has been designed to punish the saver.

Abolish taxes on interest from any source which has been designed to punish those who choose to invest rather than spend.

Abolish taxes on dividends which has been designed to punish those who have faith in private enterprise.

Abolish the estate tax which has been designed to punish those who die.

And make the corporate tax into a straight business tax, a corporate tax having been designed to punish those who create and maintain businesses not owned by government.

Imagine that all those taxes have been abolished, the current tax code has been thrown away, and in their place the flat rate tax has been adopted, and it takes only minutes to figure out the information for the postcard. Now project 20 years forward. It's hard to believe there would be a single person outside of government who would say, "Gee, I wish the good old days were back when the federal tax code was 9,306 pages, and we had a capital gains tax, and taxes on savings, and taxes on dividends, and an estate tax, and all those other taxes, and I wish I would again have to hire an accountant to figure out my yearly income tax."

So how do we dump the present code and adopt the new one?

Just do it.

Dr. Alvin Rabushka and Dr. Robert Hall of the Hoover Institution set the guidelines a long time ago with the presentation of two post cards, (1992 figures follow) one for the individual, one for business:

POSTCARD #1   Individual Wage Tax:

1. Wages and Salary (No tax on interest or dividend income) $ _____
2. Pensions $ _____
3. Total (Line 1 plus Line 2) $ _____
4. Personal allowance $ _____
     a. $11,440 for married $ _____
     b. $ 5,720 for single $ _____
     c. $10,192 for single head of household $ _____
5. Number of dependents not inc. spouse $ _____
6. Personal allowances for dependents (line 5 multiplied by $2,250) $ _____
7. Total personal allowances (line 4 plus line 6) $ _____
8. Taxable wages (line 3 less line 7, if positive, otherwise zero) $ _____
9. Tax (19% of line 8) $ _____
10. Tax withheld by employer $ _____
11. Tax due (line 9 less line 10 if positive) $ _____
12. Refund due (line 10 less line 9, if positive) $ _____

POSTCARD #2   Business Tax:

1. Gross revenue from sales
2. Allowable costs $ _____
     a. Purchases of goods, services & materials $ _____
     b. Wages, salaries and pensions $ _____
     c. Purchases of capital equipment, structures, and land $ _____
3. Total allowable costs (sum of lines 2(a), 2(b), 2(c)) $ _____
4. Taxable income (line 1 less line 3) $ _____
5. Tax (19% of line 4) $ _____
6. Carry-forward from previous year $ _____
7. Interest on carry-forward (10% of line 6) $ _____
8. Carry-forward into this taxable year (line 6 + line 7) $ _____
9. Tax due (line 5 less line 8, if positive) $ _____
10. Carry forward to next taxable year (line 8 less line 5, if positive) $ _____

The Congress hated the idea. The Congress hated it because of seven things wrong with such a single flat rate tax:

1. It would be much too simple.

2. The tax code would then prohibit any prejudice towards any specific people.

3. Hidden loopholes would no longer be able to be used.

4. The Internal Revenue Service would have to end its policing powers, cut its staff of 100,000 employees, forego most of its $6.5 billion budget, and lose the ability to impose almost all its 150 civil penalties.

5. Borrowing would be discouraged and saving would be encouraged.

6. People would always know how much they are going to have to pay in taxes with only profit and loss used as their financial criteria.

7. Power would be taken away from the federal government in the determination of rewards and punishments.

Admittedly, there would surely be those taxpayers who wouldn't want specific deductions taken away. But they might not protest if they only knew the truth: the government may give you something visibly but it takes away more than it gives — invisibly. The home mortgage deduction is the clearest example.

"If that mortgage deduction is taken away I couldn't buy a house," is a common cry. But does the one weeping about it know that the house would cost him or her a good deal less without the deduction under the flat-rate tax plan? Here is why: the government currently gives the visible, which in this case is the deduction. But there is a steep charge made that is invisible to the homebuyer and the homebuyer is paying it every month without knowing it. When the homebuyer's payment is sent to the bank, the bank then has to send a large amount of that check to the federal government. It has to do that because the check sent to the bank by the homebuyer is an interest payment, and interest is taxed. What if the bank didn't have to pay taxes on interest? (No one would under the flat-rate plan.) The monthly payment sent to the bank by the home-buyer would come way down, and the buyer would spend less on the purchase of the house. Hundreds of thousands of renters would become homeowners.

Under the Hall-Rabushka Plan, if a homebuyer prefers, the home-buyer can retain the deduction for interest on a home mortgage loan throughout the transition period to the flat rate tax, but that means the bank would then have to retain the present system of paying taxes on the interest received from the homebuyer. (The plan calls for the home-buyer getting a 90% deduction while the bank pays taxes on 100% of the interest it receives from the homebuyer.) It would be to the advantage of both the bank and the homebuyer to forego the deduction. Although it would be the homebuyer's choice during the transition period, a homebuyer would be foolish to opt for the old system, since the new system would appreciably lower the cost of the house. Home-sellers and home-buyers would sell and buy houses based only on the free market. Sellers would no longer have to pay taxes on capital gains. They would not have to quickly purchase another house to escape an inordinate payment.

As for other IRS granted gifts that do not have an invisible penalty paid by the taxpayer involved, the penalty *has* to be paid by another taxpayer or taxpayers. *Every* time one taxpayer is rewarded by a deduction or a credit of any kind, another taxpayer or taxpayers are punished by that amount. It can be no other way because the federal budget isn't lowered to make up for the money the government would have received if the deduction didn't exist. That money "credited" to taxpayer "A" is taken from taxpayer "B" who might not even be alive yet but is waiting, unborn, to receive the bill. Never applaud a credit, a deduction, a reward given by government, it's always stolen merchandise. The government cannot give a taxpayer anything but stolen goods because it doesn't have anything to give. All it can do is demand that some taxpayers give other taxpayers something. In fact our tax system is socialism — a system of transferring earnings of one person to another.

Our nation should return to capitalism.

Many of those who call themselves conservatives are just as guilty as liberals in their advocacy of using the tax code to give tax incentives for businesses if they build in inner cities. Such Enterprise

Zones may sound good to both sides of the political spectrum, but the whole idea rests on the giving of rewards with the tax code. Enterprise Zones would be magnificent if they were not plural but instead singular, and the Enterprise Zone was called the United States of America. Our federal government has no business giving tax incentives to *selected* commercial establishments or regions or individuals. A government that has the power to give selective incentives, has commensurate power to give selective disincentives, and must do so by definition because a tax credit for one taxpayer must come from another taxpayer. To be true to conservative philosophy rather than provide bait as liberals provide bait, conservatives should not perpetuate the myth that government can dole out fortune from an empty cup. True conservative, constitutionalist philosophy is the uncorrupted concept of governance that was born by our Founders.

At previous Senate Finance Committee hearings about a flat-rate tax, the argument for retaining a sliding scale of rates upwards (called "progressivity") was that although a flat rate would ensure that the wealthier pay more because they earn more, they should also be fined a higher percent because they can afford a higher percent. But afford it by whose standards? Fairness should dictate that everyone in this nation has the right to pursue what ever ambition they may want without unequal treatment by government because of the choice of that ambition.

If someone's ambition is to become a millionaire, why should that ambition be disproportionately punished? Senators want to be Senators and after winning an election they don't want the government saying, "Since you have a six year term, we are going to take two years away and give those two years to the candidates who did not win the race." Becoming a Senator is their ambition. Becoming a millionaire is someone else's ambition.

Within the testimony of the "progressivity"-advocates, the word most frequently used was "compassion" as reason for that progressivity. But, in truth, they advocated a continued use of theft, in this case theft by taking a disproportionate amount from those who sought and won a particular goal of their choice.

In fact the advocacy of "progressivity" could just as easily be called an advocacy of "regressivity" depending on whether computations are started on the bottom of the wage scale or the top of the wage scale. It is progressive if envy is an admirable human characteristic. It is regressive if success should not be punished. Even by the envious, "regressivity" could well be more accurate, since those on the higher rungs of the income level can afford the best accountants money can buy to keep their funds from being mailed to the government, while those on the bottom rungs of the income level must simply surrender to the IRS.

If we are worthy of our country and worthy of our time on earth, then we should ensure that those Americans who follow their legitimate pursuits and those who are not yet born are free from chains attached to a tax code written in greed of government.

Let's assume that the members of the U.S. Congress in a unique moment of true public service rather than personal service, agree on being logical and capitalistic and enact a flat-rate tax. What should the percentage be?

To make the plan revenue-neutral (the same amount the government is receiving now), the amount would be 19 percent, with the poor (a family of four making $16,000 or less) paying nothing. The tax begins on Dollar Number 16,001.

But this percentage should only be for the transition period. After the transition is done, it should be a Balanced Budget Flat-Rate Tax by abolishing departments, agencies, and programs of the federal government so that we stop our thievery. With a Balanced Budget Flat-Rate Tax, there would be tremendous *political* incentive to cut departments, agencies, and programs because the instant reward for the politician who advocates such cuts would be a lower tax rate to offer the voters. A politician could run on the platform of what the tax rate would be by his or her advocacies, and what the taxes generated would buy and not buy for the nation. Does the politician prescribe a budget that would call for a tax rate of 19 percent? 27 percent? 10 percent?

With a flat rate covering the budget, could the Congress keep spending more and then just raise the rate of the tax? That is exactly what we have now but we don't know it. The present tax code gives the public no way to figure out the horror of government-spending because such spending only touches them as taxation later on. It's why the public allowed the Congress to get the nation in over four trillion dollars worth of debt. But if we pay-as-we-go, the public will demand reductions in government-spending because such reductions will be the only way to reduce our taxes. We will feel it immediately — as we should — to control it.

Through our current budget process we are using money that we don't have and passing on the debt as a negative inheritance to the next generation so we can spend it while we are alive. We act as though we are in the "Chosen Generation." It is as though we have a credit-card stamped with the unborn's name on it. The credit card company keeps charging interest heaped on interest but that doesn't bother us. "The unborn kids to come will take care of that." Not fair but that is what we continue to do.

In actuality, it is worse than being a *common* thief. A common thief can be captured and prosecuted and punished and the possessions stolen can be recovered. But this generation won't be captured or prosecuted or punished; nor is there a plan to return the stolen possessions, nor will the victims have the opportunity to even try to get those possessions back from us. We will go uncaptured, because they will find out what we did to them after we're dead.

Because of those services we wanted to buy while we were alive for which we didn't have the money, we are causing a mess ahead. It's a dirty trick and should be on the conscience of every one of us since we know that we will face no more than a posthumous indictment and prosecution, and that we can enjoy what we steal. We are making our time on earth easier by making their time on earth more difficult.

We should at minimum thank the generations to come that while we lived we had periodic smiles on our faces, smiles from enjoying those things of which we were told by politicians, we were entitled. That is the word that covers the crime. The stolen goods "are nothing more than entitlements. Elect me and I'll give you more things to which you're entitled."

Why do we continue this?

We choose to blind ourselves to the obvious truth. And the obvious truth is continually evaded by government. Those in government achieve and retain their power by hiding from us the performance of their crimes. Rather than demanding that we see ourselves use our hands to steal from the wallets of the yet unborn to give to government, they launder the thievery through their taxation and budget processes.

Compounding the incomprehensibility of those processes is that there is also no shortage of those who want power so badly that they are willing to run for office on promises of more stolen goods given to you. And most unfortunate of all is that there are enough thievery-advocates capable of electing them.

One of the reasons people don't seem to be conscience-ridden is because of the terminology that government uses. We should never use the term "deficit," when in fact we are talking about a delayed tax: when you receive a monthly bill from a department store or from Visa or Mastercard, there are generally two figures on top of the bill. One of them is the amount of the payment they want right now. The other figure is what you owe in entirety. No one calls it a deficit. It's a bill, and if you don't pay that second figure this month, a heavy interest will be added to it on next month's statement.

The amount owed on our national debt is now so high that if we paid back one dollar every second, it would take longer to pay back than the length of time recorded in the history of civilization. It is such an unimaginable figure that it also becomes unimaginable to think of paying it.

Are we to die as thieves? The Balanced Budget Flat Rate Tax, once past the transition period, will stop any further theft. And adding a small percentage to the flat rate will start paying back the next generation from the debt already incurred, along with the sale of government-owned assets. (See next Chapter.)

Even those who think we owe the next generation nothing, surely can't believe that they owe us so much of their own time on earth.

What if some day the debt is paid and we have budget surpluses rather than budget deficits? At best we would lower taxes. At worst, even with irresponsible Congresses, the United States would be *earning* interest rather than *paying* interest.

The Balanced Budget Flat-Rate Tax would give, all at once, no more deficit spending, balance the budget without the requirement of a constitutional amendment, end government-created inflation, stabilize interest rates, simplify the tax code, reduce pork barrel expenditures, and make every taxpayer part of the budget process as well as the taxation process.

And it would give the nation what Congress knows to be the previously mentioned seven diminishments of their power, and beyond that a dreaded Number Eight which would come about if the flat rate was based on a balanced budget — a dreaded Number Eight that is more frightening to the Congress than the combination of all seven items previously listed.

The eighth point is that the Congress would have to be honest. The disguise worn by Congress would be shredded, the mask gone, the mystery of the budget and taxation would be over. This is what it would do:

Near the beginning of each year, the President presents his budget to the Congress and to the nation. Look backwards to a year in which the President proposed a budget of one trillion, five hundred twenty billion dollars. Did one person lose one wink of sleep that night because of the amount the President requested? Would it have made any difference if the President presented a budget of three trillion, eight hundred sixty four billion dollars? There wasn't one person in the United States including the President and including all the members of the Congress, who understood what the requested figure meant. Couldn't. Can't. Won't be able to. Its immensity is beyond comprehension.

But with a Balanced Budget Flat-Rate Tax the President of the future would say, "I propose to the Congress a budget of 14 cents." Every single person from the homeless to the billionaire would understand that figure. Fourteen cents out of every dollar of wages and salary will go to D.C.

Never again would the word "millions," "billions," or "trillions" be used except in the Budget Appendix. The President would go on to say, "Your bill of 14 cents breaks down this way: you will be spending two and one-half cents on the Department of Defense, four cents on the Department of Health and Human Services, a quarter of one cent on the Department of Transportation" and so on. "And I am proposing the abolition of 44 departments, agencies and programs to bring the rate down to 14 cents from its present rate."

Does the taxpayer today know if the Environmental Protection Agency should have a budget of six hundred twenty eight million dollars or ten billion dollars or one hundred twelve million dollars? Of course not. Yet people have demonstrated for or against the amount of money that's being budgeted for the Environmental Protection Agency without having any idea what the right figure should be. They don't even know if they are for or against what they are demonstrating for or against because the figures involved are beyond comprehension.

But what if we could ask this: is it worth another cent to be taken away from every dollar that each wage-earner receives to have an increased budget for the Environmental Protection Agency? Another half-cent? Another tenth of a cent? If you make $20,000 a year, do you want to spend $200 more for that agency? Or is it too much or too little?

The nation's work-force is presently involved only in the taxation process while the spending process is intentionally held as Congress' own. But with a Balanced Budget Flat-Rate Tax everyone will know what every figure in the budget means, and there will never be an excuse for an unbalanced budget, and no politician, no candidate, no office-holder will be able to advocate $74,840,688 to spend for some program while the public doesn't know what that politician is talking about and, in fact, the politician doesn't know what that politician is talking about. Instead, the politician will have to ask the wage-earners of the nation to contribute a set amount from each dollar they earn for the project the politician advocates.

National Health Insurance or National Defense, no one will be able to make it sound as though federal funds will be used since the term "federal funds" will be extinct. And the truth of that will hit like dynamite every time a politician sounds compassionate or sounds cold-blooded. For once we will all be talking the same language. To a person currently wanting National Health Insurance it doesn't make much difference if the projected figure is 5 billion, 50 billion, or 500 billion dollars. Where does it come from and who pays? But it would make a tremendous difference if the figure is 5 cents or 15 cents out of each dollar the taxpayer will earn. We are currently buying in a giant store with no knowledge of the merchandise purchased or the amount charged. That will stop.

Nothing has provided better evidence of the validity of a Balanced Budget Flat Rate Tax than the economic plan advocated by President Clinton shortly after his entrance into office. Its complexity was a horror of statistics and projections leaving the public with nothing to do other than to guess as to its bottom line. That plan was the ultimate example of how a politician in power can confuse the electorate. Among the thousands of provisions included within that plan:

Raise the corporate tax two percent from 34% to 36%. Raise the top individual income tax rate five percent from 31% to 36% for individuals with incomes of $115,000 and couples with incomes of $140,000.

Establish a 10% surtax on families that earn more than $250,000. Impose an energy tax. Extend the research and experimentation tax credit for the computer industry costing $6.4 billion dollars. Restore $207 million dollars to the National Science Foundation. Add $272 million for the Environmental Protection Agency's private industry development of environmental technology. Provide $17 billion on non-polluting automobiles and a national computer "superhighway." Limit to one million dollars the deductions corporations can take for pay to an individual executive unless the pay is linked to productivity.

Invoke price controls on pharmaceutical products. Give an investment tax credit for the purchase of new equipment. Initiate a job training program for the conversion of defense workers. Federal workers should skip one raise. Slow down the spending on the space station. Cut defense another $76 billion beyond the $50 billion cut of President Bush. The 100% credit for wages paid to workers in Puerto Rico would be reduced to 65%. Increase taxation from 50% to 85% on Social Security funds received if the recipient makes over $34,000, or a couple makes more than $44,000.

Increase the alternative minimum tax rate on upper income individuals from 24% to 26% for those with incomes of less than $175,000 and to 28% for those with incomes of $175,000 or more. The maximum amount of income exempt from the tax would rise to $37,500 for single taxpayers and $45,000 for couples.

And that was the simple stuff.

So would government spending be reduced or increased? How much more would you be taxed? Will the deficit be eliminated, reduced or increased?

Complexity is the device that government uses to take away the economic system of the free market in steps, and replace it with an economic system of government management. Capitalism remains at risk of being molested by the dismemberment of those things that the market should decide.

James Madison wrote, "It will be of little avail to the people that the laws are made by men of their own choice, if the laws be so voluminous that they cannot be read, or so incoherent that they cannot be understood; if they be repealed or revised before they are promulged, or undergo such incessant changes that no man who knows what the law is today can guess what it will be tomorrow. Law is defined to be a rule of action; but how can that be a rule, which is little known and less fixed?"

In the beginning (unbiblically, the beginning refers to 1913 A.D.,) the income tax didn't yet provide the confirmation of James Madison's warning. It wasn't too bad. The rules were pretty simple. There was a 1% tax on income over $3000 ($4000 for a married couple). And there was a sliding scale to 7% on incomes over $500,000. With those one-paragraph rules came the promise from both President Taft and President Wilson (it wasn't their fault) that the income tax would never be higher than 10% for anyone. It did not take long for some Presidents and Congresses and bureaucracies to recognize and act on the recognition that the power of government increases with higher taxation, regardless of previous promises, and complexity eases the acceptance from the citizens.

A Balanced Budget Flat-Rate Tax would prevent any government official from masquerading its control by using complexity as a disguise for such control. Instead each person will pay an equal percentage of earnings so that our government may pay for what we as a nation need to buy, and each citizen will know what we are buying and how much we will be charged for the purchases.

But, of course, there are seven things wrong with that plan.

Oh, that's right: eight.

CHAPTER NINE

THE POSSESSIONS OF MRS. McCURDY

Mrs. McCurdy's husband died after forty-five years of marriage. Added to the tragedy was that he left Mrs. McCurdy in debt. She didn't know how bad his finances had become until she started to attempt to pay the bills that she had never seen before. In past years, he was the one who had opened the mail and, somehow, Mr. McCurdy had managed to escape bill-collectors.

Mrs. McCurdy was fortunate enough to still have a part-time job at a child care center but it paid very little, and she was not young and not well enough to get any other kind of work to pay the bills with their ever-increasing interest. She had never asked her two children and their families, who lived across the country, for anything, and was not about to ask them to help her, or even tell them of the debt Mr. McCurdy had accumulated. She wanted them to think the best of him, and she didn't want to burden them with her financial problems; they probably had some of their own. Further, she was too proud to tell her friends her plight. They found out only when they visited her and found her home was gradually becoming more and more vacant of those things of value that she and her husband had acquired through the years. She was selling those things, one after another.

Finally, Mrs. McCurdy sold their house itself, and she moved into a small apartment. With the money she made from the selling of life's possessions, she paid every bill in full, and she was able to live comfortably, if not extravagantly.

The government of the United States of America could learn a great deal from Mrs. McCurdy.

A nation, like a person, has a number of choices to get out of debt. That person can ask for a raise from whomever is the person's employer or, if able, that person can cut back spending on any items short of necessity, or that person can borrow money, or that person can steal money, or that person can sell assets owned, if there are any assets owned that have monetary value.

Like Mrs. McCurdy, the federal government faces those five choices and has made its mind up long ago. It continues to demand a raise from its employer (who is the taxpayer), and to borrow and steal from the current and forthcoming generations. The other two options have been rejected: the federal government refuses to spend less, and it refuses to sell its assets of value.

Unlike Mrs. McCurdy, the federal government doesn't need to strip itself clean of its valuables; it owns a treasure-trove, so it can keep plenty while it sells some of those things it doesn't need.

The federal government owns approximately one-third of the nation's land, including 43% of Arizona, 45% of California, 87% of Nevada, and 96% of Alaska.

States that are located east of the 100th meridian have a far different ratio of ownership. The federal government owns less than 2% of Indiana, 2% of Texas, 2% of Pennsylvania, not even 1% of Iowa or Connecticut or New York State or Nebraska or Kansas. But moving west, its land-holdings become massive, because when the nation moved west, the federal government made sweeping claims of temporary ownership. "Temporary," however, is a word that has been eliminated from government-owned dictionaries.

The federal government owns no less than 30% of every western state, with the exception of Hawaii (10%). How much money could be made, excluding national parks, historical monuments, and other special holdings, by putting much of the unused federal land on the open market? There is no way to accurately estimate the figure because 92% of the land that the federal government owns is listed on its inventories at zero value. And that's because the government never purchased the land. It just took it.

There was a brief flirtation with the idea of selling federally-owned land during the Reagan Administration, but both the Congress and the bureaucracy, pressured by environmental and other groups, killed most of the first sales before they had a chance to materialize beyond a profit of a few hundred million dollars. Even that amount of profit didn't achieve the purpose of debt reduction because the Congress refused to put the funds received in the Treasury, but gave it to the Land and Water Conservation Fund to purchase more land.

The government retains an untapped reservoir of wealth in land holdings while our national debt gets higher every year by virtue of government spending, and by the interest rising on the debt already accumulated by government through preceding years. A combination of the Balanced Budget Flat Rate Tax and the sale of government-owned land could make the next generation of Americans closer to being debt-free.

Mrs. McCurdy's children didn't need to spend a cent to pay off the debts of their parents. No one had to spend a cent on those debts other than Mr. and Mrs. McCurdy themselves. Mr. McCurdy paid them posthumously by the sale of possessions he left behind, and Mrs. McCurdy paid them by being responsible enough to do the selling, and by simultaneously being frugal with her small income.

What a great candidate for public office Mrs. McCurdy would have made.

CHAPTER TEN

KNEELING AT THE ALTAR OF HENRY MORGANTHAU, JR.

The Great Pyramid of Cheops at Gizeh was built by slaves in the years surrounding 2600 B.C., and its site was near the River Nile. It is considered to be one of the world's seven great wonders, but it is actually one of the world's eight great wonders. The greatest wonder in the world is the Pyramid Scheme called the Social Security System that was built by politicians in 1935 A.D. near the River Potomac. How it has fooled the people all this time is a mystery unsolved by any archaeologist, scientist, mathematician, or detective.

It was constructed with giant blocks of dishonesty. The booklet issued by the government entitled, *Your Social Security* said, "During your working years, employees and employers pay social security contributions which are pooled into special trust-funds. When earnings stop, monthly cash benefits are paid from these funds."

Not true. Not a word. It was never true.

The first recipient of the system was Ida Mae Fuller who contributed $22.50 to the fund. Then she retired. Fortunately for her, she lived to the age of 100 years. And she received $20,944 dollars during her years of retirement.

Nice.

But where did the federal government get the money to give her? From her trust-fund? That's a lot of interest for $22.50.

It wasn't coming from her trust-fund. The government already spent the money she invested. Her $20,944 was coming, instead, from those who worked while she was retired, although they were told their money was only going into their own trust-funds. It wasn't. And it just got worse. In short time, the fund was paying out $17,000 more each minute than it was taking in.

At the birth of the Social Security System, one of the blocks that went into the Pyramid Club's construction was put into place by Henry Morganthau, Jr., the Secretary of the Treasury who, giving him the benefit of the doubt, probably didn't know he would be proven wrong when he said, "The worker will pay approximately fifteen cents a week. This will rise in stages until finally, beginning in 1949, twelve years from now, you and your employer will each pay three cents on each dollar you earn. And that's only on your first three-thousand dollars of income. Then it will stop. That is the most you will ever have to pay."

Hardly.

The members of the Congress, ever generous to themselves, excluded themselves from the Social Security System, recognizing that they could have a lot more in retirement funds by a wholly different retirement plan.

The public has been told that workers contribute a certain amount to Social Security and their employers contribute a like amount. How did anyone ever believe that? What if we were told that workers contribute nine-tenths and employers contribute one-tenth? Or that workers contribute one-tenth and employers contribute nine-tenths? It would all be the same. The end result would be no different if either one paid one-hundred-percent, because an employer only has a certain amount to pay an employee and it doesn't make any difference to the employer if that amount goes directly into the employee's hands or into a federal coffer in the employee's name. The rule should have been written honestly: from the wages meant to pay a worker, "x" amount will go to Social Security each pay-day rather than directly to the employee each pay-day.

After the creation of the hoax, one repair followed another. There were changes in 1950, 1956, 1965, 1972, 1974 and shortly after President Carter came to office in 1977 he proposed that "employees and employers" pay even more in Social Security taxes. When the Congress passed that 1977 bill, President Carter said, "The American people will pay more taxes into the Social Security System, but in return, they'll know that it will be there permanently and in sound condition."

Permanence and a sound condition meant a little less than five years. Then came bankruptcy and the repair crews came out again.

Why didn't candidates for office reveal the truth against opponents who lied and said that the Social Security System was solvent?

Some did, but all a candidate for office had to do was to mention the truth and it was tantamount to writing the candidate's concession speech. Social Security held the sanctity of a religion. Those few candidates who did choose to tell the truth limped around the election battlefield, having dropped their shield, giving the candidate's opponents a perfect bullseye.

In 1983, a non-partisan fifteen-person "Blue Ribbon Social Security Reform Commission" presented its recommendations to the President and to the Congress. It arrived at the conclusion that in order to correct the continuing bankruptcy, taxation for the system must increase even more than the taxes demanded at the time, and the amount of money paid to retirees must decrease. It was not a solution to crisis but rather another postponement of crisis, and a costly one before once again, taxes would raise and pay-outs would diminish. Moreover, the 1983 Commission decided that Social Security pay-outs should be open for taxation themselves, depending on the total income of the recipient.

When will bankruptcy hit next? There are any number of estimates of potential bankruptcy. By somewhere around the year 2025, the annual shortfall will be $60 billion in today's currency according to the Congressional Research Service. Disability and Medicare (which were made part of Social Security) are forecast to be bankrupt before the end of the 20th Century. In 1940 there were 220,000 recipients of Social Security payments. In 1993 the recipients reached 36 million. By the year 2013, the estimate is 70 million recipients.

On January 31, 1993, Senator Moynihan (D-NY) reported that the average male who has paid the maximum into Social Security will get back less money than he contributed. He added that ten years earlier, in 1983, that man would have received two times more than what he had contributed. (*This Week with David Brinkley*, ABC Television Network.) Such was the result of the Pyramid Scheme that only pays off early investors from money of later investors.

Senator Phil Gramm (R-TX) said on February 7, 1993, that a 44-year-old worker will get back 91 cents for every dollar that person is contributing. (*Meet the Press*, NBC Television Network.)

On August 12, 1993, President Clinton signed into law the new budget that would tax 85% of Social Security payments for couples earning more than $44,000 and singles earning more than $34,000. This time the tax increase was said to be for deficit reduction.

How could this faulty system be so sacrosanct? Who would willingly invest in such an account without interest, and a return of less than the principle, and with the government changing its ground rules every few years?

The irony is that a retirement fund, if built correctly, could mean a fortune for a person's later years. Someday the public will figure it out (it takes nothing more than a pocket calculator) and recognize how much money they could have had for retirement had they invested privately rather than be compelled to put that money into the government's Social Security System. Take a scenario of a man who gets a job when he is 18 years old for $20,000 a year in private enterprise. He has been given government permission to be excluded from the Social Security System as long as he puts away a commensurate amount of his wages into a retirement fund at a private banking institution. For the rest of his working years he does exactly that. On this privately-saved money he earns 3% interest a year. Because he is a terrible worker he never gets a raise, not even for the rising cost of living. On his 65th birthday he is still getting $20,000 a year, and he retires. His private account for retirement would be over one quarter of one million dollars, all on a consistent salary that never went one cent above $20,000 a year.

A more average worker would have over one million dollars.

The beauty of such a fund would be that the money earned by workers for their retirement would be theirs without restriction. They could leave that money as inheritance to anyone they want. They could keep the principal in the bank and live off the interest, or take the whole pot and fulfill a dream. In short, the money earned throughout working years would be theirs, as it was when they earned it. Doing this, however, requires that the government is gradually moved out of the power structure of retirement during a transition period to privatization, and because of government damage through the years, the transition period would be difficult.

First, the government must keep its promise to everyone who has made any contribution to the Social Security System. A person who has worked forty years or only forty hours must get from the Social Security System what that worker has been promised, because a government is only as good as its word, whether it means honoring its word to foreign governments by act of treaty or honoring its word to its own citizens by act of Congress. And although we have had many administrations since the start of Social Security, the continuity of promise must be kept paramount.

Second, Cost of Living Adjustments (COLAS) must be retained or the government will not be keeping its word to the retiree but, instead, the government will be keeping real money invested by the retiree.

Third, the government must stop misinforming the public by using the term "benefits" to describe what the recipient of Social Security receives on retirement. Those aren't benefits; they are the retiree's own dollars that the government is giving back to the retired worker who earned them and was already taxed on them.

Fourth, Social Security was meant as a supplement for retirement, and was not meant to discourage other income. Therefore, there should never be a "means test" to fine the wealthier social security recipient. When the person's income is used as a criterion for a reduction of payment to the retiree, then Social Security turns into a welfare system rather than the promised holding of money for the worker. Many of the wealthy were not wealthy when the Social Security taxes were removed from their paychecks. To their credit, they worked hard and succeeded. Many were simply prudent and put money away in a savings account to have in their retirement years, and they should not be punished for that. They took the federal government seriously when the federal government told the public that the retirement fund was only a supplement and the worker should plan to put away more funds for his or her retirement. What audacious thievery of government to take dollars away from those who trusted the government to hold those earned dollars for safekeeping. What if you went to a bank and said, "Hold this for me. I'll be back for it," and when you return to the bank to get your money out, you're told, "Sorry, you earned enough money in interest on other savings that we're going to keep a lot of that money you asked us to hold." Would you say, "Okay?" Would you advice your children to save at that bank?

Fifth, every person entering the work-force to whom promises have not yet been made should be required to take out a retirement fund through private enterprise at rates that guarantee pay-backs equal to or above those of the Social Security System. It will be a windfall for the worker's retirement years and for private enterprise, and therefore for the economy of the nation.

Sixth, for those already in the work-force and not yet retired, there will be a choice laid before them, a choice between continuing their contributions to the old system or starting the new system. That free choice made during the transition would be based on the age of that individual, the amount of investment already paid into the system, and the pay-back to be received. The worker could choose to pay a reduced amount of money to the declining Social Security System for reduced pay-backs during retirement, as long as the worker compensates for the reduced payment by investing the subtracted amount in a retirement program offered by private enterprise.

The transition period would be a journey to the end of crises rather than another postponement of crisis. In a generation's time, the government's Social Security System would be phased out, with that phase-out evolving into secure retirement funds for the individual.

If such a foundation is not built soon by courageous politicians, then by the end of the first quarter of the 21st Century, the American Pyramid built so haphazardly without blueprint, will lie in ruins. The ruins of that system will cause the nation's chains to tighten, leaving scars beyond repair for worker, employer, and retiree.

PART THREE

NEW TURN-OFFS FROM THE WASHINGTON BELTWAY

(THE INSTITUTIONS OF GOVERNMENT)

CHAPTER ELEVEN

THE INVISIBLE MONARCHY

The November ballots will be cast and counted, the transition period will come and go, the inauguration of the new President will take place, and by the end of January the departments and agencies of the Government of the United States will be operating under new leadership.

That is how each President-elect views the schedule from election-day forward.

But former Presidents who sit in retirement and watch current events from the distance of place and time and experience know otherwise.

They know that the November ballots will be cast and counted, the transition period will come and go, the inauguration of the new President will take place, and by the end of January the departments and agencies of the Government of the United States will be operating under the same leadership they have had for decades.

And that is because the new President will only be able to appoint less than 3% of those who work for the federal government, while some 97% of the people who will work for the new President were there before his victory.

The largest crisis evolves when a Republican or conservative President comes into the Oval Office, because the majority of those who will work for him are instinctively against his policies and have been against them long before his arrival. Washington, D.C. is a one-party city. That's true because government-as-a-career generally attracts liberals and not conservatives. Conservatives want the federal government out of their lives, and they are not inclined to put their lives into the federal government. Few conservatives have an ambition to be a permanent part of Washington's great bureaucracies. Liberals do.

The entrenched bureaucracy offers a threat of which most incoming contemporary Presidents (conservative or liberal) have not been aware: within each of those great stone buildings in the District of Columbia that house the mammoth bureaucracies, there is a secret and permanent government led by an Invisible Monarchy. The Invisible Monarchy is composed of the highest ranking civil service and foreign service careerists who stay in government while Presidents of the nation come and go. The bureaucracy regards those highest ranking careerists as Kings and Queens and Princes and Princesses within each department and agency of government.

And when the new President appoints his Secretary of a Department or the Director of an Agency, that appointee is regarded by the Invisible Monarchy as a mere temporary figure to graciously applaud and pat on the back and to whom they nod at meetings. And when the meetings are over and the appointee is pleased with the bureaucracy's reception, the Invisible Monarchy and its highest-level subjects go to the elevator talking loudly in praise of the administration, and after they enter the elevator and its sliding doors touch each other and make the elevator into a sound-proof haven, they start to laugh. The new appointee actually thinks that they will implement the President's decisions, even if they don't like them. Please.

They didn't get to be a King or a Queen or a Prince or a Princess for nothing. They will implement the President's decisions only if the President's decisions match their own. To become a real King or Queen or Prince or Princess took too many years to abdicate because of a mere election. To achieve those crowns took fighting for assignment to assignment and post to post and by maintaining, through the years, a political outlook held in common with those higher up in the royalty. The political outlook of the throne is permanent no matter the will of the voters.

The skills of those who occupy the throne must include the ability to give every appearance that it is implementing the new President's decisions which causes the President's appointees to believe, in

February and March and April and May, that they are in control of the massive bureaucracies they head.

The best of the appointees start wondering by August.

The worst of them take a much longer time.

No matter when they start wondering, most appointees of the President surrender to the bureaucracy by their second year in office. They had no idea that during the first year, they were exposing the tip of a White Flag to the bureaucrats; but more and more of the flag became unfurled as the President's appointees approved and complimented the work of the appointee's inherited staff.

By the second year, most of the President's appointees unknowingly carry the White Flag into the Oval Office and, as the President discusses the work of that appointee's department or agency, the President's appointee gives reasons why the particular department or agency he heads should not have its budget cut as the President wants. Instead the appointee attempts to convince the President that the budget should be increased. Further, "my people, who are experts with years of experience" recommend that the President can best accomplish his goals not through Policy Plan A, as the President has instructed, but rather through Policy Plan B. Policy Plan A, "you see, was tried thirteen years ago and failed," so the President is wrong. "Policy Plan B was tried seventeen years ago and succeeded." And on the lap of the President's appointee sits two bulging black notebooks filled with multi-colored lucite tabs jutting out from their pages. Black Notebook Number One documents the failure of Policy Plan A that the President wants and Black Notebook Number Two justifies the success of Policy Plan B, a plan of which the President is totally unfamiliar.

The President is sometimes overcome with the depth of the research his appointee's staff has put together. He then begins to question his own instincts. After all, the "appointee's people" are "experts."

And so most appointees find themselves advocating, not the position of the President to the bureaucracy, but the position of the bureaucracy to the President.

And, in time, the President himself, faced with the analysis of so many "experts" and faced with the winning performance of his appointee as he sits and discusses the policy with him in the Oval Office, chooses the path so capably advised for him.

It's Policy Plan B authored by the bureaucracy.

Policy Plan A, earlier advocated by the President, is out.

The President and the appointee shake hands, there is some small-talk — something about the family — and the appointee walks down the hall to the reception room of the West Wing while trying not to smile too triumphantly in victory. He strolls toward the North-West Gate of the White House bathing in what he knows will be a bigger victory to come when he gets back to the stone building that houses his bureaucracy.

Once there, he calls a meeting of his senior staff and tells them what a good job he did at the meeting with the President.

He doesn't know it but he's working for the people who are supposed to be working for him. He surrendered because he craves their admiration. He wants their praise. He wants them to know that the President listens to him. He wants them to know that as head of this giant bureaucracy, he sees the challenge just as they do — but unlike any leader they have ever had before — he can get it done. He knows that he currently lives in silent competition with his predecessors with whom he is continually compared by those who worked for his predecessors.

And they walk from the meeting shaking their heads in bewilderment, exhibiting to him as he watches their backs, how impressed they are with the way he handled the President and that they know that no one who headed this organ of government before him had achieved such a victory.

And this time in the elevator they don't laugh. They don't even congratulate themselves. It's the way they knew it would be. He's nothing. They are the Permanent Government.

Overseas in the embassies and consulates it is the same. The new Ambassador comes to the host-country as the emissary of the President. Some Ambassadors are careerists who have been in the foreign service under one President after another after another and for them it's easy. They have their own policies and they know how to put them into practice in "K.L." or "Addis" or "B.A." or whatever shorthand the foreign service uses for the host country's capital city.

Some Ambassadors are not careerists; they are friends of the President or big donors to his campaign or at least they are politically in tune with the President, and they are different than the careerists. They are like most of the appointees back home. It takes a while. Maybe until August. The Embassy Staff doesn't like the new Ambassador until he changes his ways. He generally changes his ways.

And something else happens: the Ambassador becomes an advocate of the country in which he is posted. If this miserable little country in which he finds himself isn't important, then he isn't important.

"I think that the locals love me, and I love the cottage industries of these fascinating, marvelous people." He tries to act just like "they do here." He begins to think just like "they do here." And soon he asks himself, "what's the United States doing to this place, anyway?"

And so he no longer advocates U.S. policies to the host-country. He advocates the host-country's policies to the United States.

All of this could be changed and the Invisible Monarchy could be deposed without a palace coup if the civil service and foreign service were temporarily halved by attrition, but instead of new careerists coming in as replacements at all levels of the bureaucracy to fill the open positions, new appointees (not careerists) would take their places. That would give the nation a 50-50 balance between experience and the voters'j will.

The President, regardless of party, should have the loyalty of those who work for him in the Executive Branch of Government — and at least half of those who work for him should have the political instincts of the party he represents. Admittedly, a Democrat President does not have the problem of a Republican President, but even a Democrat President may not be liberal enough for the implanted bureaucracy.

With a government staffed by an even amount of careerists and appointees, the Executive Branch would have support from within.

Even the weak appointee would be able to stand rather than crawl.

As the system presently exists, the judgment of the job done by the appointee, both at home and overseas, comes at the end of the administration. It's easy to tell if the appointee was strong and upheld the President's policies, or weak and surrendered to the bureaucracy. You can tell by the Good-bye Party that's given for the appointee by the bureaucracy. If the bureaucrats are crying because the appointee is leaving, and they tell him what a success he has been, then that appointee should have left long ago. He caved.

If, on the other hand, they act as though they're saying "good-riddance," and give him a worthless good-bye plaque reflective of their wrath, then that appointee was someone made of steel who ran the department or agency or embassy in the way the elected President wanted it run.

To be a terrible appointee in the eyes of the Invisible Monarchy is the ultimate success, but it is very difficult to achieve.

CHAPTER TWELVE

BEFORE LEAVING PLEASE CLOSE THE CABINET

The President's affiliation with his Cabinet is like some married couple's sex life. At the beginning they fool around with each other a lot. But just wait.

The couples rarely admit what's happening in the bedroom, and Presidents rarely admit what's happening in the Cabinet Room. What would happen if some President would say, "I don't want to hold any more of these Cabinet Meetings. I want a divorce!"

Almost every administration in memory started out with the President saying that power will be held by the Cabinet Members, not by the White House Staff. But as each administration progressed, the dynamics worked themselves the other way and the Cabinet Officers found themselves being subservient to the White House Staff. It happens because it should happen.

Most Cabinet Officers become victims of the geography of the District of Columbia, and victims of bureaucrats, and victims of their own weaknesses. They work in the departments they're supposed to supervise and so they are away from the White House in the separate buildings with separate staffs, and their physical surroundings as well as their psychological ones, give distance from the President.

The White House Staff, on the other hand, is where the President is, physically and psychology. They don't need strength to overcome their peers. They need strength to exceed them. They have the day-to-day knowledge of where the President wants to go, and their job is to see that he gets there. That's what the Cabinet Officers are supposed to do too, but they're the Chiefs in their own worlds. Most of them have bigger buildings and bigger staffs than the President at the White House. The President is down the block, even miles away, not knowing what's going on inside those buildings.

President Nixon tried to fix some of the mess he inherited with the structure of the Executive Branch, but the Congress didn't buy it. He proposed that the only Cabinet Secretaries to be retained would be the Secretaries of State, Defense, Justice, and the Treasury. They were the posts that started with the birth of the nation without any additions to the Cabinet Secretaries for sixty years. (The Postmaster General was also included at the birth of the nation and successfully discontinued as a Cabinet Post during the Nixon Administration.) It was 1849 before the additions starting coming: Interior, Agriculture, Commerce, and Labor. It wasn't until 1953 that the Department of Health, Education and Welfare came into existence. It quickly became the recipient of the third highest budget in the world, only exceeded by the budgets of the United States and the Soviet Union.

To please some particular constituency, most contemporary Presidents have established more cabinet departments, rather than less. President Johnson added the Department of Housing and Urban Development and the Department of Transportation; President Carter added the Department of Energy and the Department of Education, changing the Department of Health, Education and Welfare into the Department of Health and Human Services (the word "welfare" became taboo). President Reagan added the Department of Veteran's Affairs, and President Bush agreed to a forthcoming Department of the Environment, endorsed by President Clinton.

Cabinet Departments mean the creation of a Secretary and a Deputy Secretary and an Under Secretary and usually a number of Assistant Secretaries, a Special Assistant, a Chief of Staff of the department, a Controller, a General Counsel, and a raft of directors. The physical cost to the nation is high.

The psychological cost to the President is equally enormous.

If you were President, would you call frequent meetings of your

Cabinet? Why would you want the Secretary of Housing and Urban Development sitting there while you discuss an overseas conflict? And why would you want the Secretary of State slumped in his seat while you discuss a new Interstate Highway?

President Nixon's idea was not to eliminate all functions of the displaced cabinet officers, but to consolidate the abolished departments into four separate agencies dealing with human needs, community needs, the physical environment, and the economy; and instead of having Secretaries, the appointed heads of those agencies would be White House Counselors. Good idea. It would have been a better idea to just dump them, but even his more modest proposal was met with horror by the Congress. The bigger the government, and the more department heads the Congress can torment with their hearings, the happier they are.

The ideal Executive Branch of our government would be to have only the original four Cabinet Secretaries and have them working in the White House Complex.

This organizational change would also end the need for a National Security Adviser, as the Secretary of State would have the authority of that office (as he should) and that would end the repeated conflict between those two appointees; the Secretary of State being confirmed by the Senate, while the National Security Adviser, as a member of the President's staff, goes unconfirmed.

The only other high ranking officer who would be working in the White House would, of course, be the Vice-President.

Even the best of Vice-Presidents presents a problem to the President. The Vice-President was elected and so he can't be fired, and even if the President thinks the world of the Vice-President, what does he do with him? He's waiting in the wings to become the President, and his staff feels he would be a much better President than the current President and they are convinced that the current President doesn't use the Vice-President up to his capabilities. The Vice-President's staff always hates the President's Chief of Staff because he delivers the bad news about what the Vice-President is expected to say, the funerals he will attend, and generally the President's Chief of Staff acts more powerful than the Vice-President because he is more powerful than the Vice-President.

The solution to the "Vice-President Problem" would be to make the Vice-President the President's Chief of Staff. The President and Vice-President would then have to work as a team, there would be no inter-staff rivalry, and the Vice-President would know more about the presidency than the President himself. That's because the Chief of Staff selects what the President sees, hears, and reads, and therefore knows what the President does and does not see, hear, and read.

Further, it would tempt — not demand, but tempt a presidential nominee to select a vice-presidential nominee with whom he could work well, rather than select one on the grounds of political expediency alone.

Some day a President will come into Washington who recognizes that the Executive Branch of government has become a haven for bureaucrats that have created a power structure throughout Washington, D.C. that is much too big, too cumbersome, too sloppy, too independent of the President, much too costly, and diverts Presidents to deal with the petty. To return to governance, the President should reorganize the Executive Branch by eliminating the departments that have purposes in conflict with the purpose of the federal government, put the remaining Secretary's offices in the White House Complex, and make the Vice-President his Chief of Staff.

Presidents have to battle the Congress, state governors, city mayors, the national media, and hundreds of lobbying groups. But often it is their own Executive Department that wears them out and kills their grandest goals.

CHAPTER THIRTEEN

THE BACCHANALIANS WITH ZIP CODES OF 20510 AND 20515

Dionysus and Bacchus used to sit around ancient Greece drinking wine and eating grapes that were held by the fingers of beautiful women. They didn't do a great deal more than that, but I guess they figured it was enough. Those jobs are very difficult to get these days. In fact they're rationed with only 535 people in the United States able to get those kind of jobs at one time.

The Bacchanalia is enjoyed under and around the U.S. Capitol Dome, and the modern Dionysuses and Bacchuses are now referred to as members of the Congress who have given themselves 41,000 assistants, which is more than Dionysus and Bacchus put together, and the number of those assistants equal more people than are currently populated by eleven state capital cities. Those assistants cost 5.5 million dollars a year for each member of the Congress, with the people of the nation charged for them. And the ripe grapes that are fondled in these days are a health spa, free physical exams, free laboratory work, X-rays, prescription medicines, reduced cost for life insurance, magnificent retirement pensions, swimming pools, saunas, masseurs, gymnasiums, free Christmas package wrapping, photographers, tax advisers, car washes, barber shops and beauty parlors.

What makes their jobs even a greater joy is that as they create laws for the rest of Americans, they regularly exclude themselves from those laws. They need not obey wholly or in great part: the Age Discrimination in Employment Act, the Americans with Disabilities Act, the Civil Service Reform Act of 1978, the Civil Rights Act of

1964, the Employee Polygraph Protection Act, the Employee Retirement Income Security Act, the Equal Pay Act, the Ethics in Government Act, the Family and Medical Leave Act of 1993, the Fair Labor Standards Act, the Federal Service-Labor-Management Relations Statute, the Freedom of Information Act, the Independent Counsel Act, the National Labor Relations Act, the National Labor Standards Act, the Occupational Safety and Health Act of 1970, the Privacy Act, the Rehabilitation Act of 1973, the Social Security Act, the Worker Adjustment and Retraining Notification Act, and a myriad of other laws they passed for the rest of the people of the country.

James Madison wrote that Congress "can make no law which will not have its full operation on themselves and their friends, as well as on the great mass of society." In contrast to that, two centuries later, Senate Majority Leader George Mitchell admitted that, "it has been said here many times tonight...we want to treat Senators the same as everyone else...Mr. President, not a single Senator believes that. Not a single Senator." One law (or amendment if the courts find it necessary) should be made stating "All laws passed by the Congress shall apply equally to the Congress."

But how about the amusements? What do the modern-day Bacchanalians do for fun? Where are the laughs?

The amusements, the fun, the laughs are in the appropriation committees, provided through the funding they give to the bureaucracies for projects that the public knows little if anything about.

The National Institute of Health found that there was a village in Spain where the residents had married a little later in life than the average couple had married throughout the rest of Spain. Those late marriages took place between the years 1873 through 1983, 110 years. Too bad that the National Institute of Health found out about that village because U.S. taxpayers were fined $74 ,561 to find out what was going on for those 110 years in Spain.

I don't know how you feel about Bennington College but I have no great desire, no secret passion, to track the political attitudes of women who graduated from Bennington College in the 1930s. The taxpayers, five decades later, had to pay $242,508 to see what those attitudes were all about.

Here's something you might care about: the Ache Tribe in Paraguay. As we all know there are about 600 Aches living in Eastern Paraguay. Ever wonder how they gather food? The U.S. taxpayers paid $163,254 to find out how they collect that stuff. If you're interested write the Department of Commerce.

Here are some other uses of your money, but the following two studies only cost about $60,000, surely worth it: one of them was to analyze private banking institutions in London between the years 1720 and 1800, and the other one was to study agriculture and economic developments in Russia between 1750 and 1860. Good to know, just in case.

Then there is the question that undoubtedly has kept you bewildered throughout most of your life: what on earth causes the aggressive behavior of Siamese fighting fish? Why don't they cool it? Can't they simmer down those tempers of theirs? Finally there is a report on this, and it only cost $55,000. A bargain.

Then there's the Department of Housing and Urban Development. It has a program called Urban Development Action Grants. One grant of $15,000,000 went to Detroit in 1986 for the purpose of clearing a site for a new Chrysler Plant to be built there. It wasn't that Chrysler was impoverished. (And even if it was, so what?) Chrysler had earned 21.1 billion dollars that year. Ford and General Motors had to clean their own new sites. Fair is fair.

The next time you go to St. Petersburg, Florida, you can see how well your tax money works. You did your part in paying the $3,400,000 to help the Harbour View Hotel Corporation renovate a 337 room Hilton Hotel and build a swimming pool and tennis courts there. But that's practically nothing compared to what you worked for in Memphis, Tennessee. That's where you chipped in for a total of $9,700,000 for a seven-story office building with a shopping mall and 1200 parking spaces.

Then there's the $60,000,000 for which you chipped in for the anti-U.S. Government of President Garcia of Peru. At the time it sounded to the general public that our federal government gave your money to Peru for a worthy cause since Peru needed relief and rehabilitation and reconstruction of homes and roads and other necessities due to floods and droughts. But that $60,000,000 didn't go for any of those things when all was said and done. The U.S. Agency for International Development allowed the Government of Peru to use that money to pay off bank loans. Being opposed to the United States often pays off. Great gag, huh?

And here's a project that I can't help but get pretty excited about on a personal level. At last — at long last, a study on how Haitian ethnic organizations are formulated. Only a little over $250,000 for that.

My favorite project takes care of a problem I have had ever since I began traveling on commercial airlines. On every flight I ever had, I looked at the stewardess and thought, "I wonder if her nose is bigger or smaller than an average stewardess' nose?" You've probably had that experience. We all have. But, if you're like me, you didn't know if her nose was bigger or smaller than the average stewardess' nose because you didn't know the size of an average stewardess' nose. It's 2.8 inches. The government found that out. So the next time you take a plane, take a ruler with you. Measure the darned thing and see if she stacks up. That only cost the taxpayers $66,000 to find out that key information and you might as well take advantage of it since you paid for it.

Unfortunately that study was made just before deregulation of the airlines and before terms were changed from stewardesses to flight attendants, and a lot of new airlines have cropped up and old ones went bankrupt since then and so the average nose-size is probably different now. So, in fact, we don't really know if that information is still valid. And we call ourselves a Super-Power?

How do these great amusements get passed into law? Sometimes the bureaucracies just surprise the Congress like a jester, saying "look what we did last year!" and they have amazing ways of justifying them. But often those projects are in appropriation bills that include so many things that most people aren't able to discover them until they have long-since passed into law. Many of the members of the Congress don't know what they're voting for or against.

The epitome of this trickery is what's called the Omnibus Bill.

Keep in mind that near the beginning of the year the President submits his budget proposal to the Congress. There are strict rules that set down the time-limits the Congress has to work on each phase of the budget, and by law, everything should be in line; signed, sealed and delivered to the President and sent back to the Congress by October 1, the beginning of the new Fiscal Year. (By a law enacted in 1974 and that went into effect in 1976, the President has to submit to the Congress his budget within 15 days after the Congress convenes in January. By April 1, the Congressional Budget Office must submit a report evaluating the President's budget. By May 15, both the Senate and the House must complete action in adopting the initial Budget Resolution. By September 15 a final budget must be adopted. Between May 15 and September 25, individual appropriations for every Cabinet Department are supposed to be completed and sent to the President. The President can sign or veto those individual appropriation bills separate from one another.)

Most often when the new Fiscal Year begins on October 1, the Congress is late on its appropriation bills and there is no budget, so the Congress quickly passes what's called a Continuing Resolution keeping the Government in business with appropriations on a week-to-week or month-to-month basis until they get their work done. While these Continuing Resolutions are in effect, the Congress puts together an Omnibus Bill that runs thousands and thousands of pages filled with appropriations that the Congress should have completed in individual bills throughout the year. Come the end of the year, they put everything into this massive Omnibus Bill with a lot of things included that they know the President doesn't want as well as things that they know he does want. They also include things they want for their own individual states and districts, including bills they tried to push through the Congress unsuccessfully earlier in the year.

Some members of the Congress wink at each other in a trade-off of one personal interest for another. One Omnibus Bill included Senator Inouye's (D-HI) item to give $8,000,000 to a parochial school in France. (A political contributor to Senator Inouye requested that it be done.) Senators Kennedy (D-MA) and Hollings (D-SC) put in an item that would prohibit the Federal Communications Commission to grant an extension to Rupert Murdoch's ownership of particular media holdings. (Senators Kennedy and Hollings didn't like the conservative Rupert Murdoch.) Congressman Charles Wilson (D-TX) inserted an item that would take away two airplanes from the Defense Intelligence Agency after that agency had denied Congressman Wilson and a companion air transportation. There was an item included for the U.S. Government to buy sunflower oil but no government agency requested it; another item was included for $500,000 to pay for a bridge over Mud Creek in Eufala Lake in Oklahoma; and there was another $6,500,000 allocated for a ski resort in Idaho.

An Omnibus Bill allows legislators to justify voting for something they claim to be against, by saying they were for "other" things in the bill and they had to take the bad with the good.

After going through the two Houses of Congress and a Conference Committee and back to the two Houses they shoot the bill down Pennsylvania Avenue to the President and they say, "We did our work, here's the budget, now it's in your hands." The President is left with a decision to either sign the bill with everything that's in it, or veto it, throwing the whole massive volume back to the Congress for them to start the procedure all over again. But by vetoing it he brings about a virtual catastrophe for the federal government because by this time of the year the Congress has allowed the federal government to run out of money and will remain out of money unless the new appropriations bills (included in the Omnibus Bill) are passed into law. Federal workers will have to be laid-off just before Christmas, because there will be no money appropriated to pay them until there is an approved budget.

The President is in a mess. If he signs it, the taxpayers' money will be used for a lot of junk. If he vetoes it, many services expected by the citizens will be ground to a halt. The press has a field-day interviewing federal workers on the streets of Washington, worried about losing their jobs just before Christmas. Somehow the television cameras are always able to find pathetic characters who look like they've been authored by Charles Dickens, while the President is in the warm and comfortable White House being perceived as a stand-in for Ebenezer Scrooge.

The U.S. Constitution clearly calls for the President to be able to sign or veto a bill. The authors of the Constitution did not think that the members of the Congress would put practically every appropriation into one massive bill and put the President on the spot with a take-it-or-leave-it bill with federal workers and services held hostage. But that's what often happens towards the end of the year.

A responsible Congress would pass a law to prohibit Omnibus Bills and allow the President to sign or veto year-end legislation not as a bundle, but as separate appropriations. It should make that limitation upon itself because it has been clearly subverting the intent of Article One, Section Seven of the U.S. Constitution that tells the step-by-step process of how bills should be created, signed, vetoed, and overridden. (The legislation of 1974 tells when, but not how.) But don't expect the Congress to look for the original intent of the U.S. Constitution. Further, if the Congress doesn't submit all its appropriations to the President by September 25, the *President's* budget, unrevised by the Congress, should go into effect on October 1.

Even a law prohibiting Omnibus Bills, and a firm deadline of September 25 for a congressional submission wouldn't solve the problem completely, because the individual appropriation bills include thousands of items in themselves, and the President has to sign each bill in its entirety or veto each bill in its entirety. And so Presidents have advocated a Line-Item Veto, meaning that they would have the right to line-out those things they don't believe should be appropriated, and then sign the bills after they have made such deletions. (The Congress would, of course, be able to override the veto by a two-thirds majority of each House, as they can over all Presidential vetoes.)

Ulysses S. Grant was the first President who asked for a Line-Item Veto, followed by Rutherford B. Hayes and Chester Arthur, all three of them advocating a constitutional amendment to give the President that power. (Not that a constitutional amendment is needed to bring that about, since a simple statute could do it.) FDR wanted the Line-Item Veto, President Eisenhower wanted it, and Presidents

Nixon, Ford, Carter, Reagan, and Bush wanted it. Their pleas were in vain. The Congress has never given the power of a Line-Item Veto to any President, although 43 State Governors have that authority over bills passed by their individual state legislatures. The Congress knows that if bills include a massive amount of expenditures and riders with subjects separate and apart from the thrust of a bill, that the President would line-out those items, and he would thus reveal to the electorate the wasteful expenditures the Congress wanted.

Many Presidents have inaccurately given the impression to the public that if they only had the Line-Item Veto they would be able to balance the budget. Not true, since contemporary Presidents haven't *submitted* balanced budgets to the Congress, and it is most unlikely that a President would line-out those items that he, himself, had authored.

There is a solution that falls well short of a Balanced Budget Flat-Rate Tax, but during the transition period into the Balanced Budget Flat Rate Tax this idea would give both branches of government greater incentive to balance the budget: pass legislation that gives a Line-Item Veto to a President only if that President has submitted a balanced budget for the particular Fiscal Year in question, and give the Congress the authority to send him bills he cannot line-out if he hasn't submitted to them a balanced budget for that Fiscal Year. That would give incentive for the President to submit a balanced budget, and incentive for the Congress to be more responsible in those things it puts in its own budget proposal. It would give both branches of government true checks and balances.

The Congress has other tricks to get the power and money it wants:

This one was invented by those in the Congress who aspired to be President and, although most will deny it, almost everyone in the Congress has such an aspiration. A law was passed that seemed innocent enough. The law created a Check-Off Box on the top of every 1040 form that goes to the taxpayers of the nation. The box designates, by the taxpayer's mark, one dollar to go to the Presidential Election Campaign Fund to pay for the next Presidential campaigns. Along side of the Check-Off Box is this note: "Note: Checking Yes will not change your tax or reduce your refund."

Then from where will the money come?

If the IRS has discovered a way to pay for something without having taxpayers charged, why not have check-off boxes for funding child-care centers, missiles, social security payments, or a hamburger for everyone?

They haven't discovered a way to pay for something without charging the taxpayers, and the IRS's explanation of the box is absolute deception. Those boxes that have been checked are counted in Washington, and taxation or the national debt is increased a like amount. When the box is checked-off by some, we all pay now or later. In the 1992 election, Bill Clinton and George Bush's campaigns each received 55.2 million dollars as established from the marks in the check-off boxes. In the year following that election, the Congress quickly ordered the IRS to increase the one dollar check-off box to a three dollar check-off box. The Congress justifiably believed that anyone gullible enough to check-off one dollar would check-off three dollars. (Why not just give that money to the candidate of your choice?)

That Check-Off Box is even more serious than a deception; it establishes a precedent in allowing the public to determine the budget of an expenditure without knowing that the item will be billed to present and/or future taxpayers, and without the taxpayer having any idea how many other dollars are or aren't going to that fund. It is a new way of funding.

With the giant success of fooling so many taxpayers, many in the Congress are advocating that the same kind of check-off box be used for a Fund for Senatorial and Congressional Elections.

All check-off boxes should be prohibited on income tax forms. (Second best would be to prohibit the boxes unless the contribution checked-off increases the individual taxpayer's bill by the amount the individual checks off.)

As more and more citizens began to recognize the ways in which the Congress was operating and deceiving the people, there came an avalanche of calls for term limitations, the idea being that those in the

Congress should be prohibited by law (either by statutes or by a constitutional amendment) from serving beyond certain years in office.

But instead of term limitations, we should rid the U.S. Congress of its privileges and perquisites that spark the worst of their natures, rather than the best. For the unprincipled, make a seat in the U.S. Congress unappealing.

Term limitations would not even be a discussion, let alone a constitutional debate, if the salaries for the members of the Congress were very low, and if the personal privileges and perquisites were very few, and if the federal government wouldn't tax and pay for those things that are not federal (interstate) in nature, other than those few areas that are itemized in the United States Constitution.

How could we bring this about and make the members of the Congress lower their own salaries and abridge their own perquisites and privileges and observe the U.S. Constitution to a degree they have long-since ignored? Vote for those candidates who advocate those views, and keep in office those who have proven and acted upon such beliefs. If the citizens of this country are unwilling to do that, then so be it, we will simply have the government we deserve. Term limitations currently exist by will of the voters with the ballot box serving as the trigger for term limitations, rather than a federal law providing that trigger, automatically pulled. In reality, such a law would be a voter limitation. Why should anyone support limiting his or her own ability to vote for or against any candidate?

Should term limits be put into effect, unelected bureaucrats in the federal government and congressional staff members and lobbyists would have far greater power than they have currently, (which is already more than enough) because they would be the only ones who would have no limitation on their D.C. tenures. Moreover, elected officers in their last year or more, would be lame-ducks, and lose influence while still in office, as unelected Washingtonians would fill the void.

It is for sure that some voters want to keep in office particular representatives because they "bring home the bacon," which is another way for saying they bring home stolen goods. The people must understand what "the bacon" really is — theft from their own children.

Rather than the people winking at those representatives, it is up to the people to demand the end of such theft, along with the end of the privileges of Capitol Hill, and that end should come not through a new limitation of the ballot-box, but through the old limitations placed on the federal government, now ignored, written into the United States Constitution.

Until the people recognize their own responsibility, the Congress will continue its rip-offs. Ripping-off the taxpayers has become a high art, the Congress' masterpiece being the ways they have devised to give themselves pay-raises. This is their chief Bacchanalian pursuit, since a pay-raise gives them more of the wine and grapes and fingers that only money can buy. The history of that pay-raise pursuit is a fascinating study of conspiracy and meticulous labyrinthine schemes. Read it slowly because the steps taken from the simple to the complex are integral parts of their masterpiece:

It all started in December of 1981 when the members of the Congress wanted to have a raise in their salaries, so they incorporated the raise in the "Black Lung Disease Benefits Bill." If the President wanted benefits to go to those who had Black Lung Disease, he had to sign the whole bill, which meant the Congress would receive a large raise. That ploy was much too simple; it received immediate public attention and scorn, and so a new plan was devised:

When no one was looking, the Congress set up a procedure to get raises without voting for those raises — in fact without any piece of legislation giving them a pay-raise. Someone or ones had to spend a lot of time to come up with this one. The system they established was that the President, under the advice of an independent committee (the committee consisting of lawyers, corporate executives, and former members of the Congress appointed by the leaders of the three branches of government), would submit to the Congress an amount of money for a pay-raise for the Congress and other federal officers. Then, unless the Congress passed a Joint Resolution against the raise, and submitted their Joint Resolution within 30 days from the time of the recommendation, the raise would be set into law. In other words if they did nothing for those 30 days, just talk about other things, the pay-raise would come into effect. In that way they could tell their constituents that they didn't vote for a raise, they weren't for it — but they got it. That trick was passed into law in 1984.

Two years later, a wait of what they considered to be a respectable amount of time, the committee that had been established under the new system, recommended a raise for the Congress. President Reagan agreed, although he lowered the amount of the raise. The recommendation then went to the Senate and the Senate passed a resolution against their own raise. To the unknowledgeable it seemed as though the Senate was being responsible, but the Senate leadership was involved in a deal made with the leadership of the House of Representatives. In order to terminate the pay-raise, the resolution had to go to the House of Representatives to make the resolution joint between the two Houses. And this is what Speaker of the House, Jim Wright, conspired with the Senate leadership to do: nothing.

Day Number 30 came around and Speaker Wright adjourned the House early without any mention of the raise. What an oversight! He forgot to mention that it was the last day they would be able to join the Senate in a Joint Resolution against that pay-raise.

Then Day Number 31 came and he called for a vote on the resolution. The House voted the raise down, knowing the vote would mean nothing. They had the raise automatically by having let the 30th day come and go. So both the Senate and the House received the raise while they could say they voted against it. That one was for a 16% raise giving each member $12,100 more each year.

At least that might hold them.

But only for a few years.

In three years they got hungry again. This time for a 51% raise. Another $45,000 a year was proposed for each member of the Congress with the Speaker of the House getting a raise of $60,000 a year.

Having been successful before in the way one House voted and the other House didn't vote on time, a repeat was planned. Senate Majority Leader George Mitchell (D-ME) conspired with Speaker Jim Wright (D-TX) to have a vote in the Senate and not have a vote in the

House of Representatives. That meant that Senators again could freely vote against the raise knowing their vote wouldn't prevent their wallets from bulging, because the House wouldn't vote on it in time.

But some of the best-laid plans do not always go well. After the Senate voted the raise down and the Resolution was in the hands of the House of Representatives, Congressman Bill Dannemeyer (R-CA) of California pulled off a coup against the raise. On the 30th day, he called for a voice-vote to see if the House should adjourn. It meant that the vote would tell the public who was for or against the raise; those who wanted the House to adjourn were, in fact, voting for a raise. Under such pressure they voted not to adjourn, which meant they would have to vote on the pay-raise and under such public scrutiny they knew they had to vote the raise down.

They did.

It was a very short-lived victory for the taxpayers. Another scheme was developed within weeks and it was rapidly passed into law:

The pay-raise previously rejected was re-written with new provisions added, and it was called an Ethics Bill. An Ethics Bill? That name took more nerve than demanding a raise. The reason they gave for calling it an Ethics Bill was that the bill stated that with the raise, they would not be allowed to accept honoraria for speeches. They claimed that accepting honoraria for speeches was unethical because it catered to special interest groups who paid members of the Congress for giving speeches. But the Congress, obviously, did not think it was unethical enough to stop accepting honoraria *without* a pay-raise. By their own criteria, the taxpayers would have to pay them to be ethical. The "Ethics Bill" was enacted into law. The pay-raise was theirs.

And the Bacchanal went on and on and on and on.

Pass the grapes, please. No one but the taxpayers will be charged for them. Nice fingers.

CHAPTER FOURTEEN
WHY BORK
BECAME A VERB

Independence Hall is the Mount Sinai of our nation. And just as the Ten Commandments were not given to the people with a wink from God to interpret broadly, our Constitution was not written with a wink from its authors to interpret broadly. God wrote moral law. The authors of our Constitution wrote national law.

God did not say that if succeeding generations didn't like something in His commandments they could interpret His laws in terms of their own trends and times. Nor did the authors of our Constitution say that if succeeding generations didn't like something in their document, they could interpret it in terms of their own trends and times. But because they recognized they were not dealing with the law of life but with the law of government, the authors included within their document an amendment process; one that guaranteed massive and contemporaneous majority support for any amendment, so that whims or designs of the few could not become national law. Had they wanted, they would have written that amendments were unnecessary, and the Supreme Court, which was and remains an oligarchy appointed for life, could change it at will. Instead, they didn't include the Supreme Court in the amendment process at all. An amendment has to be proposed to the states by two-thirds of both houses of the Congress, or recommended by a Constitutional Convention called by two-thirds of the states and then, either way, be ratified by three-fourths of the states.

The Supreme Court has, however, become the first among equal branches of government, since the Supreme Court can judge the Executive Branch and the Legislative Branch, but neither of those two branches of government can judge the Supreme Court. Any case brought before the Supreme Court can be rejected, dismissing it back to the lower court from which it came, or receive a final judgment by the Justices of the Supreme Court. Those Justices use and interpret the Constitution to arrive at their decisions.

On June 21, 1989, a decision was made by the United States Supreme Court that, if studied, could tell any student of our judiciary exactly what the United States Supreme Court should be at its best. Moreover, it could tell any United States Senator the right and wrong questions to ask at confirmation hearings for Supreme Court nominees.

It was a decision that most conservatives scorned instantly and most liberals celebrated just as instantly, but the quick appraisals by both political elements were emotional rather than thoughtful. If the reactions had been thoughtful, the firestorm over the decision would have been far different.

The Supreme Court, in a 5-4 ruling, determined that flag-burning as a form of political protest, is a First Amendment guarantee as a right of freedom of speech — freedom of speech applying to freedom of political expression. One of those who was part of that majority opinion was Justice Antonin Scalia, one of the most conservative members of that court.

If he was so conservative, why did he rule that way? Surely he believed the flag of the United States to be much more than a cloth. He wisely ruled that way because he wasn't reflecting his political belief, he was reflecting his judicial belief. No matter how politically conservative or liberal a Supreme Court Justice may be, the task of that Justice is to make determinations based on the U S. Constitution as it reads, not as a Justice may want it to read. The definition of a conservative Justice is far different than the definition of a conservative legislator, whereas the definition of a liberal Justice is very much the same as a liberal legislator.

It is entirely likely, even probable that if Justice Scalia was a member of the Congress rather than a member of the Supreme Court, he would have authored or ardently supported an amendment to the Constitution for the states to have the authority to prohibit flag-burning. But as a member of the judiciary he could not knowingly misinterpret the Constitution without such an amendment so as to satisfy his own political instincts. (Such an amendment was proposed one year after the Supreme Court decision but, unfortunately, it was defeated in the House of Representatives, 34 votes short of the two-thirds majority necessary. The proposed amendment read, "The Congress and the States shall have power to prohibit the physical desecration of the Flag of the United States.")

The error of liberals is to think of a conservative justice in the same way they think of a conservative legislator. That is because they correctly believe that liberal Justices will generally act the same as liberal legislators. Conservative Justices are generally strict constructionists who mandate that the legislature is the branch of government to make laws, and the judiciary is the branch of government to interpret them, and interpret them without political bias. Very often political liberals would be better off with conservative Justices rather than liberal ones, but they don't know it.

A true conservative Justice will find it vital to base his or her rulings based on original intent, as one would do for the words of a deceased's last will and testament; and to meddle with that would mean that the Justice would be placing him or herself above the authors of the Constitution, which to a true conservative, would be untenable. Most often a liberal Justice will base his or her rulings based on the Constitution, but in tandem with liberally oriented "current trends and times," something for which the amendment process was created, not to be decided by the political beliefs of the Justice.

The Robert Bork confirmation hearings were to a great extent, a debate over the sacredness or non-sacredness of the Constitution. Senator Specter of Pennsylvania argued with Judge Bork over whether or not the intent of the Constitution's authors was paramount. Judge Bork said it was, and Senator Specter (R-PA) said that the matter wasn't really that simple and that a Justice has to rely on "the needs of the nation." If the Senator was right then the judiciary would become a second legislature.

Hodding Carter, who had been President Carter's State Department spokesman, admitted what most other liberals wouldn't admit: He said that Judge Bork's nomination "forces liberals like me to confront, which is that we are depending in large part on the least democratic institution, with a small 'd' in government, to defend what it is we no longer are able to win out there in the electorate."

Robert Bork's insistence on original intent of the U.S. Constitution and the disagreement and lack of knowledge by the majority of the members of the Senate Committee on the Judiciary sealed Judge Bork's doom as an Associate Justice of the Supreme Court. The confirmation process turned into a circus of personal charges, forecasting the worst to come in the confirmation hearings of Clarence Thomas, who endured and rose above the most evil charges by evil people against a Supreme Court nominee of great character. In the period between the hearings of Robert Bork and Clarence Thomas, Bork's name became a part of the American political vocabulary, with the use of personal, irrelevant, misleading, exaggerated, and false charges against a judicial or political figure, becoming known as the "Borking" of an individual. Clarence Thomas was "Borked" to an extreme that even Judge Bork was spared.

On what criteria should an individual be judged for the U.S. Supreme Court? President Clinton said that he made a decision on his first nominee for the Supreme Court based on three criteria. First, the person was progressive in outlook, wise in judgment, balanced and fair in opinions. Second, the person had a record of achievement in the finest tradition of American law and citizenship in behalf of women. And third, the person was a force of consensus building so that our judges can become an instrument of common unity.

President Clinton, other than his advocacy of the nominee being wise in judgment, exhibited an embarrassing set of wrong reasons to nominate any one for the United States Supreme Court. In addition to being wise in judgment, the reasons for nominating a particular person to serve on the Supreme Court should be based on the nominee's knowledge of the Constitution, whether or not that person will interpret the Constitution to the best of his or her ability, that the nominee has the competence to research fully the background of the Constitution and previous Supreme Court decisions, and most of all, the capacity of the person to use self-discipline in restraining that person's political beliefs in favor of the original intent of the authors of the Constitution.

Judge Bork was accused of taking a "narrow view" of the Constitution rather than a "broad view" favored by liberal legislators. What a marvelous accusation! The narrow view is exactly the one that should be made. The "broad view" means the Justice will use his or her own political biases. For a liberal to advocate a "broad view" is an admission that the Constitution is, to that liberal, not satisfactory, and the liberal knows the representatives of the people would not amend the Constitution in the way the liberal would like to have the Constitution read.

Thomas Jefferson said, "On every question of construction we should carry ourselves back to the time when the Constitution was adopted; recollect the spirit manifested in the debates; and instead of trying to find what meaning may be squeezed out of the text, or invented against it, conform to the probable one in which it was passed." If we no longer believe that and if, instead, we believe that times and trends should be enough to change interpretations of the Constitution by the judiciary, then the Constitution's supremacy is void. Why not, then, have a nine person body examine current times and trends and make laws without elected lawmakers?

Future Presidents of the United States and members of the Senate Committee on the Judiciary should have as an obligation to nominate and confirm for membership in the United States Supreme Court, only those who consider the Constitution of the United States of higher importance than themselves, and of higher importance than any political judgment they may desire to put into law. For those without such restraint of their political passions, the other two branches of government are open to them for elective office.

CHAPTER FIFTEEN

AT THE TWIGHLIGHT'S LAST GLEAMING

Drug dealers on the playgrounds of public schools.
Vagrants.
Gangs.
Riots.
Drive-by shootings.
Teen-age pregnancies in massive numbers.
Scrawled graffiti on private and public property.
Mothers and daughters begging on street corners.
Forbidden public parks.
Violent crime an every day event.

How could the United States of America have come to this? This isn't the way the United States used to be. What happened? When and where did it start?

November the 22nd, 1963. Dallas.

November the 21st of that year was the last full day in which the United States walked without a limp. Then came the incredible bullet. No matter what the Warren Commission concluded, the bullet that went in and out of President Kennedy, then went in and out of every one in the nation, wounding them all.

From November the 22nd, 1963, forward, America was different.

It was, at the time, seemingly impossible to have happened. Assassinations were far back in the American past in a different kind of world with a different kind of people. Assassinations were in costume and they happened in an unreal "then," not a real "now." This tragedy had no place in the times of thin lapels and Chubby Checker, the Twist, Andy Warhol, John Glenn, Freedom Marchers, Boeing 707s, Ingemar Johansson, Hula Hoops, Listerine Mouthwash, and Kellogg's cereals. It was impossible. He would be okay.

But Air Force One brought back his body, not his life.

Black crepe was hung above the north portico of the White House. There is still pain to think about it, and there is still that limp even when we don't think about it. To those who heard the drums of the following Sunday and Monday, the sound is still a continuing rhythm that repeats over and over inside of us.

The greatest damage was done to the young who were suddenly witness to all this — witness to the assassination of a man whose imminent death was not even a glimmer of public probability before that moment. If life could be taken from him, and it was, then the youth's own mortality became a predominant thought.

Our military involvement in Vietnam, which was known to be an heroic effort on November the 21st with its Green Berets and Americans fighting for the freedom of others, became perceived as immoral and unjust as 1963 ended. Drugs that were taboo on November the 21st became inviting and inhaled and injected before the end of 1963. Sex acts that were only whispered about by the young on November the 21st became a challenge before the end of 1963. The overwhelming quest was to do everything and to do it now because tomorrow, life may be gone.

Why hadn't that happened in previous times when other leaders died, or at least when other leaders were assassinated?

Because of something unique to the early 1960s.

Television coverage of current events was new and made the 1960s the first public decade in the history of the world.

How many people attended the funeral of President Lincoln, or of any other President before the death of President Kennedy? There hadn't been a death of a President since 1945, before the age of television, while the funeral of President Kennedy was held in practically every American's home, and his assassin was shot in millions of living rooms.

And in war, how many people saw the bombardment of Fort Sumter in 1861? But shortly after President Kennedy's assassination, American's homes were invaded with the horror of battle in Vietnam, and above the noise of boiling water from the kitchen's pots came the blasts of gunfire and the noise of helicopters landing.

And even the city streets were in everyone's homes. Haight-Ashbury drug-addicts, and Pennsylvania Avenue demonstrators were as close as Mom and Dad's channel selector.

Television was on the minds and lips of everyone: Marshall McLuhan, Theodore White, the President of the United States, the organizers of demonstrations, the Queen of England, and Tiny Tim.

Never before had any medium held the world, and particularly the youth, so spellbound by its power, though the medium was still in its own adolescence.

It was death that invaded its adolescence and made it seem mature. As celebrities and lesser knowns and many warriors passed from earth, death became a frequent visitor to every home. Pictures of a horse that once amazed theater audiences because the horse's hooves seemed to rise and fall, were replaced by horses that pulled the caissons of Kennedy, Churchill, and Eisenhower through the homes of the nation. Before the decade was done, those closest to Dr. Martin Luther King, Jr. and Senator Robert Kennedy were grief-stricken before millions of Americans.

Through television, the new generation was continually experiencing what past generations had not known until much later in most people's lives.

In 1942, before the age of television, Carole Lombard was killed in an airplane accident. Half a year later, her last motion picture, Ernst Lubitsch's "To Be Or Not To Be," was released in theaters throughout the country. The release of the film was controversial. Many didn't see the film because they felt it was disrespectful to release a film showing someone who so recently had died. That feeling was in no way unusual — for those times.

But with the acceptance of television, it became common to view living images of those who had passed away within months of their death, within days, within hours, and even within minutes of their death. It also became common to watch the living pass through the barrier of time. A famous actor would be 80 years old at 7 o'clock on Channel Two and 30 years old at 11 o'clock on Channel Thirteen. Children became witnesses to aging in new time zones out of the chronology of life. And then the assassination, and it compounded television's perverse juxtaposition of age, and there came the desire to live life in a hurry and see it all and do it all. Quick.

Sex? Now. You may not be here tomorrow. Drugs? Try them for a quick fix. Experiment. Now. Anything. There was the television commercial for Pepsi Cola that headlined "The Now Generation." There was an ever-present and ominous threat that "Now" was close to "End." Television imbued that generation with a feeling of urgency as it played strange games with the calendars of life and age and beginnings and ends.

If that wasn't enough to change the nation, something else happened forty-seven days after the assassination of President Kennedy. On January 8, 1964, President Johnson made a radical change in the purposes of the federal government. Measures meant to be temporary by President Franklin Delano Roosevelt during depression and war and retained by Presidents Truman, Eisenhower, and Kennedy, were codified by President Johnson, and he added to them a litany of new powers for the federal government over the lives of the citizens. In contrast to the duties specified in the U.S. Constitution, he told the nation that his administration "today, here and now, declares unconditional War on Poverty in America, and I urge this Congress and all Americans to join me in that effort" by calling for expansion of the Area Redevelopment Program, enactment of a government youth employment program, broadening of the food stamp program, creation of a domestic National Service Corps, higher unemployment insurance, special school aid, and federal allocations for libraries, hospitals and nursing homes. He proposed "the most federal support in history for education, for health, for retraining the unemployed and for helping the economically and physically handicapped."

He then submitted to Congress a program for his War on Poverty which would cost $962,500,00 the first year, to be carried out by an Office of Economic Opportunity. "For the first time in our history, it is possible to conquer poverty," he said. "We have the power to strike away the barriers to full participation in our society. Having the power, we have the duty."

To help pay for The Great Society he called for reductions in defense. "We must not stockpile arms beyond our needs, or seek an excess of military power that could be provocative as well as wasteful. And it is in this spirit that in this fiscal year we are cutting back our production of enriched uranium by 25%; we are shutting down four plutonium piles; we are closing many non-essential military installations." He recommended a $1.1 billion cut in defense that year, close to the amount of his War on Poverty's first year allocation.

The majority of the Congress agreed and the major legislation was passed and the federal government was embarked on a changed course of purpose, taking responsibilities away from state and local governments. New federal departments and agencies and enlargements of selected bureaucracies were to carry out that change. The federal enclave became more powerful, and as is true for every government in any nation throughout history, each increase in power of the government to bring about the personal security of the individual brought a commensurate lessening of liberty for the individual.

Simultaneously the U.S. Supreme Court was acting as a legislature, changing the laws of the land rather than interpreting them, permitting vagrancy to flourish, giving rights of criminals beyond the rights of victims, and handcuffing local police forces. Social legislation that had even been defeated in the liberal Congress was passed in the Courts.

All three branches of the federal government were closing their eyes to the philosophy and the purpose of the federal government.

The new generation was living in a changed America, and the common belief of that new generation was that they were entitled to those things that went well beyond Constitutional limits. That word again, "entitlement," seemed to apply to anything wanted, and any difficulty in life that was encountered that displaced a person's personal pleasure was considered to be a fault of government, and to be corrected by government. Duty of the individual was considered to be a relic of the past. Instant gratification was far more important than the permanent good. There was no permanent good.

It was the assassination of President Kennedy, and the new medium of television, and the changing role of the federal government enacted by all three branches of the federal government, that provided dependence rather than independence and provided acceptance to the unacceptable.

The immoral became moral.

The moral became immoral.

Heroes became fools.

Fools became heroes.

The United States of America was on a path that had no visible off-ramp. And so it wasn't long until it came to other things that were attracted like magnets to that path:

Drug dealers on playgrounds of public schools.

Vagrants.

Gangs.

Riots.

Drive-by shootings.

Teen-age pregnancies in massive numbers.

Scrawled graffiti on private and public property.

Mothers and daughters begging on street corners.

Forbidden public parks.

Violent crime an every day event.

Once-great cities where daydreams of so many became realities in the pre-November days of our history, were transformed in one generation's time into living nightmares. And there is no way for our once-great cities and our once-great responsibilities and our once-great creativity and our once-great values to become great again until the citizenry recognizes what has happened, and we start carving a path away from the one on which we are blindly running.

PART FOUR

THE RIGHT OF WAY THROUGHOUT THE LAND

(DOMESTIC POLICY)

CHAPTER SIXTEEN

THE LONGEST ASSEMBLY LINE IN THE NATION

There is a recent phenomenon that was created by masters of temptation. It's the proliferation of mail-order gift catalogues with slick paper and colored pictures and each competing catalogue seems to have at least one thing in it that looks good and is totally unnecessary to own. The phenomenon reaches an annual crescendo in the weeks before Christmas when the bulk and quantity of those catalogues bend out the sides of a mailbox.

Those catalogues provide the dessert of capitalism.

Whatever it is that's irresistible in one catalogue or another, is probably available at a local store, but there is something about buying it from a catalogue that's more fun, so you send for it and what a torrent of joy when the brown box arrives. When you carry it from the mailbox to your residence you are no longer a regular human being, but an uncivilized animal enveloped in impatience. It isn't heavy but you're still breathless. "How come I can't open this thing? What kind of tape is this anyway? How come it doesn't just rip off? Where the devil is a knife or a scissors?" Absolute ecstasy.

Let's say you see one of those items in a catalogue and the price seems reasonable enough — in this case about $30. And the shipping and handling fees seem reasonable too — just a few dollars. But what if that $30 item has a shipping and handling fee of $70 for a total charge of $100?

Then there would be no temptation, no irresistibility, no impatience, no ecstasy; it's a rip-off. "Are they kidding? I could buy more than three of those items for that cost. I'll buy it at a place that's close to home, and not pay those exorbitant shipping and handling fees." That's exactly the dialogue we should be saying every day of our lives as Washington, D.C. charges for those things we could buy close to home: "Are they kidding? I could buy more than three of those items for that cost. I'll buy it at a place that's close to home, and not pay those exorbitant shipping and handling fees."

If, for example, welfare was treated close to home, as a local effort rather than far from home as a federal effort, its costs would be greatly reduced. With the provider close to the provided, it would be very difficult for those administering the welfare to use fraud and trickery. And the legitimate costs to the locality would be far less expensive than the costs of the federal government, because of its close oversight and because there would be no shipping and handling fees. But when the federal enclave runs welfare for the nation, fraud and trickery and shipping and handling fees run rampant. The Federal Welfare Industry that has grown in Washington, D.C. is the largest industry in the nation, and over the years Congresses have provided guarantees that the industry will continue to prosper. That prosperity of the Federal Welfare Industry is guaranteed through fooling the public.

On orders from the Congress, each year the U.S. Census Bureau releases a report of new poverty statistics. Generally the report is that one out of every eight Americans is living below the poverty line. The common reaction of the public is that such a figure is unacceptable and there is no excuse for that in the United States, and the federal government has to do more.

What the public doesn't know is Washington, D.C.'s welfare-secret: the figures will always be high, because under the Congress' orders, willingly obeyed by bureaucrats, the statisticians are not allowed to account for the bulk of things that poverty-level Americans receive in non-cash benefits. And so food stamps aren't counted as income, aid to families with dependent children isn't counted, Medicare isn't counted, energy assistance isn't counted, school breakfasts and lunches aren't counted, public housing isn't counted, and a litany of other benefits go unrecorded in the report that is released to the nation. Therefore no matter how much welfare benefits are increased, or new ones invented, those living below the poverty-level will not statistically be raised from below the poverty level. Conceivably, those receiving welfare benefits from the federal government could have the value of their welfare benefits raised to one billion dollars a year per person and they would still be listed below the poverty-line. Such statistics make the whole dilemma solutionless, which is exactly the way the majority of the members of the U.S. Congress want it because it gives the Congress power, and it's exactly what the bureaucrats of the Federal Welfare Industry want because it gives them life-time jobs.

The statisticians are given another order from the Congress that corrupts the figures: any asset owned by those below the poverty-level cannot be taken into account. In the figures of 1990, it was discounted that 38% of the people identified as poor owned their own homes, and 62% owned a car. The false statistics are the ones on which welfare budgets are based. The budgets are now so high that every person could be raised above the poverty-level and the taxpayers would save billions upon billions of dollars if the federal government would simply send checks to the recipients, rather than continue programs — the amount of the checks determined by what each of those people needs to rise above the poverty-level. But that would end the Federal Welfare Industry.

What our Federal Welfare Industry has done is make living below the poverty-line appealing, not only by giving awards of those things for which most others have to work, but also by giving the welfare recipient every-day holidays. The Congress is not about to correct those flaws by allowing local jurisdiction over welfare.

Waste is a minor crime contrasted to the destructiveness of the Federal Welfare Industry. Throwing the money away would be a comparatively positive function rather than the dispersal of benefits that have become the lifeblood of the industry. The War on Poverty that was started on January 8, 1964, has, over the years, turned into a War *for* Poverty: rewarding the woman who chooses to have an illegitimate child well beyond those who have a child in marriage, rewarding the father who chooses to abandon his mate and child well beyond those who choose the responsibility of devotion and support, and rewarding the non-worker well beyond the low-wage worker.

The choice is clear for those without experience at a craft: either work eight hours a day at one wage, or don't work at all and receive benefits totaling a higher standard of living than would be received with a job. For the woman with an illegitimate child, if she marries a man who is working, or lives with her parents, the penalties are severe, because her major rewards stop.

Shortly after the beginning of "The Great Society," illegitimacy became a "life-style," not a crisis, with the amount of illegitimate births rising year by year, until in many urban inner-cities, illegitimate births outnumbered children conceived in marriage.

The men who were nothing more than sperm-donors quickly left the women, and did not seek employment, but went to the corners of their neighborhoods, and on those corners they looked tough and acted tough, and were rewarded with benefits from the Federal Welfare Industry. Further, they received daily and nightly prestige by their peers, while they took and sold drugs, and engaged in urban warfare.

Why not?

Because it was wrong?

Society no longer determined right and wrong. Right and wrong were "moral judgments" that should not be made. Not in the Great Society.

Even in the courts, if they ever got there, there was little for criminals to fear. Convicted criminals found the penalties for their crimes negligible, with nine and out of ten convicted felons not going to prison, with convicted murderers being released from prison having served less than six years for the murder, and with rapists serving three years or less.

To make the War on Poverty palatable, the word "welfare" became "human services" with those living off the taxes of others becoming sacrosanct from criticism, even if the recipients were healthy and able. Their unemployment would be perceived as consequences of society rather than the fact that some preferred to live off the public dole, since that course was not only more lucrative, but because those who chose that course were treated with empathy rather than scorn. Poverty was a status symbol.

Before the War on Poverty (the longest war in American history as it continues to give weapons to the enemy,) homelessness was unknown in the United States, other than those drunks on stoops who were usually picked-up by the police. There was a distinction made between the legitimately poor who were helped, and the urban bum who was hauled off to jail. But with the inauguration of the War on Poverty, distinctions were erased and homelessness became an option of residence, with those on the streets regarded by liberal-lawmakers as the victimized heroes of America.

One night, members of the Congress, along with Hollywood celebrities, slept on the streets of Washington, D.C. with the homeless, spending the night with them to exhibit their support of more federal help. Instead of sleeping at the outdoor "home of the homeless," why didn't they invite the homeless to *their* homes? Wouldn't that have shown greater empathy?

The legislators and Hollywood celebrities were not empathetic; they were grandstanding. They could easily endure one night on the streets, rushing to their homes and hotel rooms the following morning to watch themselves on national television as the Morning Shows played videotapes of their night of compassion.

Soon, liberal federal lawmakers allocated funds for the homeless, those funds getting larger with each year's budgets. If the allocations continue to increase, the homeless will be permanent in America, as a bureaucracy will be created whose jobs will be dependent on the crisis. There will be a Secretary for the Homeless with a Department of the Homeless, and a giant stone building will be constructed in D.C. to house, not the homeless, but the new department of government.

The real victims of the War on Poverty are the urban-poor who choose to be married-parents, and choose to work, and have to face the dangers of the neighborhood on a daily and nightly basis.

There are poor people in the United States who, through no fault of their own, have become indigent. Before the Federal Welfare

Industry came into existence, friends, neighbors, charities, and localities took care of the truly unfortunate with both physical and psychological help in reversing their crisis. It worked.

But when something local in nature works, what makes it work is rejected in D.C., and in self-protection of the federal enclave, there is a quick turn towards a federal take-over and a federal take-over means its traditional investment in failure.

Failure loads the federal coffers and packs the stone buildings with bureaucrats in the federal triangle. When a department of government is successful it is stripped of funds. The War on Poverty and the War in the Persian Gulf collectively prove the rewards of failure and the punishments of success. As the War on Poverty creates more and more poverty, it is given more and more funds. When the Persian Gulf War was won, the Department of Defense was scalped.

The United States of America has been known as the most charitable and compassionate nation in the world. But that was before the Federal Welfare Industry created the longest assembly line in the nation, churning out benefits to all corners of the nation, paid for by taxpayer's funds, giving incentives to idleness, and giving disincentives to the prospective recipient's sense of responsibility.

Today, those in the nation who are worse off than others are not those who live in economic poverty, calculated by a scarcity of dollars. The worst off in the nation are some of those who work in D.C. who live in moral poverty, calculated by a scarcity of honor.

CHAPTER SEVENTEEN

YOU ARE CORDIALLY INVITED TO LIVE HERE ILLEGALLY, REGRETS ONLY

Throughout history, governments of one nation after another dealt with problems of emigration as their citizens attempted to leave their national borders. To keep their citizens in, walls were built and watchtowers were erected and armed guards were posted along the borders.

The United States, however, has never known an emigration problem. It has known and continues to know the most flattering problem of nationhood — the problem of immigration. People want to come in, and the United States accepts more legal immigrants than all other nations of the world combined.

But the United States also accepts more *illegal* immigrants than all other nations of the world combined. The difference between legal and illegal immigration can mean the future of a nation.

Illegal immigration is a term that is self-defining, and so those unwilling to be honest about it have called illegal immigrants "undocumented workers." By their failure to use the accurate term, they manage to cloak the crime. A refusal to use self-defining language is the sure sign that the speaker or writer does not want to deal with truth.

Illegal immigration could, of course, be controlled by giving the Border Patrol enough funds to patrol the border. But government invariably rejects logic. In the early 1990s, there were more people patrolling Capitol Hill in Washington, D.C. at night than were patrolling the southern and northern borders of the United States at night. At any one time there were no more than 650 people guarding our entire southern border, and even with that small amount, an average of 1000 illegal immigrants were turned back every night — but an average of 2000 a night were successful in avoiding the Border Patrol. In addition, the Immigration and Naturalization Service had no record for the departure of over 10% of the nine million annual visitors to the United States. The whereabouts of some 900,000 annual visitors were unknown.

Border control does not mean the building of a wall; and we should never have one. Border control does not mean that the military must be assigned to the southern and northern borders of the United States; they shouldn't be there. Border control does not mean that we need a suspension of all immigration; that would extinguish the welcome to those truly seeking liberty. What we do need is to effectively turn back illegal immigrants at our borders, and to know who we are allowing in, and where we can find the foreign visitor after arrival. And that solution should be implemented immediately, before a Pearl Harbor of terrorism wakes the nation into that policy after the fact.

Sheik Abdel Rahman, the terrorist leader from Egypt, received a U.S. tourist visa in 1989, a U.S. multiple-entry visa in 1990, and permanent residence in the United States in 1991.

Any nation that does not maintain jurisdiction of its borders, cannot guarantee its sovereignty.

The boldest action we could take would be to repeal more immigration laws than we enact. We have passed laws that give incentives to foreign nationals to leave their homes and enter the United States illegally. Our laws have had the same effect as an engraved invitation.

By law, illegal immigrants receive MedicAid, housing assistance, public education, school breakfasts and lunches, aid for families with dependent children, Home Energy Assistance, Emergency Medical Care, and other federal and state services paid for by those who are American citizens. In addition, illegal aliens receive an average of $23 in Social Security benefits for every $1 they pay into the system. In California the problem is acute. Over 70% of all births in Los Angeles

County Public Hospitals are to illegal alien mothers. "Cross the border, have a baby, and you have a United States Citizen in the family, who can receive all benefits of such citizenship." There is little wonder why so many expectant mothers rush to cross the border into the United States.

The illegal immigrant is not only rewarded by unprecedented benefits, but by a codified discouragement to learn the language of the United States. Bilingual education has become a federal law. And for those new citizens (sometimes with the citizenship proceedings in a foreign language) they can receive ballots in a language of their heritage which de facto overrides our previously made law that to become a citizen you must be able to "read and write and speak English in ordinary usage."

Our bilingual laws are not only an encouragement to reject the English language, the bilingual laws are an affront to all those immigrants who comply with the rules of citizenship, and a guarantee that the non-English speaking citizen will encounter hardship after hardship throughout life in the United States. Moreover, what degree of common sense would dictate that someone should vote who cannot read or understand what the candidates say?

Surely a child of school age is in the best position to learn the English language. With every passing year the ability to learn a language diminishes.

The states, taking their cue (and orders) from the federal government have enacted laws that have rejected all degrees of common sense:

California demands that its public schools offer education in 42 different languages. A federal district court judge in Arizona ruled that public employees cannot be required to speak English on the job. Bilingual education costs Texas taxpayers 51 million dollars a year according to the Texas Department of Education. Many states within the United States administer drivers' tests in multiple languages although traffic signs are in English.

We are erecting a new "separate but equal" element into the life of the United States, and at the same time laying the foundation for a crisis to come: divisions as extreme as secession and civil wars in other nations have erupted because of nothing more than language differences.

The United States, with its unique diversity of heritage of its citizens, has been the most successful country in the history of the world. There has never been a country in the world like it. It is the diversity of heritage, not the insistence of remaining a foreigner, that has made the United States successful, with our common language being the glue that has held those diverse heritages together. Bilingual laws soften the glue and cause the pieces of our unique fabric to break apart.

In the late 1970s and early 1980s, there was a U.S. Senator from California who advocated that English be made our national language; and he warned the nation that if such an action was not taken, the United States could be in peril, separating into blocks that would be at each other's throats because of a failure to communicate as one people. That prophecy has already come true in some areas of the country. In the last year of his Senatorial career he was serving with Senators whose names alone told the richness of the United States: Abdnor, Boshwitz, Deconcinni, Durenberger, Kennedy, Laxalt, Metzenbaum, Sarbanes, Tsongas, and Zorinsky. And his name was Hayakawa. What other country in the world ever had a legislative body with names of such ancestral diversity? None. What if those Senators had grown up without learning the English language? What if they rejected the American way of life in favor of remaining strangers among other Americans?

What talented people are we wasting today by discouraging their use of the English language and American culture?

Every federal law regarding bilingual education and bilingual ballots should be abolished. And welfare payments and other benefits to illegal immigrants should be abolished.

The laws that have thus far been enacted as ways to stem illegal immigration have been dismal failures:

Congress authorized an amnesty provision for those who have been in the United States illegally for five years, which was a further affront to all those immigrants who sought and worked for and attained legal status in the United States. Further, such amnesty, once given, only encouraged prospective illegal immigrants to come across the border and wait it out until a new amnesty would be enacted that would cover them. They recognize, justifiably, that if the United States Congress did it once, the United States Congress can do it again.

Congress authorized a law that employers would be punished who hired illegal immigrants. Such laws turned employers into police and such sanctions enhanced prejudice. Under such law, employers look carefully for a skin-tone that is different than their own, and they listen carefully for an accent that is different from their own. Those without prejudice have been encouraged to adopt prejudice.

In addition, a National Identity Card has been suggested for legislation in almost every session of the Congress. But such documentation would allow government-control over movement of our own citizens that should be untenable in a free society. The better idea is to use what is already available: The Immigration and Naturalization Service already maintains a list of legal residents of the United States through a computerized system called SAVE, an acronym for the Systematic Alien Verification for Entitlement. If the welfare request comes from someone not listed in the SAVE system, the benefits should be denied.

There have been other factors that call for correction:

A new case must be brought through the courts in an attempt to overturn the weird 5-4 decision made by the Supreme Court in 1982 called "Plyler v. Doe" which requires the states to provide public education to the children of illegal immigrants.

"Sanctuary Status" that cities have given themselves in defiance of federal laws, must be prosecuted. Such "Sanctuary Cities" have held themselves above U.S. law, and promise illegal immigrants safe havens from the United States Immigration and Naturalization Service.

What should determine whether or not a citizen of another country should be granted residence in our country? Our system of immigration should be based, first, on the degree of persecution from the country of origin, and whether or not the government of the country accused of persecution is friendly or unfriendly to the United States. If the government of the country condemned by the emigrant, is a government that is friendly to the United States, the requested immigration should be denied in favor of the prospective immigrant going to a nation that harbors that person's own political appetite. The Refugee Act of 1980 allows anyone from a foreign nation, once here, to file for asylum in the United States as long as there is fear of persecution if they return to their native home. Almost as soon as that refugee act was put into law, prospective immigrants arrived from El Salvador and Guatemala claiming such refugee status. But there were "safe haven" refugee camps sponsored by the United Nations Organization close to where those people had lived. The U.N. refugee camps were located in El Salvador, Costa Rica, Honduras and Mexico.

If those people had legitimate fears of persecution in El Salvador and Guatemala they could have claimed refuge status in any one of those camps. More questionable was that since the governments from which those people claimed persecution, were friendly to the United States Government, why didn't those people escape to Cuba or Nicaragua where the refugee's political beliefs would match the political beliefs of their new host-government?

Why did they choose to come to the United States, whose policies the refugee opposed? In those days refugees from East Germany did not attempt an escape into the Soviet Union, they attempted to reach West Germany; and refugees from Laos did not attempt to go east to Vietnam, they went west to Thailand. Why would any true political refugee escaping persecution, want to escape to the country that is the benefactor of the country the refugee has elected to leave? Our acceptance of any such immigrant took accommodation away from someone who wanted to come here who embraced the United States.

The Refugee Act of 1980 should be amended to define refugee status with more political clarity and precision. The person we classify as a legitimate refugee for legal residence in the United States should be one who seeks liberty, escaping from a government that is in opposition to the United States.

The next line of factors for legal residence should be the prospective immigrant's skills and the guarantee of being taken care of in this country by relatives or friends who accept such responsibility.

In our lack of doing what should be done about illegal immigration we have encouraged hostility among so many American citizens that a cry started to be sounded for an end of *all* immigration, illegal and *legal*: "Stop!" voices yelled from within our borders. "We have enough. It's time to close the gates."

Isn't it fortunate then, that those who yell for such closure of the gates had ancestors that made it here before such a closure? How they forget (if they ever learned), that there were always people in the United States who were warning the government to close the gates and let in no more immigrants because, it was said, there were enough. With wisdom, the government did not stop legal immigration, and the open gates provided this country with talent and energy that helped those previously here to embark on the greatest economic expansion of any nation in the history of the world, to say nothing of the greatest national morality in the history of the world.

Has it reached its limit?

Will new immigrants be taking from "us"?

Who is "us"?

If the nation remains true to its purpose, "us" are those who crave liberty above all, and are willing to live and die for such liberty. Of all criteria, "us" should not mean those who met a deadline imposed by others already here.

But national committees have been organized, and spokespeople of those committees warn the nation of what they consider to be the crisis that will be created by a further influx of refugees and other legal immigrants. Those committees and spokespeople are echoes of selfishness that are heard around the world: beyond the shores of the United States, international forums convene with regularity to discuss population control.

The bottom-line of both the national committees and the international forums is that the world faces the risk of "too many people." It should be noted, however, that in all cases, without exception, the line that is drawn to establish the stopping-point comes after the speaker's own birth. The speakers at such committees and forums do not say, "Kill me. That will help solve the population problem."

There is, instead, the overwhelming belief of such speakers that "I'm here and you can see how valuable I turned out to be" but "the unborn won't be as good as me. They will be a burden." Never mind that in the last 200 years the world population grew six-fold while the world output grew eighty-fold. Never mind that three-tenths of one percent of the earth's land is being used for human settlements. Never mind that food production has outpaced population, and with the doubling of the world's population in the last fifty years, food production has tripled. Never mind that the arable land in India alone could feed the world.

In 1960 Hong Kong had a population of three million people. That small urban center was packed and it seemed as though there wasn't enough room for one more person on those crowded streets. From Victoria Peak that overlooked the city, there was a view that allowed the top of the city's buildings to be seen, and on top of every commercial building, squatter's huts were highly visible; little rotten run-down shacks by the thousands built on the roof-tops of those buildings. What a miserable sight. What a sure sign of poverty and overcrowding. Something had to be done, it was said, to stop the immigration from the Chinese mainland. And all kinds of attempts were made. Some were successful for a short time, but the refugees didn't stop. Nor did people stop having children.

And the population kept rising and rising until it near-doubled in thirty years. But the view from Victoria Peak was no longer inhospitable. There was not one squatter's hut on the top of any building, and Hong Kong had a far more vibrant economy than it had thirty years before. Hong Kong prospered beyond 1960s imagination.

People were an asset — because the people had talent and imagination and creativity and values and had passion for liberties they were denied north of the border, in China.

An ocean away, the United States of America has been the inspiration for all those who sought liberty. It was the Goddess of Democracy, a representation of our Statue of Liberty, that was erected in Tiananman Square by those who sought liberty within the borders of China.

The fabric of our country has been made strong by the joining together of uncommon heritages into a common nationality with a common language and a common passion for liberty.

Often the greatest patriots in this nation are those who were born in distant lands run by totalitarians. Those who lived in an absence of liberty are generally the ones who treasure most the opportunity to be free.

I remember vividly a day in Washington, D.C. when a member of the Congress who was a jerk with no convictions, confided to me that he plans to be the President of the United States. Under the Constitution, he qualified for the U.S. Presidency. Within hours I spent time with a U.S. citizen born in Moscow. With tears in his eyes, he told me the virtues of the United States and how liberty is sometimes under-appreciated by those who have always known such liberty. Under the Constitution he did not qualify for the U.S. Presidency. The United States Constitution allows every advantage to the legal immigrant who becomes a citizen of the United States as one who was born here — except that it prohibits those who were not born in the United States from becoming President of the United States. That exclusion is the only prejudice in the U.S. Constitution. Since the U.S. Constitution also prohibits anyone under 35 years of age from becoming President (wisely), it would only be proper that an amendment to the Constitution be enacted allowing the foreign-born to become President, but only after 35 years of citizenship. That would make the criterion of eligibility consistent, calling for 35 years of citizenship rather than using the quirk of fate that might have determined birth; and such an amendment would remove the psychological barrier that separates a foreign-born citizen from all other citizens. The amendment should read, "United States citizens born outside of the United States shall be eligible to occupy the Office of the Presidency after 35 years of United States citizenship."

This nation's power of magnetism comes from the world-known knowledge that a government can exist whose purpose is the liberty of the citizen.

People in foreign lands often use shorthand in the title they give the United States of America. They say "The U.S.," "The U.S.A.," "The States," and "America." But the name this nation is called by those who choose the challenge of liberty is the name this nation appreciates most:

Home.

CHAPTER EIGHTEEN
D.C. STANDS FOR DOMESTIC CONTROL

Although the Founders of the nation used only 52 words to set into writing the purpose and functions of the United States Government, two centuries later it took federal regulators 11,400 words to set into writing one directive for growing olives in California.

There are 41,000 federal regulations for a Big Mac Hamburger and any other hamburger made at McDonalds or Wendy's or Burger King or any of the other commercial hamburger outlets of the United States. Number 32,674 states that the catsup has to be Grade A fancy and it must flow no more than nine centimeters in thirty seconds at sixty-nine degrees Fahrenheit — or else.

The Code of Federal Regulations governs almost every phase of the lives of U.S. citizens, costing taxpayers 461.4 billion dollars a year (1992) and at least double that number of headaches. One by one, each regulation may seem innocent enough, and some may appear to be virtuous, but they provide links in the chain that is strangling the nation.

Private enterprise is the heart of capitalism, and regulatory agencies have become daggers into that heart. If you want to start a business of your own today, the IRS will tell you what earnings you must surrender, the EPA will tell you where you can and can't build, OSHA will dictate safety requirements, the EEOC will tell you whom you must hire and whom you can't hire, if you transport inter-state the NHTSA will tell you what vehicle you can use, the ICC will tell you what routes you must take, the SEC will tell you what you must disclose financially, and after 78 more policing bureaucracies tell you how to spend your life in business, the IRS will come back and tell you how much of your business you can't leave for a loved one to inherit.

The pharmaceutical company, Eli Lilly and Company, estimates that it fills out 27,000 forms each year for the federal government, at a cost of five million dollars to fill out those forms, and its total cost of compliance with the regulations is fifteen million dollars. Eli Lilly and Company's application for government approval of a new arthritis drug weighed more than one ton.

The Sohio Petroleum Company abandoned a project to build a pipeline for transporting California oil to Texas, which could have eased the nation's energy needs with the use of the pipeline substituting for shipping the oil in tankers through the Panama Canal. Sohio gave it up because after spending more than 50 million dollars for 715 government licenses, and still encountering more regulatory obstacles, it just wasn't worth it to Sohio anymore.

General Motors has more than 20,000 full-time employees doing nothing but working on government regulations compliance. Goodyear Tire and Rubber Company spends more than $38 million a year in compliance costs. The Chairman of DuPont said that if his company were attempting to start today, it's likely that DuPont would not get to the starting gate, due to current licensing procedures and regulations.

But it isn't private industry that's the chief victim of all this; it's the citizen. Since private enterprise is unequipped to be a charity for government use, increased regulations cause a private enterprise to either go out of business, or lower the wages or number of employees, or lower the quality of its output, or increase the price of its products and services. By 1993 the approximate cost in regulatory burdens to the average American family was $12,500 per year.

Unlike other charges, the customers are most often not told when or how they must pay for government regulations. The price of an automobile includes an average of $700 in easily identifiable regulatory fees. The average hospital patient's bill is increased by 42% because of government regulations. Health Insurance Companies have to obey over one thousand government regulations. (If government did less rather than more, health costs would come down dramatically.) The cost of a new home is increased around 19% because of regulations.

And the cost of regulations goes unmeasured when it comes to those items that are not tabulated in economics, but in other costs in daily life:

A government regulation ordered the schools in Oak Ridge, Tennessee, to ensure that both boys and girls sports teams were cheered equally by their cheerleaders.

A rancher was ordered by a federal government agent to label his two private bathrooms "men" and "women" even though he lived alone.

The Bureau of Land Management wanted to buy some fire equipment for two pick-up trucks. They issued 155 pages of requirements, including 23 fold-out diagrams. The low bid was $31,000 which included $24,000 for processing the regulations. The cost of the equipment itself was only $8,000.

The Department of Energy ordered Washington, D.C. to allow right turns on red lights, therefore costing $300,000 to put up signs forbidding the right turns at more than 80% of the city's intersections.

The state of Wyoming turned down a juvenile-justice $20,000 grant from the federal government because it would have cost $500,000 in paper work to obtain the $20,000 grant.

In California a ten year old boy opened a bicycle repair shop. He did so well that he hired three of his friends to help him. He had to close down, however, when the Labor Relations Board cited him for employing minors.

Cowboys were ordered by the Occupational Safety and Health Administration to work within a five minute ride (by horse) to a toilet.

The Occupational Safety and Health Administration ordered backup alarms on vehicles at construction sites, while it simultaneously ordered employees at those sites to wear ear plugs, making it virtually impossible for those employees to hear the alarms.

The ones who prosper from the army of regulators are those in the army itself. By the early 1990s the army consisted of 122,400 regulators. With each new regulation, the number of bureaucrats and the scope of the bureaucracy increases, and its enforcement powers grow, while the private sector diminishes. The Consumer Product Safety Commission had a budget of less than $1 million in 1973 and within six years after its birth, its budget increased to $40 million which was an increase of 4000%. Every time a new federal law is passed, that law has to be administered and enforced and the bureaucracy's regulators spring into life and write up the ways in which the new law must be attended:

"No person shall prune, cut, carry away, pull up, dig, fell, bore, chop, saw, chip, pick, move, sever, climb, molest, take, break, deface, destroy, set fire to, burn, scorch, carve, paint, mark, or in any manner interfere with, tamper, mutilate, misuse, disturb or damage any tree, shrub, plant, grass, flower, or part thereof, nor shall any person permit any chemical, whether solid, fluid, or gaseous, to seep, drip, drain or be emptied, sprayed, dusted or injected upon, about or into any tree, shrub, plant, grass, flower, or part thereof."

All of this started in 1899 when Michigan ordered horseshoers to have licenses.

Two years later, in 1901, New York State demanded that villages have licenses for the running of public carriages, cabs, hacks, carts, drays, express wagons, auctioneering, hawking, the keeping of billiard saloons, the doing of a retail business in the sale of goods of any description, and we were on our way.

In 1930, three years before he became President of the United States, Franklin Delano Roosevelt said, "If we do not halt this steady process of building commissions and regulatory bodies and special legislation like huge inverted pyramids over every one of the simple constitutional provisions, we shall soon be spending billions of dollars more."

Power grows every time a new form leaves a bureaucrat's office. The Clean Air Act of 1990 meant that small companies would be compelled to spend more than $10,000 each for pollution permits.

In 1977 President Carter initiated the U.S. Department of Energy and said at its inauguration, "I want to point out that the department can now, I think, begin to deal in a much more aggressive and effective way, not only with the needs of supplies to increase the production of oil, gas, coal, solar and nuclear powers, but also to make sure that consumers of our country are treated fairly, that prices are adequate and not excessive." Enter $10 billion for the first year of the new department, and 20,000 bureaucrats. Enter regulations on energy beyond anything known in the past. There were new regulations on the price of old oil versus new oil, regulations on allocations, even regulations on how much a gasoline station could charge. If those gasoline station operators did not comply with the new regulations, he or she could be fined ten thousand dollars and be put in prison. The only way for gasoline station operators to stay in business (and many didn't) was to offer less services. Self-service gasoline stations became predominant with the customer responsible for filling the gasoline tank, checking water and oil under the hood, and cleaning the windshield; services that had previously been customarily provided by gasoline station attendants.

In two years time the Department of Energy developed over one thousand, five hundred new regulations. Regulations made it more advantageous for the U.S. oil industry to abandon many investments in the United States and invest more overseas. It was not long until the United States had to rely more on foreign oil than at any time in U.S. history, importing 56% by 1993.

OSHA became law as the Occupational Safety and Health Act and the "A" in OSHA quickly changed from the word "Act" to the word "Administration," and it immediately started defining everything that could be found in a place of business. Do you know what an "exit" is? "That portion of a means of egress which is separated from all other spaces of the building or structure by construction or equipment as required in this subpart to provide a protected way of travel to the exit discharge." Once defined, regulators could inspect exits in businesses all over the country to see if they lived up to the code. Do you know what a ladder is? "A ladder is an appliance usually consisting of two side rails joined at regular intervals by crosspieces called steps, rungs, cleats, on which a person may step in ascending or descending." Then various types of ladders are described in detail, with this added: "The angle (a) between the loaded and unloaded rails and the horizontal is to be calculated from the trigonometric equation: Sine (a) equals difference in deflection/over ladder width." Within its first three years of operation OSHA cost the citizens of the country $26 billion in new regulations. Was it worth it? The percentage of job-related injuries and illnesses didn't decrease, they increased.

Has the environment improved since the birth of the Environmental Protection Agency with its host of regulations? Have the inner-cities improved since the birth of the Department of Housing and Urban Development with housing regulations? Has education improved since the birth of the Department of Education with its regulatory oversight of local schools? Have the roads become safer and better since the birth of the Department of Transportation with its expanding code of regulations? But each year those departments of government are rewarded with bigger and bigger budgets.

How can the regulatory labyrinth of bureaucracies be put under control? Every regulatory entity of government should live under a Sunset Provision written into its ongoing legislation, which would mean that the government entity would go out of business unless it could prove success, and prove either a neutral or positive economic impact, and prove non-violation of constitutional rights of the citizens.

James Madison warned that he believed "there are more instances of the abridgment of the freedom of the people by gradual and silent encroachments of those in power, than by violent and sudden usurpations."

Thomas Jefferson told the government to leave the people free "to regulate their own pursuits of industry and improvement" and within the Declaration of Independence, he wrote a litany of charges against King George the Third, stating that he "has erected a multitude of new offices, and sent hither swarms of officers to harass our people and eat out their substance."

Today it is our own federal government that is abridging the freedom of the people by gradual and silent encroachments, and our own federal government that regulates the citizen's industry and improvement, and our own federal government that has erected a multitude of new offices, and sends hither swarms of officers to harass our people and eat out their substance.

CHAPTER NINETEEN

RETROACTIVE MORALITY

I don't remember the date, not even the year, but it was some time in the 1940s when the *Reader's Digest* published a paragraph near the bottom of a page, regarding a particular slice of life. It was when southern states were segregated. The paragraph told about a family that moved from the south to the north, and the boy in the family came home from school and asked his mother if he could bring a new friend over for lunch later that week. His mother said "sure," but then began to think about it. The family was now in a northern state, and so the school her son was attending was integrated. She asked her son, "Is your new friend that you want to bring over — is he a negro?" The boy looked at his mother with a confused expression and he pondered the question. After a while he answered, "I don't know. I'll look tomorrow."

The boy had not been educated yet into the world of prejudice. Oscar Hammerstein II put it best in the song from "South Pacific": "You Got To Be Carefully Taught," whose lyrics told that no one is born prejudiced, but prejudice is educated into a person, by a child being "carefully taught, before you are six or seven or eight, to hate all the people your relatives hate. You got to be carefully taught."

And taught they are, with the most prestigious educators of prejudice practicing their craft from Washington, D.C. Just as Paris was once the fashion capital determining the latest styles in clothing, Washington, D.C. has become the fashion capital that determines the latest elitist prejudice for the nation.

It was in 1993 at a party in Georgetown that, like a new wardrobe, the prejudice of the times was on display. While the party-goers stumbled over the word "mankind" and quickly corrected themselves to make it "humankind" so as to prove they believed in equality for women, and while they carefully counted the races and religions and ethnicities represented in the room, conversation was thick with the prejudice that was "in": Prejudice against the rich.

The trend-setters at the party were, themselves, by almost any definition, well above the median income but they considered themselves to be "the good rich" in the same way that years back there was always "the good negro" and "the good" of any minority ethnicity. This night the conversations were interspersed with love for minority races and hatred for the rich which, one supposes, had to mean that no person of minority ethnicity is rich and no rich person is of a minority ethnicity or there would be too much confusion in the new prejudice-advocacy.

This prejudice came all the way from the White House and Capitol Hill where it was quite acceptable for the President and members of the Congress to speak publicly with rancor and scorn against "the fat cats" and "the well-off." No one could get away with speaking that way about any other minority, but there is an acceptability about throwing epithets at the rich. And the reason is simple; most people would like to have more money, so the rich are envied. Probably very few people hope that some day they will be in a racial or ethnic minority to which they don't already belong, but they do hope they'll become millionaires. There are often lines waiting to buy lottery tickets because maybe, just maybe, buying a ticket will make the purchaser one of the minority of millionaires. I would doubt that there would be lines if the lottery offered a grand prize of becoming a minority, other than the minority of holders of wealth. Therefore, they say, "they must be taxed a higher percentage than the rest of us." That should make the envious happy. In truth, if those making above $200,000 were taxed on 100% of their earnings, the government would be able to operate for only 108 days. (If the 100% tax was limited only to those who earned one million dollars or above, the government would only be able to operate for 33 days.)

Those who are prejudiced against the rich have the capability to be prejudiced against anyone, since prejudice is nothing more or less than taking one characteristic held in common by a number of people and making that characteristic more important than the individual. The evil is not determined by the group chosen, but by the fact that any group can be chosen.

Nowhere is prejudice more evident than in political campaigns, and those statements often made by the candidates, by the pundits, by the analysts, and by the poll-takers, when they talk about "The Black Vote" and "The Jewish Vote" and "The Italian Vote" and one "Group Vote" after another.

Are they, in fact, saying that those who qualify to be in one of those "groups" are no more than cattle going into a voting booth marking the ballot the same as "others within that group," whereas those not in the defined groups are diverse and free-thinking and individualistic people who may vote for just about anyone since they look at all the issues?

It's as though candidates must talk only about Affirmative Action Programs when talking to someone whose ancestors came from Nigeria or Togo, and must talk about Israel when talking to Jews, and must talk about abortion when talking to women, and must talk about immigration laws when talking to those of Mexican descent.

Prejudice will be on the way out when candidates talk to one audience as they talk to other audiences without any pandering, and prejudice will be gone when candidates go to South Central Los Angeles and talk about oil-imports, when candidates go to the B'Nai Hayim and talk about China, when candidates go to The Women's Civic Organization and talk about deficit-reduction, when candidates go to Olvera Street and talk about Bosnia.

Buddha said, "When a man speaks the truth he speaks to all men equally. Only the liar chooses his audience with care."

Liars whose careers dwell in political life are often influenced to choose their advocacies with care by those on the outskirts of elective office who claim to be "Hispanic Leaders" and "Women's Leaders" and "Black Leaders" and other "something" leaders whose only credentials are their egos. Unelected by the group over which they claim leadership, they regard themselves as the voice and image for all who bear the same race or religion or heritage or sex, although there are no records of competitions they won to attain that leadership, and no ballots that can be produced to show the choice of the people they claim to represent. Such self-proclaimed leaders find their power is not with the "group" they pretend to lead, but with candidates from outside such a "group" who fear that perhaps that person has the power that he or she claims.

That self-proclaimed leader then extracts from the candidate a slate of promises, and that "leader" takes those promises back to the "group" as proof of his or her ability to influence the mighty.

What the "group" does not recognize is that any candidate who promises some favor to one group must rob from another to grant such favor.

Prejudice provides a market-place full of material for candidates. How is it possible that in the most advanced civilization in the world, close to the end of the 20th Century, there is still prejudice that is so real that candidates for office get trapped by it and, at times, seize it? How come this absolute stupidity continues and its evidences are seen so often?

It is because of the instinct of too many politicians to trade prejudices, one for the other, rather than end prejudice itself. Politicians take the clay of prejudice, and unwilling to let it dry and be smashed into oblivion, consistently keep the clay of prejudice wet, and in its wetness, their clay is reshaped into new images. And too many people follow.

As soon as the word "nigger" became unacceptable, the word "wasp" was established.

When alcohol became denounced, the taking of narcotics became acceptable as experimental and recreational.

When criminals were dealt with as subjects for rehabilitation, the police were condemned.

When new poverty programs were initiated by the government, hostility against the wealthy became acceptable.

Prejudice is not considered to be wrong as long as the prejudice isn't aimed at yesterday's target.

Affirmative Action programs have become the epitome of such transformations. They didn't begin that way; they began with the clearest justification and the cleanest motivation. The beginning came in President Kennedy's Executive Order 10925 to end racial discrimination by government contractors. Then in 1965 the term became prominent by way of Executive Order 11246 signed by President Johnson and supported by Dr. Martin Luther King, Jr. The order instructed government contractors to take "affirmative action to ensure that applicants are employed without regard to their race, creed, color, or national origin." In other words, no prejudice. Color-blind.

But if we are in favor of the original concept of affirmative action, then we should oppose practically every Affirmative Action Program of more recent years, because the definition has been changed to mean that applicants are employed, not *without*, but *with* regard to race, creed, color or national origin. It has become prejudiced to be unprejudiced.

Affirmative Action has become one of the most insulting, degrading, and demeaning programs for those it professes to help. It indicates an assumption that those helped do not have the right stuff by talent or ability alone. It brings about a suspicion on the part of others that a particular person may have a job or position, not because of that person's qualifications over other applicants, but because of the employers need to accommodate an Affirmative Action Program.

But what if, for example, a person of African or Caribbean heritage that has been hired is much better qualified than any person of another heritage who applied for the job? As an observer, how would you know? Bill Pearl, the brilliant commentator of California, put it in terms of an emergency room at a hospital. I'm paraphrasing his example, but what if someone you loved needed to go to an emergency room in a hospital, and you brought your loved one there, and you found two doctors, and one was of Nigerian descent, and you knew the hospital had an Affirmative Action hiring program. Wouldn't you be suspicious that the one who was Nigerian (and you could tell because of his complexion) might have been hired because of race? Wouldn't you be more inclined to choose the doctor whose skin was lighter? If there was no Affirmative Action Program and there were two doctors with different complexions, it would make no difference which one you would choose, the complexion of their skins would be an asinine criterion on which to make a judgment. As long as there are Affirmative Action Programs that demand that the person who obtained the job be granted the position because of being a group-designate, there will always be suspicion on the part of those who must entrust that person.

(Other than when necessary, I refuse to use the terms "black" and "white" because such use suggests that complexion is important. The term "African-American" is worse, because it not only suggests complexion, but it sanctions hyphenated Americans and makes heritage as important as citizenship.)

Making up for history only breeds revenge for revenge, in an endless repression, and calls for retroactive morality. Therefore, what should have been the abolition of prejudice has become the perpetuation of prejudice. Past injustices cannot be corrected by imposing current injustices. Further, the Fourteenth Amendment of the U.S. Constitution demands equal protection of the laws. U.S. Supreme Court Associate Justice William Douglas, an acknowledged liberal, admitted that there "is no way to reconcile a quota system with the Fourteenth Amendment."

Still, hands of too many politicians are grayed from working with the clay and enjoying it. Affirmative Action Programs should be abolished because they have skewed the true definition of affirmative action. Some day this nation is going to look at a person as a human being, period — not as a part of a group of "different kind of people."

It was during the second gasoline-shortage that I stumbled across a new "different kind of people," a "new group," and a new desire for a new affirmative action program for a new minority. It makes as much sense as any of the previous and current prejudices. In that spring, some states adopted the policy of allowing the filling of automobile tanks with gasoline only on alternate days.

Those with license plates that ended in an odd number could have their tanks filled only on odd-numbered days, and those with license plates that ended with even numbers could have their tanks filled only on even-numbered days.

My license plate ended in "9."

In time I began to notice that there was something different about those people who had plates that ended in an even number.

A lack of humility. A little arrogance. A chip on their shoulders. I didn't want to start open hostility of the odds against the evens, but those evens did seem to drive at a somewhat faster speed than us odds; they had little smirks on their faces, and for some reason it always seemed to be an even-numbered day. Upon waking up I would discover that it was the 4th or the 6th or the 10th of the month and the odd-numbered days were coming less and less frequently.

And on even-numbered days the lines of cars at the gasoline stations seemed to be much shorter than they were for the people whose license plates ended in 1's and 3's and 5's and 7's and 9's, on odd-numbered days. And the evens were content to wait in line without impatience as though they knew some secret that the odds hadn't been told. While they were waiting in line at the gasoline stations, they were always outside their cars having coffee and doughnuts being served by pretty women in shorts and everyone was laughing together. On odd-numbered days there were no pretty women in shorts and everyone stayed in their cars looking grim; it was very serious in line, and it was very hot.

At the time I was considering the introduction of legislation for the state in which I lived (California), canceling all even-numbered days for a period of time. June would go from the 1st through the 59th and, if necessary, while the rest of the country started August we would continue on until June the 121st.

In suggesting that idea, however, I was accused of being prejudiced. But I was certain that I was not prejudiced and, in fact, some of my best friends had even-numbered plates, but after going through this crisis, I did not want them parking in the garage next door.

The legislation never came to pass and I know now where I made my mistake. As an odd-numbered leader I did not search out a politician and tell that politician that I represented a tremendously large group that could bring that politician victory. I should have done that, assuring that politician that under the conditions of my representation, I could deliver half the votes in my state.

If there are any young readers, all that is written in the few paragraphs above tells you everything you'll ever need to know about prejudice.

CHAPTER TWENTY

COMPASSION BY COMPULSION

Georgetown is not normally visible from Capitol Hill, but it was not a normal night. In the summer of 1828 a huge fire in Georgetown lit the sky, and a number of Congressmen, including Congressman Davy Crockett, were walking out of the Capitol Building down the giant west staircase, when they saw the reddened sky and flames leaping above the north-western horizon. They rushed to Georgetown in a hack to help put out the fire.

The following day, some of the same Congressmen offered a bill to the House of Representatives to appropriate $20,000 for the victims of the Georgetown fire in an effort to help them rebuild. In comparison with the damage sustained, it was a small amount of money.

When Davy Crockett was running for re-election he was reminded of that fire by a constituent, Horatio Bunce, who said he would never again vote for Congressman Crockett.

As recorded in Edward Ellis' *The Life of Colonel Davy Crockett* published in 1884, the constituent said, "Your understanding of the Constitution is very different from mine...The Constitution, to be worth anything, must be held sacred, and rigidly observed in all its provisions...You voted for a bill to appropriate $20,000 to some sufferers by a fire in Georgetown...It is not the amount, Colonel, that I complain of; it is the principle...The power of collecting and disbursing money at pleasure is the most dangerous power that can be intrusted to man, particularly under our system of collecting revenue by a tariff, which reaches every man in the country...If you had the right to give anything, the amount was simply a matter of discretion with you, and you had as much right to give $20,000,000 as $20,000. If you have the right to give to one, you have the right to give to all and, as the Constitution neither defines charity nor stipulates the amount, you are at liberty to give to any and everything which you may believe, or profess to believe, is a charity, and to any amount you may think proper. You will very easily perceive what a wide door this would open for fraud and corruption and favoritism, on the one hand, and for robbing the people on the other. No, Colonel, Congress has no right to give charity. Individual members may give as much of their own money as they please, but they have no right to touch a dollar of the public money for that purpose...The people of Washington, no doubt, applauded you for relieving them from the necessity of giving, by giving what was not yours to give...I have no doubt you acted honestly, but that does not make it any better, except as far as you are personally concerned, and so you see that I cannot vote for you."

That is not the end of the story:

The effect on Davy Crockett was indelible and it came to public attention two years later when a naval hero died in Washington, D.C. The naval hero and his wife were well known and highly respected among the Washingtonians of the time. The day after the naval hero's death a bill was proposed in the House of Representatives to award the naval hero's widow $10,000. Dozens of Congressmen lined up on the floor of the House of Representatives to go to its Well and deliver a speech in support of the appropriation for the widow of the naval hero. Congressman Davy Crockett listened to those speeches skeptically as he remembered the constituent who talked with him two years earlier.

When it came to Congressman Crockett's turn to make his speech he did not repeat or paraphrase the words of his colleagues who had talked about "so small a figure for such a worthy act of compassion." Instead he said, "Mr. Speaker, I have as much respect for the memory of the deceased, and as much sympathy for the sufferings of the living, if suffering there be, as any man in this House, But we must not permit our respect for the dead or our sympathy for a part of the living to lead us into an act of injustice to the balance of the living. I will not go into an argument to prove that Congress has no power to appropriate this money as an act of charity. Every member upon this floor knows it. We have the right, as individuals, to give away as much of our own money as we please in charity; but as members of the Congress we have no right to appropriate a dollar of the public money...We cannot, without the greatest corruption, appropriate this money as payment of a debt. We have not the semblance of authority to appropriate it as a charity. Mr. Speaker, I have said we have the right to give as much money of our own as we please. I am the poorest man on this floor. I cannot vote for this bill, but I will give one week's pay to the object, and if every member of this Congress will do the same, it will amount to more than the bill asks."

None of them, not one of them other than Davy Crockett would offer his own money. Although Davy Crockett would be known to future generations, not for his years in the House of Representatives, but for his heroism in other fields that ended in his death at the Alamo, this little known incident was to be one of the most heroic days of his life.

After 163 years passed, in July of 1993, the caretaker of the Lincoln Memorial died. He had been the caretaker for seven years on temporary status. That temporary status did not entitle him to the benefits given to permanent workers. The day after the caretaker's death, a bill was proposed in the House of Representatives to help other long-term temporary workers like him achieve benefits, and the bill also appropriated $38,400 to the widow of the caretaker. Members of the House of Representatives, one after the other, spoke in support of the appropriation for the caretaker's widow. The bill passed the House and went on to pass the Senate. Delegate Eleanor Holmes Norton (D-DC) who initiated the legislation, called the proposal "small and compassionate" and "seized the imagination and touched the hearts of the members" of the Congress.

Had everyone in the House of Representatives in 1830 given a week's salary to the widow of the naval hero, she would have received a total of $13,000. Had everyone in the House of Representatives in 1993 given a week's salary to the widow of the caretaker of the Lincoln Memorial, she would have received a total of $1,083,317.31.

Shortly before the caretaker's death, the Congress had appropriated 7.6 billion dollars for the victims of Hurricane Andrew in Florida and Louisiana, and victims of a volcano in Hawaii, and victims of a typhoon in Guam, and 1.3 billion dollars for victims of a riot in Los Angeles. The federal government is heavily into the business of charity with the Congress deciding what is and what is not a charitable appropriation by use of the public purse. Further, the tax code directs that if a taxpayer gives to a charity of his or her choice, there is a tax deduction for the giving of that money, the deduction automatically meaning that the money has to be taken from other taxpayers who did not give as much to a charity.

Under most conditions the Federal Emergency Management Agency uses taxpayer's money for 75% of a relief effort. In the case of Hurricane Andrew, the agency paid 100% of relief. There is no question that emergencies dictate emergency help, and the federal government's organ for that, the Federal Emergency Management Agency could serve a necessary but *restricted* purpose: to do what the locality and other closer entities may not be able to do, depending on the emergency, such as providing food, water, tents, communications and other vital necessities that are common to practically all large disasters, but it should not provide rebuilding efforts other than the rebuilding of federal facilities and interstate roads. If the federal government continues to be the organ for rebuilding of private property, why should any citizen buy insurance for such emergencies? Insurance Companies paid $7.3 billion for the victims of Hurricane Andrew, yet many of the uninsured were the smartest of all because the federal government acted as a premium-free insurance company with taxpayer's money. Insurance companies paid $3.5 billion to victims of the Los Angeles riot. But many of those who didn't have insurance were the victors, receiving premium-free recovery. The federal government receives a request for emergency aid an average of once a week and most requests are granted.

Individual states have individual risks. Floods are frequent in states that border the Mississippi and Missouri Rivers, hurricanes hit the Gulf states, tornadoes are destined to strike in the mid-western states, earthquakes hit California, volcanoes are possible in some states but impossible in others. Each state should have reserves set aside for their own individual risks to their own state property, but most states don't have those reserves because they know the federal government, with funds from taxpayers at large, will come to their rescue. Florida, a certain host to hurricanes, has no state sales-tax, therefore there is no adequate emergency fund set aside for that certainty. In 1992 Indiana received $2,000,000 from federal taxpayers because of a mammoth flash flood, yet Indiana had a budget surplus of $138,000,000.

States and cities have no incentive to do the things logic would dictate they should do. During the great floods of the Mississippi River in 1993, Davenport, Iowa was immersed in water. Davenport hadn't built levees which would have called for taxing the local residents by local taxation. Five miles up the river was Bettendorf, Iowa whose city government had elected to build levees, and so the damage to Bettendorf from the same flood was minimal.

The Great Society programs included federal flood insurance at uncompetitively low costs. The average policy offered by the government cost an annual premium of only $252 for coverage of $105,770.

Such low-cost government subsidization of insurance through the National Flood Insurance Program (NFIP) encourages property-purchasers to build in areas of great risk, therefore adding to each disaster with increased casualties.

President Clinton told the victims of the Mississippi River Flood of '93 that his administration would not let them down, and he would be "forceful, coordinated, and effective." He should have warned the nation, "You taxpayers will pay for this!" They did. Taxpayers spent 4.7 billion dollars. That led his political adviser, Paul Begala, to say that President Clinton "is the most empathetic man God ever made." But President Clinton's empathy was not evident by a reduction of the contents of President Clinton's wallet.

There is one other great liability to the giving of money through Washington, D.C. The non-victim feels no reason to give his or her own donation to help the victims when the federal government is going to take taxpayer's money to provide mammoth amounts of aid. After the Los Angeles riots there was a feeling of unity in Los Angeles never before known in that large metropolis. People from all over L.A. and beyond were going to areas of L.A. they had never visited before, to bring supplies and help the rebuilding efforts, and private enterprises were pledging millions of dollars worth of help. But when the announcement came that the big Amtrak train would arrive with federal funds, that marvelous feeling of community disappeared. The federal government provided a disincentive for individual compassion.

President Grover Cleveland said that "the friendliness and charity of our countrymen can always be relied upon to relieve their fellow citizens in misfortune...Federal aid in such cases encourages the expectation of paternal care on the part of the government and weakens the sturdiness of our national character, while it prevents the indulgence among our people of that kindly sentiment and conduct which strengthens the bonds of a common brotherhood."

Generally, both liberal and conservative members of the Congress from a state experiencing a crisis join together to advocate bills of massive federal aid for their constituents, trying to outdo each other. But it is only another version of unconstitutional charity by the ongoing theft from others in the nation, that causes federal taxes to rise for those things that are not federal in nature. The California earthquake of 1994 set a new high in demanding such involuntary charity from the nation's taxpayers. The bill to the states was nine billion dollars. Instead of the President of the United States using his office as a bully pulpit, asking the people of the country to voluntarily contribute to the relief effort, he chose involuntary taxation, receiving applause for his compassion.

$60,000,000 of the bundle of that earthquake aid was for Exposition Boulevard's right of way lane, $140,000,000 was for the economic impact on local bus services, $245,000,000 was for local school rebuilding, $500,000,000 was for housing assistance, and on and on went the list of local needs. It isn't simply that those funds were to come from a waitress in Maine, a dock worker in Louisiana, a nurse in Nebraska, and a coal miner in West Virginia; those funds would come from the waitress in Maine, the dock worker in Louisiana, the nurse in Nebraska, and the coal miner in West Virginia of the *next gen-*

eration, all of whom will not even remember the California earthquake because it occurred before their births.

Too bad, but the likes of Davy Crockett are all too rare, and every American pays a tremendous cost for the lack of Congress' interest in emulating his responsibility to the taxpayer, and the sanctity in which he learned to hold the U.S. Constitution.

CHAPTER TWENTY-ONE

DISTANT THOUGHTS
OF LUCY ZANDINI

It used to be that the worst thing you could do in high school was smoke a Lucky Strike behind the bleachers at a football game, or drink a Lucky Lager outside the senior dance, or date Lucy Zandini who, it was rumored, fooled around a lot.

Teachers were on the lookout for someone who might be hiding a pack of chewing gum.

And there used to be some kid who sat in the back of the class who was taller than any of us, and he needed a shave before any of us, and his voice was lower than any of our voices that were still cracking between soprano and alto. The reason he was so tall and we weren't and he had stubble when we didn't and his voice was low and ours weren't, was because he was older than anyone else in the classroom, having failed a grade twice. He was not allowed to move on to the next grade until he was able to perform the curriculum assigned to his current grade. And his very presence provided incentive for the other kids not to fail. No one wanted to be that tall guy in someone else's class.

Decades after those days, I visited a local junior high school at night, to take part in a debate. I arrived early and walked the halls and I was hit with a wave of potent nostalgia. There were the classrooms with the rows of chairs and the blackboards and the brown bulletin boards, and it all seemed so good and pure. There were the rows of green lockers lining the halls with their combination locks. (After all these years I still have dreams — maybe one, two, or three a year — in which I'm trying to find my locker, and after finding it, I spin the dial on it in hopes that I can remember the numbers of the combination.) And there was the smell of school — that musty smell of innocence that has never changed through the years.

But then I walked out of the building to look for the auditorium and I suddenly saw something that jarred me out of that nostalgic trance. There was a large sign on the fence of the school-grounds that read: "REPORT WEAPONS ON CAMPUS." And next to the fence was a metal detector.

The acts of disobedience now are not a quick cigarette or a secret beer or a fast girl. The current acts are taking cocaine or crack, and a concealed knife or gun, and a conscience-less rape or murder.

Now no one is that tall guy who sat in the back of the class, because now no one fails. They just move on, grade after grade no matter how poorly they may do on tests, and they can graduate as illiterates. Worse than that, some are able to enter college as illiterates or even graduate from college as illiterates and, apparently, some can even become members of the Congress as illiterates.

During the Presidential campaign of 1976 the National Education Association made a deal with candidate Jimmy Carter. They would endorse him for the Presidency, although they had never endorsed a presidential candidate before. In return, should he win, he would propose a separate federal Department of Education.

They both kept their sides of the deal in an agreement that flew against the spirit of the U.S. Constitution. The authors of the U.S. Constitution, who were some of the best educated people of their time, and perhaps of all time, intentionally did not put the word "education" in the U.S. Constitution because they felt that giving the central government a role in the teaching of children could bring about a tyranny, as had happened in other nations. Education was to be the business of the parents and their localities.

That didn't stop the President and the Congress of 1979. The Department took off like all bureaucracies take off, into expanding budgets and expanding powers. "I don't know what history will show," President Carter said, "but my guess is that the best move for the quality of life in America in the future might very well be this establishment of this new Department of Education, because it will open up for the first time some very substantial benefits for our country...It will increase the nation's attention to education...It will make federal education programs more accountable...It will streamline administration of aid to education programs...eliminate unnecessary bureaucracy, cut red tape, and promote better service for local school systems...A Department of Education will save tax dollars. By eliminating bureaucratic layers, the reorganization will permit direct, substantial personnel reductions...It will make federal education programs more responsive...A Department of Education will ensure that local communities retain control of their schools and education programs."

Wrong on every count.

Each state would be fined for the Department's upkeep. Americans did not recognize that they would have more money for education if the department had not been created.

California, as the biggest state and, at the time, recognized as having the best public schools in the nation, lost big, both in educational quality and in money, and was symptomatic of what was happening to other states. It came about that Californians would send approximately four billion dollars to D.C. for the Department of Education in an average year, and receive three billion dollars back. The three billion dollars that would come back to California would be received with a list of specifications and regulations and directives on how it must be spent, including $66 million for bilingual education. If an increment of money would not be spent on its Washington-assigned purpose, the money for that increment would be withheld. Therefore, no increments were rejected by California. By the fifteenth year of the Department of Education, California tied with Mississippi as the worst state in the nation in the ranking of reading ability for fourth graders, even though California was spending $1000 more per fourth grader than Mississippi.

Why can't Californians decide how to spend their own education dollars? Why not allow California taxpayers to send those education dollars to Sacramento rather than D.C.? Or better yet, send those education dollars to City Hall rather than Sacramento? Or better yet, send those education dollars to the School District rather than City Hall? Or better yet, send those education dollars to the individual school rather than the School District? Why is there the assumption that Washington D.C. knows best?

The Washington bureaucrats in the Department of Education look at a student from anywhere in the United States (other than the District of Columbia itself) as a number, a statistic, a fact — not a face, not a name, not a boy or a girl. In those first 15 years of the Department of Education, literacy among young Americans took a downward plunge never experienced in the history of the United States. By the early 1990s 25% of high school seniors in the United States were functionally illiterate.

There was a D.C. celebration back in 1979 when the Department of Education was inaugurated, and the public was unaware of the kind of changes in schooling that was ahead for their children. Schools in many urban centers would soon come to mean a place of danger for children — physical danger as well as psychological and emotional danger, as children would be compelled to go to a place of fear every day, to say nothing of what would happen to teaching, with classes devoted to subjects of multi-culturalism, condoms, environmentalism, and condemnation of the United States.

In 1983 the National Education Association, along with the Union for Concerned Scientists, developed a 144 page curriculum which was a teaching plan dealing with nuclear war, encouraging children to gather signatures for petitions so as to place referendums on ballots regarding nuclear policy. Even *The Washington Post* called the plan "political indoctrination." The plan was called *Choices: A Unit on Conflict and Nuclear War.* One of the suggested quizzes for teachers to give their students was a multiple choice question on Page 88: "An MX Missile is about as powerful as how many Hiroshima Bombs?" There were four choices. Three were fictitious, one was actual. They didn't make any of the fictitious answers higher than the actual number, which is sophisticated propaganda, designed to make the reader or, in this case, the quiz-taker, feel the amount is the highest it could be. There were no questions on the power of the Soviet SS-17 or SS-18 or SS-19 Missiles aimed at the United States.

Another multiple choice question asked, "The U.S. Government spends more of its budget on (a) military programs (b) social programs (c) foreign aid or (d) environment." The answer designated for the teacher to tell the students was (a) military programs. They were misinforming the students. The truthful answer was (b) social programs. A commentator on television pointed out that inaccuracy, and soon an errata sheet was sent in the mail to change the question, not the answer. The question was changed to read: " In Fiscal Year 1987 (this was still in 1983) the U.S. proposes to spend more of its money on (a) military programs (b) social security (c) energy (d) education. The answer was (a) military programs. They changed "social programs" to "social security." More important is another inaccuracy: the United States was not proposing that defense exceed education, since the amount to be spent on education (federal, state, and local) would be more than defense. Instead of the National Education Association simply correcting the answer which would have called for a one-letter change from (a) to (b) they let their agenda show, by changing the question. The child in school, not knowing this background, would simply be left with the inaccurate impression that military programs were the biggest item of United States spending. The truth was unimportant to the National Education Association.

The National Education Association issued its policy statement of purposes including: "The Association urges the United States and all other nations to adopt verifiable freezes on the testing, development, production, upgrading, emplacement and deployment of nuclear weapons and all systems designed to deliver nuclear weapons."

The Association was not so adamant on the excellence of teachers, opposing merit pay for teachers, stating, "The National Education Association believes that competency testing must not be used as a condition of employment, license retention, evaluation, placement, ranking, or promotion of licensed teachers. The Association also opposes the use of pupil progress, standardized achievement tests, or student assessment tests for purposes of teacher evaluation."

Nor did the Association believe in the free market system for educators stating "The 'market value' means of establishing pay cannot be the final determinant of pay scales since it itself too frequently reflects the race and sex bias in our society."

The National Education Association has spent millions and millions of dollars (raised by dues from its union members) to fight state referendums that would allow parents the right to send their children to a school of their own choice, public, private or parochial, with some of the money citizens are compelled to spend through taxation for education. The National Education Association is justifiably fearful of competition, and holds on tight to the jurisdiction of the tax money used for public schools.

There is a private school, Marcus Garvey Private School, in South-Central Los Angeles, an area where there had been life-threatening and life-ending riots. Marcus Garvey had an enrollment of 500 children with 600 on the waiting list. The owner of the school said that if a referendum passed that would allow school-choice with vouchers, some six thousand children would be in line for enrollment the day after the passage of the referendum. That would mean new private schools would be built for such a massive overflow, and the public schools would have to become safer and better in order to compete. The President of the National Education Association, in fighting against such a referendum in California, admitted that schools in inner cities "are absolutely terrible, they ought to be blown up," but he went on to say, "but I don't think the solution is to let some kids escape." The President of the National Education Association-affiliated California Teachers' Association said in reference to school-choice, "There are some proposals that are so evil that they should never even be presented to the voters. We do not believe, for example, that we should hold an election empowering the Ku Klux Klan, and we would not think it's undemocratic to oppose voting on legalizing child prostitution." He equated school-choice with the Ku Klux Klan and child prostitution.

The *New York Times* had a front page story by William Celis III, (October 6, 1993) regarding a school in Baltimore: "A year ago, the Harlem Park Community School here seemed to represent the worst of what was wrong in public schools: graffiti covered the halls, crack vials littered the grounds, students did not have enough textbooks and, because the toilets did not work, the children sometimes defecated or urinated in stairwells.

"Today the building is clean, attendance has improved and, while it is too early to see conclusive results in test scores, there are early indications that students are learning faster than expected, and with more enthusiasm. One mother, Pamela M. Brown, said last week: 'A lot of the parents say their kids come home singing. Kids are excited about going to school.'

"The difference: Harlem Park and eight other Baltimore public schools have been taken over by a private company that runs them for profit."

Although President Clinton was sending his own child to a private school, he supported the National Education Association in its fight against allowing parents to have school-choice through vouchers, which would make it easier for *all* parents to send their children to a private school.

When Governor Clinton was attempting to be the nominee of the Democrats for the Presidency, he told the screening panel of the National Education Association, "If I become President, you'll be my partners. I won't forget who brought me to the White House. " He won their endorsement, and their power was exhibited at the Democrat's National Convention at which almost one out of every eight delegates was a member of the National Education Association. What President Clinton also would not forget is what no President has been able to forget since 1979: The Department of Education is considered to be the possession of the National Education Association.

Their cry has been that the United States must spend more and more for our schools, disregarding the fact that it isn't money that's needed, but safe schools and real education for the nation's children. The United States spends twice as much per student as Japan, but Japanese students come out of school far better educated than graduates in the United States. The District of Columbia, which spent 50% more per student than the national average, and under total federal control, had a drop-out rate that was the worst in the nation.

Each year a huge presentation is prepared by the bureaucracy of the Department of Education to give to the appropriation committees of the Congress to justify more and more power for that department. The presentation is hundreds of pages with charts and graphs and pictures and statistics. That presentation should be one page with three words, "Abolish This Department." Whomever makes that presentation will be known as the greatest educator in contemporary America.

Some day the children of the United States will have the kind of education they deserve. The educational system this country used to have, worked. That was when kids were taught to read and write and were taught history and geography and mathematics and science, when schools were safe because criminal acts were not allowed to start — before political indoctrination became an agenda of schools, before the National Education Association had federal power and before we had a Department of Education. That's when the United States of America was the best educated society in the world. We could do it again if we want to. The curriculums to use are still in the Library of Congress — dusty, but still there.

There's just one further statement about those old days in school:

Lucy, honest, I never believed those stories.

Back then at least, such stories were seldom true.

CHAPTER TWENTY-TWO
HOW DO YOU FEEL ABOUT CHOICE?

Throughout the month of January, 1973, while the Vietnam Peace Accords were signed, while President Nixon was inaugurated for a second term, while Senator John Stennis was mugged outside his home in Washington D.C., while wage and price controls were ended, while the Super Bowl was played between the Washington Redskins and the Miami Dolphins, and while a Soviet space probe landed on the moon, the flags of the United States were at half-staff. The event-filled month started that way because President Truman had already died, and just days before the flags in mourning were scheduled to rise and furl normally again, the news came from Texas: President Johnson was gone.

It was the 22nd of January, and the avalanche of events didn't stop with the tragic announcement from Texas. Within hours of his death, the U.S. Supreme Court released a decision called Roe v. Wade.

Through the years that followed, Roe v. Wade became known as the ruling that made abortion legal.

It wasn't.

Roe v. Wade was the ruling that made it *illegal* for a state to make its own decision regarding abortion, by its elected State Representatives under the Tenth Amendment of the United States Constitution. Prior to Roe v. Wade, abortion was as legal as it is today in New York State, in Washington, D.C., in Washington State, in Hawaii, and in Alaska, while 15 other states had different degrees of legality with different restrictions. Liberalized laws covered 41% of the U.S. population by states making their own choice.

What Roe v. Wade did was cause abortion to be a dividing force in the United States by putting the federal government into the act.

Prior to Roe v. Wade there were no huge protests and demonstrations for abortion or against it, there were no questions on the subject addressed to Supreme Court nominees by the Senate Judiciary Committee. Abortion had been the business of the states, as the death-penalty was the business of the states.

The Roe v. Wade decision of the Supreme Court of 1973 did not interpret a law, it created a piece of very intricate legislation, deciding what could and could not be done in each of the trimesters of pregnancy. The Supreme Court wrote that during the first trimester the woman's right is absolute. In the second trimester the states may intervene to protect the health of the woman (the word "health" became so widely interpreted that, in practice, the ruling made the second trimester equal with the first trimester), and in the last ten weeks of pregnancy the states could proscribe abortion except when necessary to preserve the life or health of the mother (the word "health" again became so widely interpreted that the distinction became transparent). The decision was based on "the right of privacy suggested by the 14th Amendment" (words not found in the 14th Amendment or elsewhere in the U.S. Constitution). Associate Justice Blackmun wrote that the right of privacy "is broad enough to encompass a woman's decision whether or not to terminate her pregnancy."

No one could answer if this right of privacy would allow any and everything else to be decided or accomplished in private. Could an American legally decide, in private, to commit incest, or abuse drugs or do anything? What would the right of privacy permit or prohibit?

Many of those who agreed with abortion on demand were, nevertheless, opposed to the ruling of the U.S. Supreme Court in Roe v. Wade because the Court had taken over the duties of a legislature. *The New Republic,* nationally known at the time for its liberal editorials, opposed the decision based on that overreach of the court. The sanctity of the three branches of government with their separation of powers had been obfuscated. Constitutional scholars had to ask (both liberal and conservative), "Why do we have three branches of government if the court was, in fact, able to legislate? What then, does the Congress and state legislatures have as their exclusive prerogatives?"

All of that was and remains a Constitutional argument.

The moral argument of abortion was separate and apart from that, and it escalated to new heights after the Roe v. Wade decision:

Those who advocated abortion on demand, or more accurately, abortion on desire, used two major arguments: "a woman has the right to do with her own body as she chooses" and "the government should get out of the bedroom." Those two sentences became as common as "Hello. How are you?"

Without emotion or wild-eyes on either side, those two lead arguments should be considered seriously, one by one:

"A woman has the right to do with her own body as she chooses." True. Of course. All human beings, male or female, should have the right to do whatever they want to do with their own body. If a woman wants to chop off her arms or legs, it may be painful and a crazy thing to do, but that's her right. But a woman doesn't have four arms, four legs, four eyes, two noses, and two hearts. Nor does a woman have two genitalia, one of a female, and the other of either sex, female or male. The issue of abortion involves a second set of arms, legs, eyes, genitalia, and heart. Does one human body have the right to do whatever that human body wants to do with another human body?

In recent years it has become common for a woman in India to have an abortion after an ultrasound test that reveals the baby is a girl. Is that abortion a decision defined as a woman having the right to do what she wants with her "own body"? It's clear that it is the other body that is being defined.

"The government should get out of the bedroom" is even a more self-defeating argument than the one regarding a woman's body, since "the government should get out of the bedroom" is a statement of admission that the time of choice occurs in the bedroom in sexual encounter. The government, after all, has not been, is not, and seeks not to be in the bedroom. The statement is made as an argument for abortion — an argument that, in fact, defeats its very purpose because sexual encounter, not abortions, take place in the bedroom. To be accurate, the phrase of advocacy should be "the government should get out of the clinic." That, however, lacks the drama wanted, and would also bring about an immediate answer that if government should get out of the clinic, then government should not be required to allocate funds for the clinic.

There is a third statement used by those who advocate the choice of abortion: the accusation that "conservatives claim to want the federal government to be less involved in the life of individuals, yet they want the federal government to be involved in the decision of abortion."

No.

It was Roe v. Wade that put the federal government into the act of abortion, and it's liberals who want that ruling to remain the law of the land. Moreover, many liberals want taxpayers funds to pay for abortions. Throughout the history of the abortion debate it has been liberals that have wanted federal government involvement.

"But conservatives want an amendment to the U.S. Constitution making abortion illegal." Some conservatives do advocate such an amendment. Some conservatives (including this one) do not because the U.S. Constitution does not include a list of those things the people cannot do, but rather those things the government cannot do. The U.S. Constitution does not make murder illegal, or kidnapping illegal, or rape illegal, or theft illegal. Only treason and slavery are itemized by the U.S. Constitution as federal crimes.

The question could then logically be asked that "since conservatives want decisions made as close to the individual as possible, why do conservatives want the state governments to be able to legislate restrictions on abortion, rather than allow the woman to make her own restrictions or lack of them?" It's because, in the unborn, there may be a third human life involved beyond the Mother and Father.

Since there may be another human life involved, there should be laws governing the potential ending of that life by another. It is not simply up to each individual whether or not to harm any other human life — not even to harm an animal. (Some flies and a roach are protected under the Endangered Species Act.) And this gets to the heart of the question: on what day of pregnancy is the day that life begins?

Since conception "starts it" and nothing else is needed, common sense would dictate that this is when life *begins*. But there is no scientific or medical or public agreement on this, except that life begins somewhere between conception and the end of the ninth month. But is it Day Number 1, Day Number 26, Day Number 144, Day Number 202, Day Number 270, or some other day? Since it has not been established beyond argument, wouldn't it be logical and rational to err on the side of life? Surely the Supreme Court did not and does not have the knowledge to know beyond the arguing experts when life begins — but it made its decision without that valuable piece of information. None of the seven Justices who agreed to the majority opinion of Roe v. Wade claimed such knowledge. Justice Blackmun, who wrote the majority opinion admitted that, "When those trained in the respective disciplines of medicine, philosophy and theology are unable to arrive at any consensus, the judiciary, at this point in the development of man's knowledge, is not in a position to speculate as to the answer."

Trimesters are imprecise, using guesses. During the first trimester there is a heartbeat, brain waves, blood circulation, fingerprints, footprints, pain receptors. If life is said by some to begin on Day Number 91 (the first day of the second trimester), is it inconceivable that it could begin on Day Number 90? (The last day of the first trimester.) If, in the future, there is empirical evidence released by, say, the Mayo Clinic that life begins on Day Number 83, would both sides of the abortion debate agree that abortions before Day Number 83 would be the choice of the woman, and from Day Number 83 forward would be forbidden except in highly restricted conditions? On both sides that would be the test between fanaticism and common-sense.

The day of uncontested proof has not yet arrived, and in the interim there is a valuable fact that gives evidence to the reality under which the leaders of abortion-rights think: They will ask, "How do you feel about choice?" rather than "abortion." They will not volunteer the use of the word "abortion," and generally have to be forced into using the word they are talking about.

Why not ask, "How do you feel about abortion?"

Why is that so difficult?

It is so difficult because the ones asking the question do not want to raise the specter of the visualization of the act they address. The word "choice" is palatable; it's positive; it's good. But the word "abortion" fits none of those criteria, and so the word is intentionally avoided.

If any point has to be disguised, something is wrong with the honesty of those addressing the point. And in this case something is wrong with their thought-process regarding abortion because they are not proud of their own conclusion. The anti-abortion respondent who falls for the disguised question, "how do you feel about choice?" with an answer about abortion is foolish, caving in to the deception of the one asking the question. The answer of the one being asked should be that he or she is for choice of any and everything as long as it does no harm to another, but very much opposed to choice when it comes to theft and kidnap and rape and murder and drug selling and bodily injury.

The dishonesty in replacing the word "abortion" for "choice" is absolute because the advocates of abortion-rights do not organize demonstrations for the choice of anything *except* abortion. This nation has never seen the National Organization for Women (NOW) organizing their members to demonstrate for choice of school vouchers, or choice-of-adoption, or choice of employees to join or not join a labor union, or choice-of-cyclists to wear or not wear helmets, or choice-of-drivers to wear or not wear seat-belts, or choice of smokers, or choice of a person to own a gun, or any other act of choice — except abortion.

By both constitutional and moral criteria, Roe v. Wade should be overturned and the decisions on abortion should be given to the separate elected state governments, since we have representative government in this country.

During this period of arguing over when life begins, the federal government's duty should be to "promote the general welfare," and promotion would indicate that the government should campaign as a bully-pulpit; that as long as the Supreme Court decision on Roe v. Wade is law, the individual should recognize that abortion is a Supreme Court given choice, but it is a terrible choice rather than a political cause, and the government should try to influence and persuade people not to make that choice, just as government has helped influence public opinion against drugs.

On January 22, 1973, the flags of the nation were at half-staff because of the death of two former U.S. Presidents. Since 30 million abortions have been performed in the first 20 years after Roe v. Wade, those flags might well have been flying at half-staff for more than former Presidents. That January they might have flown at half-staff for someone or ones who would have held that office in the future, had their time on earth been granted.

CHAPTER TWENTY-THREE

HOW COME THE WORLD IS STILL HERE WHEN NO ONE RECYCLED BEFORE?

In January of 1928, *Time Magazine* started a tradition of having their cover story of the first issue of each year devoted to their choice as "Man of the Year." As the years went on, sometimes it was a woman, and on occasion, a group of people, but the tradition took a very strange turn for their first issue of 1989. That was the year when *Time's* cover story was their choice as "Planet of the Year."

When I saw that New Year's cover, I was very glad that our planet won against the other eight planets. Admittedly it was a parochial gladness since I have lived on this planet ever since I was born and if Pluto or Mars would have won I would have been angry. I was so proud of my home-planet that I bought the magazine to read about how it won the award. I didn't want to laugh at the other planets — it was just a normal feeling of a competition won.

But then in reading that issue, it became apparent that *Time Magazine* wasn't giving our planet a compliment after all. The articles were filled with one warning after another about the imminent dangers facing our planet, and it made the reader wonder if the earth would last long enough to allow a subscriber to receive every issue for which he or she foolishly paid in advance.

Some of those articles suggested that our planet was being poisoned and stripped of natural resources, and we were making the world fall apart. Moreover, the articles suggested that the earth wasn't meant to maintain Man but that Man was put here to maintain the planet for some reason never offered. If Man is less important than the planet, for whom are we saving it?

Twenty years prior to the *Time Magazine* cover, in 1969, Paul Erlich wrote that the oceans would be dead by 1979 resulting from pesticides, oil spills, and other environmental crimes. In his book, *The Population Bomb* that was underwritten by the Sierra Club, he said the earth had only a few years left, and he advocated that a government agency should decree the optimum population, and there should be compulsory sterilization.

In 1970 (only nine years before "D-Day" when Paul Erlich had prophesied that the oceans would die) the first "Earth Day" was proclaimed, warning us of a coming Ice Age.

In 1972 the Club of Rome warned that the world would run out of gold by 1981, mercury by 1985, tin by 1987, zinc by 1990, petroleum by 1992, and copper, lead, and natural gas by 1993.

By 1973 Lowell Ponte wrote that "It is cold fact: the global cooling presents humankind with the most important social, political and adaptive challenges we have had to deal with for ten thousand years. Your stake in the decisions we make concerning it is of ultimate importance: the survival of ourselves, our children, our species." But it wasn't long before environmental leaders changed the threat of global cooling to global warming. By 1994, (April 21) Vice-President Gore said, "The threat of global warming is the most serious problem our civilization faces." By that time $300,000 had been spent by the Environmental Protection Agency (EPA) to study the flatulence of cows alone, to see if they were contributing to global warming, and another $500,000 was allocated to find out if perhaps the belching of cows had long-range heat-producing effects.

The warning of global warming was not retracted even though 2,300 scientists including 65 Nobel Prize winners from 79 countries signed the Heidelberg Appeal stating that there is a lack of solid data of "global warming." The net rise in world temperature during the last 100 years was about one degree Fahrenheit, most of it before 1940, and the northern oceans were getting colder. A National Oceanographic and Atmospheric Administration study of ground temperature in the United States from 1889 through 1989 found no warming at all. NASA's satellite study gave evidence of nothing more than normal fluctuations of temperature. Further, a true global warming could be beneficial, according to estimates made by Great Britain's *Nature Journal*, that stated global warming would gain U.S. farmers somewhere between 1.5 and 3.5 billion dollars more a year because of higher productivity, increasing corn production by 10%, wheat by 25%, and soybean production by 35%.

Global warming was not the first or the last scare invented by environmental leaders:

There was the Alar Scare. Alar had been sprayed on apples for years, and by eating them, we were warned we could all die. The scare made apple-growers lose 250 million dollars with many driven to bankruptcy. Then, too late for many, Alar was confirmed to be unharmful, keeping apples crisp and retarding spoilage.

There was the Asbestos Scare. The cost of asbestos removal has been estimated to be from 200 billion dollars to one trillion dollars. The danger from asbestos left alone and not removed has been compared to smoking one-half cigarette in a lifetime, with *Forbes* estimating that the forms of asbestos used in the United States is one-third as likely to be the cause of death as being struck by lightning. The most common type of asbestos (chrystotile), called "white asbestos," accounts for 95% of the asbestos used in electrical and thermal insulation, cement water pipes, brake linings, and construction materials, and is not considered to be dangerous if untampered. Judge Stephen Breyer (a federal appellate judge at the time) said "over the next thirteen years we can expect more than a dozen deaths from ingested toothpicks, a death toll more than twice what the EPA predicts from asbestos pipe, shingles and roof coatings." In 1990 the EPA completed research that concluded ripping out asbestos was a mistake, often sending small asbestos fibers into the air. The advice was changed to leave it alone.

There was the Times Beach, Missouri Scare of 1982 when its residents were moved away because of the perceived dioxin risk. It was already known that dioxin doses that killed guinea pigs had no effect on hamsters, but the order to move residents was enforced. The moving of the 2,240 residents from Times Beach cost the taxpayers 37 million dollars, buying out the town. Another 120 million dollars of taxpayers' money was spent for decontamination. After a decade, a government study concluded that none of it was necessary since there had been no danger to the people of Times Beach. Dr. Vernon N. Houk, who was the federal officer who urged the evacuation, stated that he had made a mistake.

There was the On-shore and Off-shore Oil Scares that resulted in no major oil refineries being built in the United States during the 1980s while more than one-hundred old ones were closed down. All of this was done while it was estimated that oil reserves beneath the U.S. outer continental shelf were approximately 18 billion barrels of oil and 145 trillion cubic feet of natural gas. (Absolute disaster was predicted for fish after the Exxon Valdez oil spill off Prince William Sound, Alaska, in 1989. The next year the salmon catch there topped the previous 1987 record by 38%.)

There was the Sugar and Artificial Sweetner Scare that frightened parents into believing their children could become frenetic and hyperactive and wild from any quantities other than the lowest amounts. That went on for over a decade until two scientific studies were conducted by Dr. Bennet A. Shaywitz of the Yale University School of Medicine and Dr. Mark L. Wolraich of Vanderbilt University, both finding no adverse effect on children. "And we gave them a large dose, about 10 times what any child would consume."

There was the Coal Mine Scare of toxic materials which resulted in strip-mining and smoke-stack restrictions impeding an 800 year supply of coal. Three volcanoes; Mount Krakatau in 1883, Mount Katmai in 1912, and Mount Helda in 1947 spewed more toxic materials than all of the air polluting materials made by Man since the beginning of the Industrial Revolution. Mount St. Helens produced 910,000 metric tons of carbon dioxide in 1980.

There was the Landfill Scare which resulted in the EPA setting a limit to a chemical in dirt — a limit so low that a child eating half a teaspoon of dirt every month for 70 years would still not get cancer from it. In 1993 the EPA admitted that at least half of the 14 billion dollars spent on Superfund cleanups was used for the same kind of "dirt-eating rules." Judge Bryer presided over a case that lasted over ten years and produced 40,000 pages of documentation concerning a dump that was made safe for "children to eat small amounts of dirt" for 245 days, at a cost of 9.3 million dollars. As Judge Breyer noted, "there were no dirt-eating children in the area. It was a swamp."

There was the Acid Rain Scare with billions of dollars spent by U.S. industry to minimize acid rain. After ten years of study and the spending of one half billion dollars, The National Acid Precipitation Program established by the Congress in 1980 concluded that acid rain created no real damage to crops, forests, or people, and that the acidity of lakes come from the surrounding soil and rock, not acid rain. The study further concluded that 90% of the lakes were acidic in pre-industrial times. The EPA suppressed the $500 million study until the acid rain requirements were enacted into law.

There was the Breast Implant Scare when in 1992, the U.S. Food and Drug Administration demanded a moratorium of silicone breast implants, and scared every woman who had already had them done. It was not until after manufacturers agreed to a 4.3 billion dollar settlement in 1994 that a Mayo Clinic Report concluded that those women who received implants were no more likely than anybody else to develop connective tissue diseases. Twelve other major studies reached the same conclusion.

There was and remains the Secondhand Smoke Scare that was initiated with an EPA report that secondhand smoke (which used to be called smoke) is a cancer risk to nonsmokers. The EPA report was not based on accepted scientific methodology but directed to support a predetermined conclusion. The EPA reviewed thirty studies on this question, twenty-four of which showed no increased risk of lung cancer to nonsmokers. So the EPA used selective data, re-analyzed studies, and reduced its statistical confidence standard which is customarily required for such studies. At the same time the EPA was doing this, the largest study ever made on secondhand smoke was released, sponsored by the National Cancer Institute. The study reported that nonsmokers had no significant increased risk of lung cancer from exposure to secondhand smoke. And so the EPA simply ignored this study. Also ignored were several studies of air-quality measurements in restaurants, that reported that people who frequent restaurants with smoking sections would be exposed to the equivalent of one cigarette per year. That would be far less a risk than the auto emissions likely to be encountered while driving to a restaurant for dinner. If the EPA used the same unorthodox techniques while investigating other commodities, it would have to ban hamburgers, peanut butter, broccoli, coffee, doughnuts, burning logs in fireplaces, chlorinated drinking water, and many others products as Class A carcinogens. Any government that demands that a restaurant owner seeking kitchen help *must not* discriminate in hiring a person with the AIDS virus, although that person could possibly get blood on food from a cut, while that employer *must* discriminate against employees and customers from passing on "secondhand smoke" — is nuts. (Some local governments even prohibit "secondhand smoke" in airport terminals and outdoor stadiums.)

There was and remains the Wetlands Scare resulting in five percent of the United States defined as wetlands, prohibiting thousands of private property owners from using their own property. John Pozsgai, a Hungarian immigrant in Pennsylvania, was sentenced to three years imprisonment and fined $202,000 for placing top-soil on a piece of property he owned because the EPA classified it as a wetland. Even puddles were defined as wetlands with building prohibited because of migratory birds and fish. 40% of California and 75% of Alaska, is now defined as a wetland.

There was and remains the Endangered Species Scare, where animals, fish, rats, bugs, and plants were given more protection than the private property and jobs of individuals. The protection of the Spotted Owl cost 33,000 American jobs in the timber industry and cost the nation billions of dollars in increased costs of housing. Because of a fly called the Delhi Sands Flower-Loving Fly, the U.S. government threatened a medical center from being built on the fly's habitat, and anyone killing or harming such a fly can be fined up to $200,000, and sentenced to a year in jail. Seven acres of land that do not harbor the fly are also prohibited from being developed because they might be "an important link between adjacent patches of occupied habitat." In California some one and one-half to three million acre feet of water are needed to meet the federal requirements for the Delta Smelt, an endangered fish. What that means is that the Delta Smelt is allowed to consume more water than the residents of the entire city of Los Angeles. Since 1973 The Endangered Species Act has been law. That law has given precedence to Spotted Owls and Delta Smelts and Kangaroo Rats and Snail Darters and Marble Muralets and Chinook Salmons and Gnatcatchers and Furbish Louseworts. There are, in fact, close to 700 species and sub-species listed as either endangered or threatened, including 25 species of insects, and some 3,500 other endangered or threatened species are on the waiting list for such classification, including two dozen different kinds of flies, and one roach. One of the reasons for much of the damage done in the California fires of 1993 was the quantity of scrub that was left untouched, by law, to retain the habitat of endangered species.

There was and remains the Clean Air Scare resulting in the Clean Air Act that has caused price increases in everything from gasoline to dry cleaning, costing close to one trillion dollars, with small companies spending approximately ten to fifteen thousand dollars a year on data collection and paperwork alone. Within the Clean Air Act was the "Too Many Drivers" scare, mandating employers in particular areas to be responsible for increasing the number of passengers per automobile in trips between home and work, with the EPA suggesting parking charges for employees who drive alone, employer subsidies for carpools and public transit, four-day work weeks, and employer-supplied shuttles for lunch-hour errands of employees.

There was and remains the Deforestation Scare, with thousands of jobs in the lumber industry and building industry destroyed, although the nation had more trees than at any time of its history. The renewable resource of trees became thought of as once fallen, never to be replaced. With two and one half million acres of virgin old growth already set aside, and private forests planting twice as many trees as required by law, the forests are flourishing with an average of seven trees replacing each tree that is cut down. Wildfires that once destroyed forests with regularity have been minimized by the forest industry that immediately rushes to control them, while in government-maintained wilderness areas, the trees are allowed to burn unless there are threats to other areas.

All of these scares were largely driven not by planet-lovers but by capitalism-haters.

Once, not long ago, the same political element took the words "peace" and "love" and used them as a disguise. What they meant by "peace" was surrender, from which Southeast Asia is still suffering. And what they meant by "love" was promiscuity and drugs, from which the United States is still suffering. Young people followed the word-thieves, thinking that they really meant peace and love. But with the passage of time, those words became too easily understood as having been masks, and a new word was used to bring about the same agenda:

Environment.

That word was even more encompassing than peace and love because environment includes everything — trees, air, water, aerosol sprays, tin cans, bottles, energy — everything. And what they really mean by environmentalism is socialism. They hate private enterprise, they hate private property, they hate the system of the United States.

The cost to every American by the misuse of that word, has been immense. According to the EPA, the cost to the nation for pollution control alone was 131 billion dollars for 1992, or 2.3% of the gross national product, yet pollution causes a maximum of two tenths of one percent of all cancers. The average American spends approximately half what he or she spends on shoes and clothing, on pollution controls. To make matters worse, the Brookings Institution found that the adjusted reduction rate for pollutants since the founding of the federal EPA has been slower than in the 1960s when the environment was regulated primarily by state and local governments and private enterprise.

One saving grace concerning the current batch of environmental leaders is that they have come along at the end of the 20th Century rather than at the beginning of the 20th Century. Had they come along at the beginning of the 20th Century, the United States would have been, and would still be, a third-rate third world nation.

We would still be riding around on horses and wagons for sure. Can you imagine what would have been said about those driving machines with all that exhaust pouring out of them, and with enough power to crash and kill?

And how about that madman, Tom Edison? Plug his electric wires in the wrong way and you can be a dead duck, to say nothing of the fire that electricity can start — it could kill a person or burn down a city. Besides, when Edison was a kid in Orange, New Jersey, he made a laboratory out of his folk's garage in their backyard. The EPA would have attempted to close him down the first night, and if they didn't get him that night, OSHA would have had him out of there the next day.

Then take Alexander Graham Bell. He invented the telephone and in order for his telephone to turn into a far-reaching communication device we had to cut down millions of trees, hoist up the dead trees all over the landscape: hills, plains, mountains, valleys, the wilderness, and put wires between them upon which birds could be electrocuted if they landed in the wrong places. The telephone wouldn't have made it to first base.

And the Wright Brothers? They'd be kicked off Kitty Hawk. They'd be told, "Haven't we cluttered up the Earth enough? Are we now going to start cluttering up the sky? And those flying machines can crash."

And who would have let Paul Muller get his D.D.T. on the market? Forget about containing malaria; that stuff could put poison on the world's vegetation.

There would surely be no rockets, no space exploration, no spacecraft.

And in terms of energy, no coal mines — they'd bring about Black Lung Disease and pollute the air and they could cave in. And no oil wells either. Who wants to look at big black derricks on the horizon? And then when you consider transporting oil and the damage an oil spill could cause, forget that as well.

Those warnings would have been valid in every instance. All

those catastrophes have come to pass. Worse ones are probably coming in the future. That's because we want to progress and progress is a risk. We have advanced because we have taken the risks.

Judi Bari, an Earth First Spokesperson said, "I think if we don't overthrow capitalists we don't have a chance of saving the world ecologically...I think it is possible to have an ecologically sound society under socialism. I do not think it possible under capitalism."

The *Earth First Journal* of September 22, 1989, published a suggestion to its readers: "Your doctor tells you that you have 6 to 18 months to live. Your condition will steadily worsen. You decide that rather than endure all that suffering, you'll go out in a flash — taking out say the Southeast power grid." Another quote: "The possibilities for terminally ill warriors are limitless. Dams from the Colorado to the Connecticut are crying to be blown to smithereens, as are industrial polluters, the headquarters of oil spilling corporations, fur warehouses, paper mills."

David Foremen, the Co-Founder of Earth First, who was on the Advisory Board of Proposition 130 in California (the purpose of which was to put severe limitations on the timber industry), had thoughts on foreign aid. He said, "The worst thing we could do in Ethiopia is give aid. The best thing would be to just let nature seek its own balance; to let the people there just starve there."

All of this is done in the name of environmentalism, with children being taught false information to turn them into "environmentalists."

Never again should we allow a good, beautiful word of the English language to be seized by a political element that uses it as a camouflage for an agenda — an agenda that if known, would fall from its revelation.

The EPA began in 1970 and has since become the national breeding ground for those who despise capitalism. And they mean to beat capitalism down by disproportionate licensing and regulations. The EPA's necessary functions (of which there are few) should be moved to other departments and to localities, where they can be balanced away from the super-liberals who have found in the EPA a swamp in which to multiply.

One of the many sparks of genius of our nation's Founders was their abandonment of any entity that would result in a national police force. But environmentalists have formed national police forces in regulatory agencies that march into the domain of private property and private enterprise, establishing regulations and dictatorial manifestos that are destroying our economy and ability to compete. The "Eco-Cops" as they are called, are the most feared of all.

Only Sunset Provisions could bring about the end of the national police force and the end of scares such as a coming Ice Age Scare and the Global Warming Scare and the Alar Scare and the Asbestos Scare and the Times Beach Scare and the Oil Scare and the Sugar and Artificial Sweetner Scare and the Coal Mines Scare and the Landfill Scare and the Acid Rain Scare and the Beast Implant Scare and the Secondhand Smoke Scare and the Wetlands Scare and the Endangered Species Scare and the Pollution Scare and the Too Many Drivers Scare and the Deforestation Scare.

All U.S. Government agencies should be followers of our system again, rather than the destroyers of our system, as many of them have become.

CHAPTER TWENTY-FOUR

WHAT VERY FEW PEOPLE KNOW ABOUT HARRY BECK

Labor Day is such a unique holiday because it doesn't make any demands. No one receives a gift, no one has to prepare a turkey, we are not expected to make fools of ourselves by wearing funny hats and blowing whistles, and there aren't even any fireworks to shoot-off or watch. We don't have to do anything.

No one is even expected to say "Happy Labor Day."

It's a marvelous holiday. And it's worth observing because labor has been both a necessity, and a love of Man, ever since Man was first placed on earth.

But in some of the states of the United States, no matter how talented a person may be, no matter how much a person may excel at a particular craft, no matter how long a person may strive for opportunity within that craft, that person will not be able to get a job in that particular field of the person's excellence unless that person repeatedly pays a private organization whose officers make a profit from that pay. Those are the states that compel people to pay a labor union if that person wants a particular job.

Legislatures of other states have corrected that coercion with Right to Work laws that authorize all workers to be free to join a labor union or not join a labor union depending upon the person's choice. In recent years, the greatest protection to the laborer has become the competition of wages and benefits and opportunities between free-enterprises, not the demands of labor-unions made on both employers and employees.

Many union administrators get angry when the right to work is advocated and they answer, "If some people join a union and some do not, then the non-joiner is a free-rider receiving benefits, while the payment of dues is left to others. And remember, in this country, majority rules, and it should be the same for labor. If a majority wants a union, the one who does not want to join a union must join as well."

That argument often wins because the process of thinking it through stops before there is recognition that the person who does not want to join a labor union is not asking to be a free-rider but, rather, that person rejects having to be a captive-passenger.

Thomas Jefferson wrote, "To compel a man to furnish contributions of money for the propagation of opinions which he disbelieves is sinful and tyrannical."

Majority rule does not mean minority denial. In the United States a dissenting minority is not required to contribute to the financial support of a majority private organization. Further, if a union or a guild has to force people to join, then what they offer cannot be as valuable as they claim. If the union administrators really want to protect the worker, the administrators of the union should be overjoyed that all workers, joiners and non-joiners, receive benefits. But the truth is that many union administrators are in business to protect the wages of only those workers who contribute to the wages of the union administrators.

The giant who started the labor movement in this nation, Samuel Gompers, would shudder at the current union administrator's demands, since he had proclaimed that "a compulsory institution of unionism, rather than a voluntary one, would be a menace to the citizen's liberty."

It is.

As of 1985, the U.S. Supreme Court ruled that no one has to be under the jurisdiction of a union. In the Pattern-Makers Case (#83-1894) the decision was made that "an employee cannot be discharged for failing to abide by union rules or polices with which he disagrees...Full union membership thus no longer can be a requirement of employment. If a new employee refuses formally to join a union and subject himself to its discipline, he cannot be fired. Moreover, no employee can be discharged if he initially joins a union, and subsequently resigns."

There was a "but" to all this. If an employer had an agreement with a labor union for collective bargaining, the employee (a new-hire or old-hire), would still have to pay full union dues, even without being a member. The union would have no jurisdiction over that person, no authority to demand that the person go on strike, no ability to demand other union directives, but the individual would still have to pay full union dues because of the agreement made between the employer and the labor union.

But then came Harry Beck.

Harry Beck was a member of the Communications Workers of America. Taking note of the 1985 Supreme Court decision, he resigned from the Communications Workers of America and continued to pay full dues as required. But then he found out that the union was supporting political candidates and causes with which he disagreed — and with his dues. That did it.

With the moral and financial help of Reed Larson's National Right to Work Committee, he brought his case against the union all the way to the U.S. Supreme Court, and the decision came in 1988. Harry Beck won. (#86-637) The determination was that he only had to pay the financial core of his dues that went towards collective bargaining, contract administration, and grievance adjustment. His dues were cut down by 79% because 79% of his dues went for organizing the employees of other employers, for lobbying in support of labor legislation, for participating in social, charitable and political events, and for other things separate and apart from collective bargaining, contract administration, and grievance adjustment. That Supreme Court decision meant that any worker could go on "Financial Core Status." All benefits of the employee would still be retained such as health coverage, pensions, credits, minimum salaries, because the individual would still be paying for those benefits under the financial core for which the individual would be charged.

Concurrently, the individual choosing Financial Core Status

could no longer run for office in that union or cast a ballot in union elections.

Most people in the United States do not know about Financial Core Status and that's because no one tells them. The unions generally don't tell them about it because too many employees would choose it. Employers generally don't tell their employees about it because they fear the union will think that management is trying to influence employees to leave the union. And most of the major media largely ignored the Beck decision or minimized it. The *Los Angeles Times* told its readers the news of the decision this way (reprinted here in full):

"Unions that take 'representation fees' from non-members in 'agency shops' must rebate whatever percentage of the money is used for political purposes if individual workers object." That's it. That was the entire article. That piece of writing and editing was not meant to win the Pulitzer Prize for either detail or clarity.

The new law of the land was to be ignored.

Shortly after the Beck decision, a Screen Actors Guild memo marked "Confidential–For Board Eyes Only" said, "If the Supreme Court ruling and its resultant publicity causes 150 or 200 people to request Financial Core Status, the Guild may decide to simply let those people go. However, if five or six thousand people decide to request Financial Core Status, the Guild may want to keep 85 to 90% of their dues money."

Hollywood is an example of a union-nightmare with its pretended compulsory unionization of the arts. There is something that doesn't make sense about it. To their great credit, actors, musicians, directors, film editors, truly creative people have one common bond: they want to create. They do not want anyone to tell them what to create or how to create. As long as taxpayers' money isn't involved, they should not be told what to create or how to create. If the government was to say, "You can or can't create this project even though you have private financing" there would be a creator's revolution in this country and it would be warranted.

That common instinct among the creative is one of the elements that makes them artists. And that is why it is so tragic to see those who think of themselves as artists go on strike — having established mini-governments called unions and guilds that can, in fact, dictate that a writer cannot write, a musician cannot compose, a dancer cannot dance, an actor cannot act, a director cannot direct, a film editor cannot edit, until the terms under which they work are satisfactory to the mini-government so established.

Would Beethoven have jumped from his Fifth Symphony to his Seventh Symphony because during the period of time he was inspired to write the Sixth there was a strike of Local 47? Would Michelangelo have forgotten all about that Statue of David if the Sculptors Guild of Italy was picketing? Would Shakespeare have left his *Midsummer Night's Dream* half-completed to observe the dictum of the Writer's Guild of Stratford upon Avon? And it's even hard to imagine as recent an artist as the great filmmaker, John Ford, riding out of Monument Valley to halt production in observance of a strike.

One clear exposure has come from all this: so many of those who claim to be artists and who continually advocate liberal policies, reveal themselves to want more money for themselves even at the cost of creation, and at the cost of work for grips, electricians, construction workers, dozens of crafts and talents; tens of thousands of co-workers. As they sympathetically talk about the disenfranchised, they hold no conscience while they disenfranchise others for their own financial reward.

Across the country from Hollywood and its mini-governments that dictate to its employees, is Washington D.C. with its own mini-governments operating under the country's maxi-government. While union membership across the nation continually goes down (now only 16% of workers), only government workers have increased as union members. Although they do not have the right to strike, some government employees have done exactly that, presenting a danger to the public-good because, in union, they seize the citizen's need for their specialty, and hold that need as a hostage with which to negotiate.

What if the employees of the Department of Health and Human

Services decide to strike and their computers are turned off and Social Security checks go unwritten? What if the Foreign Service Association decides to strike and our foreign representation doesn't show up for work? What if the Department of Defense should decide to strike for better working conditions?

The question then comes back from some federal workers, "Then what do we do when we have legitimate grievances and they aren't being addressed? What do we do?"

Quit.

It's legal. It's honorable. And it gets the worker out of the situation that the worker believes to be unjust. Let us assume that the grievances are much worse than have ever been claimed. Assume that a particular group of federal workers are forced to work twenty-hours a day for a dime, and they are doused with ice-water and kicked in the shins every morning when they get to work — undeniable, non-arguable grievances.

Quit.

But they shouldn't say that they have no recourse but to strike. They have given their oath: "I am not participating in any strike against the Government of the United States or any agency thereof, and I will not so participate while an employee of the United States or any agency thereof." Further, federal law states that an individual may not accept or hold a position in the Government of the United States "if he participates in a strike or asserts the right to strike against the government or if he is a member of an organization of employees of the Government of the United States that he knows asserts the right to strike against the Government."

Young people watch our respect or disrespect of the law. If we want children to observe every traffic signal, then we can't go around town knocking those signals down every time we are in a rush to get across an intersection. No one can expect both the protection of the law and the elimination of law at will.

Then the question is asked, "Why did we praise those who used the power of a strike against the communist government of Poland in the 1980s, but we prohibit such strikes against our own government?"

That question is either naive or thoughtless. In Poland, a person had no choice but to work for the government. In the United States there is the choice to work for private enterprise or the government, weighing the liabilities and assets of each.

President Franklin Delano Roosevelt is often thought of as the President who championed the sanctity of labor, and such recognition of President Roosevelt is appropriate. But his support was not without limitation. He said, "A strike of public employees manifests nothing less than an intent on their part to obstruct the operation of government until their demands are satisfied. Such action, looking towards the paralysis of government by those who swore to support it, is unthinkable and intolerable."

A striking federal employee can become as much a threat to this nation as an external force of hostility because, in good faith, the people have placed their trust in that employee.

The vast majority of workers in government and out of government who have dissatisfaction with the amount of union dues they are billed, have no knowledge of the Supreme Court decisions giving them the right to leave the jurisdiction of a labor union while retaining their jobs and benefits.

They almost found out:

On April 13, 1992, President Bush signed Executive Order #12800, instructing federal contractors to let employees know that they are not required to join unions, and that unions must specify the amounts they spend on organizing, strikes, lobbying, and political activities, under the Beck Decision of the U.S. Supreme Court.

Most of the unions paid no attention to the Executive Order, biding their time. And they didn't have long to wait. President Bush's Executive Order had a very short life. Nine and one-half months after he signed it, on February 1, 1993, President Clinton rescinded Executive Order #12800. It was only twelve days after his inauguration.

The Supreme Court decision would, by and large, continue to be invisible and inaudible and unprinted in public journals.

More people should know about Harry Beck, but very few people have been told anything about him.

It's time to talk about him, since talk is all that's left.

CHAPTER TWENTY-FIVE

FOR SOME UNKNOWN REASON WE'RE EVEN TOLD THEIR MIDDLE NAMES

Anyone who has lived through the death of a loved one knows that, other than missing the person constantly, there is something beyond endurance — and that is to re-live the moment of the tragedy. And so to restore and retain sanity, to live a normal life, to joke, to be productive, to live, you don't call on that memory. You keep it somewhere in your mind, but you build a wall around it rarely crossed. You have to build the wall to protect everyone you meet and everything you do — to protect the time you have left.

The cruelest and most unusual punishment of all would be to have to constantly re-live a moment of tragedy. And that is exactly what the implementation of our system of justice demands for some. We often sentence the innocent to such a fate when a murder of a loved one takes place because we insure, by delay and denial of the death penalty, that those who love the victim will be further victimized, re-living that moment of tragedy in years of repetition, dissolving themselves into a semi-life.

The family and friends who loved Michael Baker and John Myeski, the two boys at a fast-food place who were murdered (with the murderer eating the left-over hamburger), suffered that moment of tragedy for fourteen years before the murderer was executed. They endured those fourteen years of magnified torture, as groundless appeals for the murderer were granted. Other than for the most exceptional circumstances of new pertinent evidence, appeals of murderers have no business in a system of justice.

There is an actress who each day for seven years feared the man who once attempted to murder her. Her fear was valid since from his prison cell, he threatened that he would succeed in murdering her when released from prison. Yet there were those strangers who advocated his release, immersed in the cause of prisoner rehabilitation.

The best arguments for capital punishment were written by one of the wisest persons of our times, Dennis Prager. He comments that a little girl lies dead and Robert Kennedy lies dead and others lie dead while their murderers eat, laugh, hope, make friends, read, play, and even search for love. He says that if he were murdered and therefore not able to see his children grow up, not able to be with his wife, never again see the sky, or hear music, or read a book, or talk with friends — why should his murderer be able to do every one of those things? And Dennis Prager writes that the argument that murder and capital punishment are morally similar because they both involve taking a life, is as perverse as saying rape and lovemaking are morally similar because they both involve sexual intercourse. And, he continues, if capital punishment is state murder, then sending a criminal to prison is state kidnapping.

Worse than any other consequence of keeping murderers alive, is that we automatically reduce the value of the innocent.

In the doing of that, society often rewards the murderer, not only with life granted, but with celebrity status. Whereas the government is the culprit that keeps a murderer alive, the media are the culprits that give the murderer his reward of stardom.

Does the nation know the name of the man who tried to assassinate President Reagan? His name is well-known because it was bannered throughout the nation through the media.

The night of the assassination attempt, television reports and TV talk shows exhibited pictures of him from his high-school yearbook. Every facet of his past was examined and acquaintances were interviewed and psychiatrists and psychologists, in rapid succession, probed how he could come to commit such an act.

He received so much celebrity status that within two weeks of that assassination attempt, there were over 300 threats upon the lives of the President and the Vice-President.

The media chose the wrong person to give celebrity status. The American public should have seen and heard psychiatrists and psychologists examine what went on in the minds of Timothy McCarthy and Thomas Delehanty and Jerry Parr, when in split-seconds they risked their lives in making quick decisions on what to do to save the life of the President. Why didn't we see and hear and read their biographies on television and radio and the press? Where were their high school yearbooks? Why weren't we told what they were like in their youth? Where were their acquaintances? Where was the media interest?

Timothy McCarthy of the Secret Service and Thomas Delehanty of the District of Columbia's Police Force both became wounded that day by attempting to save the President's life. Secret Service Agent Jerry Parr forced the President down to the limousine floor. Every school-child should have known and still know those three names so well that they would be second nature.

But the major media continually make the criminals noteworthy and the heroes are left to treat their wounds.

In 1984, in San Ysidro, California, a man murdered twenty people in a restaurant. His name was told and re-told and re-told, and following the accepted pattern, his photo, his biography, and all the analysts were brought out in public view. But the one who brought an end to the massacre, risking his life, was simply called "a police sharpshooter" and a "SWAT Team marksman." No name. In order to find out his name it was necessary to phone the San Ysidro Police Department. His name was Charles Foster with a face and a biography but he didn't murder 20 innocent people like the criminal did. All Charles Foster did was stop the murderer from murdering more people at the restaurant.

In 1992 the convicted murderer of Michael Baker and John Myeski was finally executed, after those fourteen years of delay. When he was executed, his name was on the headline of every major U.S. newspaper. Why didn't they headline his execution, not with his name, but that "The Murderer of Michael Baker and John Myeski Executed." Those kids should be the ones known. Their lives were snuffed out; their names shouldn't be.

In the current urban centers of decay, the media make a habit of giving the *names* of gangs — names the gangs gave themselves. What notoriety the criminal gangs receive! And when leaders of the gangs meet, the major media refer to a Gang Summit Meeting! Summit? That's the designation we give to meetings of Chiefs of State. The gangs are given commensurate prestige.

The public would be so much better served by telling, with prominence, the names of members of the police force who lost their lives protecting the public *against* gangs. Our children, our society, should know the names of heroes, not criminals.

There is no higher morality on earth than the morality of the individual who risks his or her own life for the safety of a stranger. Local police forces and other protective services get little attention while the filth of society gets headlines.

Those who shot President Kennedy, and Dr. Martin Luther King, Jr., and Senator Kennedy, and Governor Wallace, and President Reagan, and Michael Baker and John Myeski, deserve no more than anonymity and death. They are the refuse and the debris of society — to be thrown out in the garbage.

CHAPTER TWENTY-SIX

"HEY BUDDY, WANT TO BUY SOME DIRTY PICTURES?"

L ouis Harris testified to a Congressional Committee that his polling organization discovered that the majority of Americans favor taxation for the arts as much as they do for their own social security retirement funds, and he said that a solid majority, 59% of the people, were willing to pay $15 more in taxes for the arts.

That's very good news because it means so many people are interested in the arts, and because the results of the poll speak so forcefully *against* federal taxation for the arts. That wasn't Lou Harris' intent, since he was testifying in favor of federal taxation for the arts and he was using that piece of polling data as a point in favor of such taxation. But if 59% of the people are willing to pay $15 more a year for the arts, what does a 1040 tax form have to do with it? That 59% can and should feel free to donate $15 to the arts, and by such a donation rather than a tax, they can even be selective in the art and artists they finance. And the arts would receive over five times what they are receiving through taxation. Perfect.

That should be the end of it.

But this is America and there is nothing that is the end of anything. The federal government wouldn't think of giving up such a confiscation of funds. And so the taxpayer's wages continue to be confiscated for the National Endowment for the Arts.

The N.E.A. as it became known (because all government bureaucracies are referred to by initials or an acronym or all its employees have to go to jail), financed some weird things including a celebration of the anniversary of the Sandinista Revolution of Nicaragua and the exhibition of a photographer's work that included photographs that many would classify as pornographic, and the exhibition of sacrilegious photographs including one of a miniature crucifix submerged in a glass of the photographer's urine.

Those who protested the spending of their taxes being used for such things were met with anger by others who said that stopping such financing would be an act of censorship and a breach of the First Amendment.

Is it?

The First Amendment certainly can and should be interpreted to mean that a person has the right to photograph anything a photographer wants to put in front of a camera. But how could anyone seriously interpret the First Amendment to mean that all Americans must pay the photographer?

Censorship has no place in this debate since in a free country a citizen should not only be free to buy a particular piece of art, but free not to buy a particular piece of art. Imagine that you have a blank wall and you want to put a painting or a photograph on that wall. And so you go to a gallery that has paintings and photographs for sale and you look at all of them and you decide on a particular one, and you buy it. Does that mean that you censored all the ones you *didn't* buy? Of course not. You just didn't want them. Others can buy them if they want them. Taxation for a piece of art, however, makes a demand on what you buy.

What is called the "arts community" answers that "the artist must create what that artist wants to create, and the government should have no role in the jurisdiction of the subject matter." They're right until they add the words, "Just supply the money." Does any other beneficiary of the taxpayer's funds act so arrogantly? What if Boeing or Lockheed or McDonnell Douglas said, "Hey, we're the experts at building military equipment and we're going to build whatever piece of military equipment we want with the money given to us by the Department of Defense. Maybe we'll build a bomber, maybe a missile, maybe a submarine; it should be our choice. We're the experts."

Should arts be the sole exception in the way we contract with taxpayer's money? The argument is made that many artists wouldn't be able to practice their art if it wasn't for the government (taxpayers) supporting them. And it is true that some of the greatest artists have been unsuccessful in making a living from the sale of their art. But they went on to work doing other things to support themselves and their creations. Historically, artists have created, no matter the obstacle. No artist is going to go through life without performing that creativity because of a lack of government grants. The passion for art in a real artist is too deep, and that passion is not surrendered.

Further, why couldn't the artist who has never received an N.E.A. grant also cry censorship? Why was one artist chosen over another? Is every creative effort that is not financed by the taxpayers an act of censorship? Is the *New York Times* censored since it doesn't receive a government grant for its articles of creativity? If the answer is that the *New York Times* can make it on its own, consider that the photographer who chose to photograph the crucifix drowned in his urine, made out quite well on his own, charging clients $10,000 for photographing their portraits.

Without the arts this would be a miserable, even an unlivable world. But artists become tools of government when that government, armed with the people's money, makes the decision on what is art and what is not art. Therefore, the government should be out of the arts entirely and the National Endowment for the Arts should be abolished.

Then the debate over censorship will be done.

CHAPTER TWENTY SEVEN

THE CRECHE HUNTERS OF DECEMBER

It happens every December. That month is the hunting season for the American Civil Liberties Union (ACLU) with a search employed by representatives of the ACLU going throughout the nation to find a creche or a crucifix or a menorah on public property. Once found it is targeted by the ACLU for removal. The basis for removal is the separation of church and state called for in the Constitution. But the ACLU is getting their documents confused. It is the Constitution of the former Soviet Union whose Article 52 states "In the USSR the church is separated from the state, and the school from the church." The United States Constitution does not use that language. It states that "Congress shall make no law respecting an establishment of religion, or prohibiting the free exercise thereof." Congress hasn't.

The ACLU is engaged in very weird political causes and its hunting season is only one of them. The Policy Guide of the ACLU is a catalogue of such pursuits. It is a huge volume, and the following are some excerpts:

Policy #18: "(Motion picture) Industry sponsored rating systems create the potential for constraining the creative process and thus contracting the marketplace of ideas. Despite the stated goal of providing guidance to parents, experience has shown that ratings inevitably have serious chilling effects on freedom of expression."

Policy #84 "The insertion of the words 'under God' into the

Pledge of Allegiance is a violation of the constitutional principle of separation of church and state."

Policy #120 "Military conscription, under any circumstances, is a violation of civil liberties and constitutional guarantees...The ACLU also questions the use of conscription even in war time because of the anti-democratic power it gives government to wage wars without the support of the people."

Policy #125 "The ACLU calls for a broad-based inquiry into war crimes, within the widest possible definition of war crimes against humanity and crimes against the peace, focusing upon actions of the United States military and other combatants against the people of South Vietnam, Laos, Cambodia, and North Vietnam."

Policy #133 "The ACLU recognizes that U.S. Government reliance upon nuclear weaponry as a dominant element of foreign and domestic policy, while propounded as a defense of democracy, is in fact a great threat to civil liberties. Four decades of adherence to this policy has fundamentally altered the nature of our constitutional democratic process and poses a paramount threat to civil liberties."

Policy #217 "Roadblocks where drivers are stopped for sobriety testing without probable cause violate Fourth Amendment principles."

Policy #242 "The most appropriate correctional approach is re-integrating the offender into the community, and the goals of re-integration are furthered much more readily by working with an offender in the community than by incarceration...Probation should be authorized by the legislature in every case, exceptions to the principle are not favored, and any exceptions if made, should be limited to the most serious offenses, such as murder or treason."

Strange.
Very strange.

Even stranger is that the ACLU has enjoyed a great deal of success, particularly when it has engaged itself in keeping religion out of public places. The ACLU was largely responsible for the arguments that convinced the U.S. Supreme Court to write decisions regarding the prohibition of prayer in public schools.

Such successes prompted the United States Senate to debate a proposed amendment to the Constitution that would overturn those Supreme Court decisions. The year was 1984 and the national debate was fierce, with the ACLU mounting a campaign to influence Senators to vote against such an amendment. As the debate went on in the U.S. Senate, it became mired in an avalanche of irrelevant facets. There were questions of whether or not the amendment should pertain to audible prayers or only to silent prayers or should it be called a moment of reflection or a moment of meditation? And if it was a vocal prayer, who would write it? Who would give it? A teacher? A student? Would the students take turns? The proponents fell for such a debate and concentrated on each local issue until the central point was lost. In the end that amendment fell eleven votes short of getting the two-thirds majority that was necessary, and so it was never passed on to the U.S. House of Representatives and to the state legislatures for ratification. The ACLU was in celebration.

By concentrating on whether or not school prayer should be silent or vocal, or who would write what, the goal of the proposed amendment was sacrificed. The wording of the amendment became so complex that it was destined for failure. None of the amendments that compose the Bill of Rights could have passed with such complexity. The amendment will come up again and the complexity should be discarded, and it should be made devoid of inordinate detail with the amendment simply stating that "Neither the United States nor any State has the authority to prohibit or mandate observances of religion, including any prayer, anywhere."

"Anywhere" would mean in a school or a laundromat or a restaurant. It would overturn the U.S. Supreme Court anti-school-prayer decisions of 1962, 1963, and 1985 that disallow even the suggestion that a moment of silence be used for prayer. The new amendment would let the authority for school-prayer rest with local jurisdictions and school-districts and the teachers, parents, and students themselves.

Further, it would end the hunting season of the ACLU every December.

Until that amendment is added to the U.S. Constitution, children will be able to hear lectures on "safe sex" in school, but not be allowed to display the Ten Commandments. And until that amendment is added to the U.S. Constitution the vigilantes of the ACLU will continue to get in their cars and search for creches and crucifixes and menorahs so as to get them removed from all public property, and they will continue to insist the illumination be extinguished in public buildings that have office lights in their windows displaying the collective pattern of a crucifix when viewed from outside at night.

Without such an amendment, in contemporary America, the ACLU and the government will continue to require that the taxpayers can only support a crucifix if it's soaked in urine.

CHAPTER TWENTY-EIGHT

NO LENIENCY FOR BOOKS, BEER, CASSETTE MACHINES, SKI CAPS AND SPRAY CANS

Vladimir Ilyich Lenin issued a directive: "Make mass searches and hold executions for found arms." The executions came.

Joseph Stalin said: "If the opposition disarms, well and good. If it refuses to disarm, we shall disarm it ourselves." The opposition was disarmed.

Joseph Goebbels wrote Hitler a note after two thousand Nazi S.S. troops were held off for a month from invading a Warsaw Ghetto by inhabitants with ten pistols. He wrote, "This just shows what you can expect from Jews if they lay hands on weapons." It did.

Within days of Fidel Castro's takeover of Cuba he disarmed the populace saying "Arms? What for? No longer do you need arms." But they needed them more than ever.

The wisdom of the authors of the United States Constitution guaranteed that the citizens of the United States would never have to fear such possibilities, their guarantee recorded in the Constitution's Second Amendment: "A well regulated Militia, being necessary to the security of a free State, the right of the people to keep and bear Arms, shall not be infringed."

When contemporary liberals hear the amendment they say "Ha,

Ha! You see? It says 'A well regulated militia being necessary...' They were referring to the *militia* having the right to keep and bear arms." The authors of the Constitution would have to have been sloppy writers if they did not mean the people, and they were not sloppy writers. The authors of the Second Amendment wrote "...the right of the *people* to keep and bear arms" not "...the right of the *militia* to keep and bear arms." It is very apparent that they meant that *because* a well regulated militia is necessary, the people should have the right to keep and bear arms. Further, the phrase "right of the people" also occurs in the First and Fourth Amendments, and the definition of that phrase is wholly consistent within the Bill of Rights, as confirmed in the Supreme Court decision of U.S. v. Verdugo-Urquidez. But for those who won't accept that the Second Amendment really means the right of the people to keep and bear arms, the statements of so many of our Founders may be helpful:

George Mason, who drafted the Second Amendment: "I ask, sir, what is the militia? It is the whole people...To disarm the people – that is the best and most effectual way to enslave them."

James Madison, who abbreviated the Second Amendment: "Americans need never fear their government because of the advantage of being armed, which the Americans possess over the people of almost every other nation."

Samuel Adams: "The Constitution shall never be construed to prevent the people of the United States who are peaceable citizens from keeping their own arms."

Alexander Hamilton: "The best we can hope for concerning the people at large is that they be properly armed."

Patrick Henry: "The great object is that every man be armed. Everyone who is able might have a gun."

Thomas Paine: "Arms like laws discourage and keep the invader and plunderer in awe, and preserve order in the world, as well as property."

Richard Henry Lee: "To preserve liberty it is essential that the whole body of the people always possess arms."

John Adams: "Arms in the hands of the citizens may be used at individual discretion for the defense of the country, the overthrow of tyranny, or private self-defense."

Thomas Jefferson: "No freeman shall ever be debarred the use of arms." And Thomas Jefferson quoted Cesare Beccaria: "Laws that forbid the carrying of arms...disarm only those who are neither inclined nor determined to commit crimes...Such laws make things worse for the assaulted and better for the assailants; they serve rather to encourage than to prevent homicides, for an unarmed man may be attacked with greater confidence than an armed man."

With the clarity of the Second Amendment and the advocacy of our Founders, why, then, is there the continuing pursuit of gun control without advocacy of amending the Constitution to strike out the Second Amendment? It is, of course, because striking out part of the Constitution's Bill of Rights would not be a cause that could gain popular support. And so most gun control advocates simply ignore the Second Amendment or explain it away as not really meaning what it says.

The agenda of gun control is a contemporary mind-set in which the erasure of the Second Amendment is but a part. It used to be that those guilty of committing a crime would be sentenced to a fine or imprisonment or both. But now the punishments are generally minimal while we give the greatest blame to the object the person holds rather than the person holding the object. The contemporary mind-set suggests that when a crisis of criminality occurs, sympathy and understanding should be given to the criminal. The blame for the crisis is instead directed against a thing — non-breathing — no face — inanimate — an inanimate object so as not to have to direct our passions against a human being no matter the evil of that human being. What has come about and permeates American society is a denial that criminality comes from the intentions of Man, but rather from the inventions of Man.

When Salman Rushdie's book, *The Satanic Verses* was published and there were terrorist threats regarding its sales, the immediate reaction was to lock up the books.

When there were brawls at a large football stadium, the determination was to lock up the beer and not allow its purchase.

When a terrorist's bomb was found to have been hidden in a portable radio cassette machine aboard PanAm Flight 103, the immediate reaction was a demand that the U.S. Department of Transportation and the Federal Aviation Administration mandate that cassette machines should be prohibited from being carried on passenger airlines.

When a wave of burglaries were being committed by criminals wearing ski-masks in Bridgeport, Connecticut, there was an appeal to ban the sale of ski-masks in that city.

When graffiti became an epidemic in Los Angeles, a prominent legislator proposed the prohibition of the sale of spray cans except to commercial businesses.

Disregarded in all this was the simple truth that some people are good and some people are bad and there should be punishments for those humans who are guilty of crimes without commensurate punishments for the innocent, by taking away a right.

In the 1980s, U.S. citizens used handguns approximately 645,000 times a year to stop crimes from being committed. Add the figures for shotguns and rifles and the figure expands to over one million times a year to stop crimes from being committed. During this period, 98% didn't even shoot or use warning shots, but the appearance of the firearm itself prevented the crime. In 1990 the figure of crimes prevented by gun ownership was 2.4 million.

In a National Institute of Justice study of incarcerated felons, 38% said they had decided not to commit a particular crime because of the fear that the potential victim might be armed.

The curse of gun control rather than criminal control was exhibited in Stockton, California, in 1989 when five school children were shot to death by a man who had previously been arrested seven times on charges from armed robbery to firearms violations to narcotics violations to sexual assault.

Why was he was out on the streets?

In response to the tragedy, the state legislature misdirected its passion and instead of creating laws that would keep such criminals imprisoned, they legislated a new gun-control bill.

The lawmakers did nothing to stop evil people from doing evil deeds. Instead, they took pride in thinking, "Ahhh, now we took care of that." What they did was worse than nothing because in their simplistic conscience-freeing by the false belief that they did *some*thing, they paved the way for new crimes. At the same time, their action punished those who never committed a crime and wouldn't think of committing a crime.

It is safe to say that obeying the law was not uppermost in the mind of the murderer of Stockton, therefore had he found new gun-control laws prior to going to Stockton, he would not have thrown in the towel and found a job as an accountant and become a community leader. He would have found a way to kill.

Whenever a shooting takes place that captures the attention of the nation, it can be counted on that some politicians, with eyes bulging and lips being bitten, will point their finger at the National Rifle Association (NRA), saying that the NRA is just too powerful. Again they want to focus on a faceless entity, a straw man, rather than recognizing that the power of any organization is only as great as the power of the people who believe in the cause they espouse. What those politicians fail to recognize is that an organization cannot create the people, it's the people who create the organization.

I have never thought, nor have I ever heard that feminists are feminists because of the power of the National Organization for Women, or that civil rights advocates are civil rights advocates because of the power of the National Association for the Advancement of Colored People. That would be insulting. Why can't it be believed that people oppose gun control legislation because of strong philosophical and constitutional beliefs?

Some think that people in the Congress vote one way or another to please a particular lobbying group, and then that member of the Congress gets automatic contributions or votes. I have little doubt that some are that unethical, but the fault is then with the legislator, and not with the lobbying group.

Kennesaw, Georgia passed a local law requiring all households to have a gun. Armed burglary went down 72%. Florida passed a law permitting concealed guns to those adults that have no previous record of crimes, and other law-abiding requirements. The murder rate fell 21% while the national average went up 12%. In contrast to that, Washington D.C.'s murder rate went up from sixth in the nation to first in the nation following the imposition of strict gun-control laws.

Daniel Polsby, professor of law at Northwestern University, suggested an idea of great merit, disregarded by those who feared inanimate objects rather than criminals. He suggested "to find people with the same statistical reliability as police officers; according to U.S. Justice Department crime statistics, almost everybody over 40 with a clean criminal record and no history of substance abuse would qualify. Call these citizens 'auxiliary peace officers.' Pay them some modest amount, say $50 a month, to pack a handgun wherever they go. Insist that APOs receive the same modest firing-range instruction that police officers get and the same classroom schooling about when it is proper to use a gun. But commission enough APOs so that bad guys would have to fear the presence of one or more of them on every bus, shop, street, and public space in the city. We know we can't flood the street with police officers; we should try to flood it with APOs."

On a higher level of arms, we have already verified the credibility of Professor Polsby's idea: during the height of the cold war we had no reason to fear the nuclear weapons of Great Britain and France; we wanted them to have more of them rather than less of them. We did not insist on a reduction of *their* weapons. Our justifiable concern was the possession of nuclear arms by the Soviet Union.

On April the 29th and 30th of 1992, Los Angeles became a city living in anarchy and terrorism. Rioting thugs mugged, looted, burned buildings, and committed murders. The citizens who were taken by surprise had good reason for self-defense but were faced with a state-imposed 15-day waiting period to purchase arms. They would have to wait until May 13. The rioters, however, did not wait. They simply smashed the windows and doors of gun stores for their weapons. Over 4000 guns were stolen during the riot. Fifty people were murdered, eight more died because of the riot, and 623 structures were set on fire.

The idea behind the state's 15-day waiting period, and the Brady Act's nation-wide five day waiting period, was to provide a "cooling off period" which assumes that those who would purchase guns legally might be those inclined to commit an irrational act. But those who want to commit an irrational act do not consider law-breaking irrational.

Waiting periods set precedents that could incrementally lead to the prohibition of arms. The *Los Angeles Times* now advocates "It is also our judgment that the only way to end the killing and maiming is to impose a near-total ban on the manufacture, sale and private possession of handguns and assault weapons – in effect to restrict their possession to law enforcement officers." After rhetorically asking if both criminals and non-criminals would give up their guns, the *Los Angeles Times* wrote, "The better question, we would argue, is whether we can afford *not* to find appropriate ways to collect and destroy guns." A California Assemblyman entered legislation to ban handguns within the state. The chairman of the California Democrat Party advocated the end of private gun ownership.

If gun controls become the norm, and since 96% of violent crimes are committed without a handgun (statistics of the U.S. Bureau of Alcohol, Tobacco and Firearms), why not ban knives and ice-picks and clubs and brass knuckles and bricks and sticks and stones? Criminal minds will always find an instrument to carry out criminality. With the misdirection of our lawmakers, evil becomes the victor.

That misdirection should be exchanged for dealing directly with crime, rather than dealing with inanimate objects:

More prisons are vital on local, state and federal levels since there is no use convicting criminals to a prison-term without space existing to incarcerate them.

City governments should hold protective services as their first and foremost duty, with every other city expenditure placed on a lower level of priority. After the 1994 Southern California earthquake, the Los Angeles Police Department temporarily tripled the amount of police on the streets to deter looting. More than looting was deterred as crime went down 90%. The streets were safe. For a few days in the

1990s, Los Angeles was as safe as it was in the 1950s. Los Angeles should triple police on the streets on a permanent basis. Police must come before libraries and pot-holes and garbage collection. None of them mean anything if the citizen is unsafe going to or from the library, driving on the streets, or taking out the garbage.

Those who assaulted Reginald Denny, a man who happened to be driving by the wrong intersection at the wrong time, and who was dragged out of his truck, beaten to a pulp and had a brick smashed in his face, were not found guilty of intent to murder "because intent is difficult to prove." For the future, that phrase of law should be changed from "intent to murder" to "indifference to murder." Very likely the assailants who tortured and bashed in the head of Reginald Denny didn't care whether they murdered him or not, and it was luck that he lived. Similarly, arsonists generally do not care whether or not they murder, but rather they crave to see the flames they ignited. Indifference to murder is accurate and should hold the same punishment as intent to murder.

Punishments must fit the crimes committed, and all sentences given to criminals should be carried out to their full length, with a twenty year sentence meaning the convicted criminal does not get out of prison until twenty years pass. Work-time and good-behavior should be expected, not rewarded.

It is, however, much easier to blame and imprison inanimate objects.

In the first story of Genesis, Adam and Eve did something they shouldn't have done. God had warned them against eating the fruit from a tree in the Garden of Eden. But the fruit was tempting and they ate the forbidden apple. God had a strange reaction to what they did, by contemporary standards. He blamed and punished Adam and Eve, not the apple.

It seems that God recognized, as did our nation's Founders millenniums later, that good and evil come from humans themselves, and not from the objects held in their hands.

PART FIVE

BRIDGES BEYOND THE WATER'S EDGE

(FOREIGN POLICY)

CHAPTER TWENTY-NINE

THE TOTALITARIAN'S PARTNER IS THE NEUTRALITY OF THE FREE

Once in the middle of an American night something very unusual happened. It's difficult to pin-point the date with precision because the event was invisible and because we didn't recognize its first sounds. It happened some time shortly after the assassination of President Kennedy, and it was very much like the arrival of a Trojan Horse that washed up on the shore. As we slept on the night of its ignored arrival, its doors opened, something came out, and then the doors closed before the dawn and each successive night its doors opened, something came out, and then before the dawn the doors closed again, and on and on it went for night after night until its cargo was emptied and the hollow horse washed back into the sea.

It wasn't carrying and unloading soldiers, nor was it carrying and unloading anything else made of flesh. It was, instead, carrying and emptying an "aura" — a poison that infected the nation and some welcomed the poison.

Before it arrived, America's foreign policy objectives were well known. The country had both purpose and direction and every nation was aware of what we were and where we wanted to go:

America's values were based on the belief that totalitarianism was intolerable and that we would defend and uphold liberty here and around the world. There had never have been a nation with such a sense of high purpose before, and its example was setting a new world inspiration.

President Kennedy put it clearly in his Inaugural Address: "Let every nation know, whether it wishes us well or ill, that we shall pay any price, bear any burden, meet any hardship, support any friend, oppose any foe, in order to assure the survival and the success of liberty."

No other nation's Chief of State had ever said anything like it. He was not only talking about the liberty of those citizens of the country he represented, but the liberty of people all over the world.

But then the new mysterious, invisible aura came, and it rejected all of that and cast its conclusion that we had no obligation, moral or otherwise, to oppose any spread of totalitarianism around the world. And the aura concluded that somehow, after all we had been through, it was no time for international challenges; it was the time for nothing other than holidays from the international arena. And so to many it was. No more duty and sacrifice. We had enough of that.

As the feeling swept so many in the nation, those intoxicated by its aroma said, "As far as the rest of the world is concerned, our only obligation is to stay out of it."

It became fashionable to ask, "Why should we retain friendships with governments around the world that deny many of the very ideals in which we believe?" But the question was asked with imaginary choices at hand:

In Cuba the choice wasn't between Fulgencio Batista and Patrick Henry. It was between Fulgencio Batista and Fidel Castro.

In Vietnam, the choice wasn't between Nguyen Van Thieu and Thomas Jefferson. It was between Nguyen Van Thieu and Phan Van Dong.

In Cambodia the choice wasn't between Lon Nol and James Madison. It was between Lon Nol and Pol Pot.

In Ethiopia the choice wasn't between Haile Selassie and Abraham Lincoln. It was between Haile Sellasie and Mengistu Haile-Marium.

In Angola the choice wasn't between Jonas Savimbi and

Theodore Roosevelt. It was between Jonas Savimbi and Agostino Neto.

In Iran the choice wasn't between the Shah and Dwight Eisenhower. It was between the Shah and the Ayatollah Khomeini.

In Nicaragua the choice wasn't between Anastasio Somoza and John Kennedy. It was between Anastasio Somoza and Daniel Ortega.

The reality was that most of the world was divided between totalitarian and authoritarian states with a sprinkling of democracies around the globe. During the 1980s democracies proliferated and with the end of the Soviet Empire in the very early 1990s, there was a sudden avalanche of democracies. Authoritarian and totalitarian states did not, however, disappear and although neither of the two are just, the differences, no matter how meaningful, were ignored and remain ignored by liberal activists:

Authoritarian governments generally disallow some civil liberties while totalitarian governments generally disallow all civil liberties.

Authoritarian governments generally encourage emigration while totalitarian governments generally lock their borders so their citizens cannot get out.

Authoritarian governments are self-confined while totalitarian governments are expansionist and search for conquests:

While under the Shah, Iran did not threaten any other nation in the area. The Shah was a friend to Anwar Sadat and King Hussein and King Khalid and Golda Meir. There was no thought of expansion of his territory. Whatever he did or didn't do was done or not done within the borders of Iran and he encouraged Iranians to study in other nations of the world, most particularly in the United States. Then in his place came the Ayatollah Khomeini with all civil liberties denied and emigration halted and his Islamic Fundamentalist Revolution became the leading threat to other nations of the Mideast and even to some beyond.

In Nicaragua, Anastasio Somoza posed no threat to his neighbors. El Salvador was under no danger from Anastasio Somoza; nor was any other country within the Western Hemisphere — not Honduras, not

Costa Rica, not any nation. Then the Sandinistas came into power and all of Central America trembled.

There are differences other than civil liberties and emigration and expansionism between authoritarian and totalitarian governments, major among them is that most of the authoritarian governments, like most of the world's democracies, have been friendly to the United States, whereas all the totalitarian governments have been hostile to the United States.

The significance of that depends upon how a person feels about the United States.

There are those Americans who believe that there is something intellectual about being neutral. In their quest for neutrality, there is a leaning over backwards to see events from the other side. Before the Khomeini Revolution in Iran, it was chic to see things from the side of the revolutionaries. It was chic to be against the Shah. There was no vision involved in that, and our neutrality and public accusations against the Shah ensured Khomeini's victory. Before the Sandinista's Revolution in Nicaragua it was chic to see things from the side of the revolutionaries. It was chic to be against President Somoza. There was no vision involved in that and our neutrality ensured the victory of the Sandinistas.

Neutrality became a kind of cocktail-party-understanding of world events. Somehow there came a determination that we should be a Super-Switzerland: observers, not participants in taking sides.

"After all, aren't we just as bad?" they asked and then went on to the potato chips and the dip and talked about a current movie.

A very strange phenomenon grew in the United States during those years when it came to the continent of Africa. To the liberal leaders in America there was only one country in Africa worthy of interest, rather than the 51 countries that composed that continent. The only country of interest was the Republic of South Africa. In that nation, run by an authoritarian government, there was a policy of apartheid that separated the races — where those with a dark complexion were segregated and without the rights given to those of light complexions;

where the government gave the darker people second and third class status. Those who were light ruled the country. It was for sure, a minority government.

Of the 51 African nations, it was one of 47 minority governments. (There were only four democracies: Botswana, The Gambia, Senegal, and Mauritius.) Most of those minority governments were not simply authoritarian as was the Republic of South Africa, but they were totalitarian, and some were primitive and performed such atrocities that vast numbers escaped, many to the Republic of South Africa, if they could survive the journey. Massacres of the majority in so many of those other 46 countries of minority governments, were commonplace, but only worthy of yawns from the leading American liberals.

There were the slaughters by the hundreds of thousands of the Tutsis and Hutus in Burundi and Rwanda, where 85% of both countries were Hutus (and short) and 15% were Tutsis (and tall). Height of the tribes, and other physical characteristics, rather than the color of the tribes, separated them. And there was the genocide in Uganda from one dictator after another, there was the exterminations in Liberia, there were the slaughters of one village after another and then one city after another in the Central African Republic, there were the one hundred thousand slaves of Mauritania, the house by house burnings of Cameroon, the 12,000 children sent to East Germany by Mozambique, and the 75,000 who died in its "Retraining Camps," and there were majority populations persecuted throughout the continent with few countries of exception — but there was no interest of American liberal leaders — because the victims and the perpetrators in those African nations were all of the same color.

On Embassy Row in Washington, D.C. there were no demonstrations outside the Embassies of Burundi or Rwanda or Liberia or Uganda or Cameroon or the Central African Republic or Mauritania or Mozambique — but any dawn there were lines of angry protesters outside the Embassy of the Republic of South Africa.

That is where the protesters stayed until the lighter people stopped persecuting the darker people in that nation. It mattered not at all that the slaughters in that nation were now coming from and to people of the same complexion, with 10,000 killed from 1980 through 1990 in contrast to the 8200 killed in the entire seventy year period prior to 1980 by those with a light complexion.

It must be understood that liberal Americans were more interested in the color of the persecutors than the lives of the persecuted, more interested in the complexion of the murderers than in the deaths of the murdered.

With one exception, the Republic of South Africa, American neutrality was the policy for an entire continent of 51 nations.

When an incident occurred anywhere in the world in which the United States or one of our authoritarian allies did something that was unjustifiable, something that diminished the world's perception of our foreign policy, there were those in the United States who had not a sense of tragedy or a sense of regret but, instead, a sense of joy: a joyful anger in "proving" that "the United States isn't so good." There were those in this country who reveled in such failures. "Look what we did!" Or "Look what our friends did!"

El Salvador took precedence in that thought-process regarding a friendly government that was authoritarian. How much was said and written about "Right Wing Death Squads" while rarely was a word said or written about "Left Wing Death Squads" even though the entire war was about Marxist-led guerrillas trying to take over El Salvador's freely elected government by force. That was undeniable. The Marxist-led guerrillas could not win at the ballot box, receiving only 3.085% of the vote. That was undeniable. They tried to prevent elections. That was undeniable. They murdered ten elected mayors, with 137 other elected mayors resigning under death-threats made against their families, and they murdered the Attorney General, the President's Chief of Staff, one governor, six judges, and thousands of non-government civilians. That was undeniable. The guerrillas were receiving aid from the Soviet Union and Soviet-bloc nations. That was undeniable. The majority of the U.S. national media all but ignored all of that, to concentrate on the questioning of our ally. That was chic.

Imagine that instead of El Salvador being involved in such a civil war, that it was the United States in a civil war against guerrillas, with family members fighting against the guerrillas and getting killed in the doing of it. Imagine, too, that the threat was to overturn our elected government. It would be safe to assume that many people within the United States would find it unthinkable to tolerate sympathizers and collaborators with the other side. Moreover, it is safe to assume that many people would find such sympathy and collaboration with the enemy a capital offense when the nation's fate was hanging in the balance, and the war would determine that fate. We weren't talking about anything less than that for El Salvador. Certainly the Underground of European States in World War II did exactly the same to Nazi sympathizers. Killed them. And that is totally understandable, justifiable, and under the circumstances, commendable.

What patriots in a nation at war would think differently? After World War II, some 10,000 French citizens were executed by their government as collaborators under the Vichy regime of France during the war.

As the last quarter of the 20th century went on, neutrality grew in the United States and those neutralists opposed helping people around the world who were fighting against totalitarians. Democrat liberals erased the words of President Kennedy's Inaugural Address, until they were almost invisible. The final erasure came 33 years after his Address, on April 23, 1993, when President Clinton made it official: "The United States should not become involved as a partisan in a war."

What?

Didn't we fight as a partisan in World War I? And World War II? And Korea and Vietnam and Grenada and Panama and the Persian Gulf? We always took a side. No longer as a partisan? What did that mean?

Neutrality.

It meant agreeing to fight, but not as a partisan.

We would enter a war only as a neutral — as a peace-keeper. For the first time in any of our lifetimes, we had a President who held peace higher than liberty.

He believed that as a youth in the 1960s, and sustained his belief as an adult in the 1990s. And it was the sustained belief of his chief advisors, despite the nation's heritage.

President Lincoln could have had peace and spared the states the agony of war and the death of one-half million Americans. He could have done that by removing the Union's troops from Fort Sumter and by allowing the secession of South Carolina and allowing the other states that sought confederation to become independent of the Union. And there would have been peace.

In the second decade of the Twentieth Century, France and Great Britain and the United States could have avoided World War One by refusing to pick up arms. And there would have been peace.

President Roosevelt could have brought about peace for the United States by standing before that Joint Session of the Congress on Monday, December 8, 1941, to request of the Congress, not a declaration of war to return fire for fire but, instead, a declaration of accommodation. And there would have been peace.

President Bush could have chosen peace in the Persian Gulf and allowed Saddam Hussein to keep Kuwait and to go on to conquer other Gulf States. And there would have been peace.

Surrender brings about peace, and neutrality brings about peace — the peace of the slave for the many, the peace of the master for the few, and the peace of the grave for what is left. But there is peace.

If we choose peace to liberty here and throughout the world, who would then be the obstacle to totalitarianism?

In the past it wasn't Switzerland that provided the obstacle to totalitarian expansion.

One year after the 1993 statement of "the United States should not become involved as a partisan in a war," President Clinton confirmed the meaning of those words. On April 15, 1994, in discussing Bosnia and the imminent bombardment and "ethnic cleansing" of Gorazde, he said, "The United States has no interest in having NATO become involved in this war and trying to gain advantage for one side over the other." And he said that the United States has no intention of rolling back the Serbian territorial gains, and that NATO's role is "to be firm but not provocative and not try to change the military balance."

The night before the entombment of President Anwar Sadat of Egypt, a number of U.S. delegates to the ceremonies were sitting in a small room off the side of the lobby of a large Cairo Hotel, and they were telling stories to one another about the late Egyptian President.

One of the most prominent U.S. delegates told the others, "I was in this city shortly after the Shah's arrival here," and he reminded the others of how the Shah had been forced to leave Iran, then to leave the United States, then to leave Mexico, then to leave Panama, and only Anwar Sadat of Egypt would accept the Shah. "And I said to President Sadat, 'Tell me, Mister President, it must have been a very difficult decision for you to invite the Shah, knowing that it might cause some real repercussions.'

"President Sadat was very indignant at my suggestion and he answered me by saying, 'Difficult? Why should it be difficult to decide how to treat a friend? For me there was no difficulty.'"

That incident illustrates the greatness of Sadat and illustrates that the diplomat was an ordinary man. The illustration is a tragedy in what it says about human nature. If the world was a better place, the same incident would illustrate that what Sadat answered made him an ordinary man, and the delegate was a fool. President Sadat's clear answer could have been expected because he was not a neutral. It was the U.S. diplomat's muddy question that exposed his own lack of integrity; abandonment of friends was the expected.

Dante said that "the worst place in hell is reserved for those who are neutral in times of crisis." If he was correct, then there are a lot of reserved seats waiting down there for some very famous American politicians and some prominent members of the U.S. media.

To be alive and witness events, and then to assume a position of neutrality is not the sign of a deep thinker. It is the sign of not being able to conclude a thought. Or worse than that, it is knowing what is right, and out of an overriding quest for safety, refusing to do it no matter the consequence to others.

CHAPTER THIRTY

SNOW IN
EVERY SEASON

Fifteen years after World War Two, I was in Germany, and I was young enough, and bold enough, and undiplomatic enough, and rude enough to ask many of those I talked to, "What did you do during the war?"

I received a consistent answer: "I was a ski instructor."

They said they learned what went on during the war when they returned from the mountains and, I was to assume, put away their skis in late 1945.

After hearing the same response so often, I recognized my lack of diplomacy and my abundance of rudeness, and I stopped asking. Any further questioning would not have achieved any discernible objective.

Sixteen years later, CBS presented a television show in which the reporter, Dan Rather, was walking through the remains of a concentration camp with the noted nazi hunter, Simon Weisenthal. Dan Rather looked over the fence and saw a village and he asked if that village was there when the concentration camp was in operation. Simon Weisenthal said it was. Dan Rather gave a stunned and horror-struck look, exclaiming that those people that lived there at the time must have known what was going on and didn't do anything about it. But his stunned and horror-struck appearance was not to be believed because at that very moment genocide was being committed in Cambodia and Dan Rather knew it, and the network for which he worked knew it, and the other large media of the nation knew it, but they were mute. The major media had a self-protecting need for silence since they had previously cast their stories against the actions of the

United States, not the Khmer Rouge. If the major media would have informed the public about what was happening after the war, their own credibility would have suffered.

Move the calendar forward another 16 years to the early 1990s and to Bosnia and Hezergovina. This time the media did their job.

The genocide in Bosnia was going on and on, with the quantity of the atrocities matched only by the quantity of excuses used for inaction from the government of the United States.

"These are ancient rivalries, hundreds of years old."

Most wars are ancient rivalries, hundreds of years old.

"The Europeans should do more."

In most European wars, most European countries should have done more.

"There are other horrible conflicts going on in the world."

There have always been other horrible conflicts going on in the world.

"The terrain is impossible."

Nor was the terrain ideal on the beaches of Normandy and the jungles of the Philippines and the mountains of Burma and the sands of Iwo Jima.

"Bosnia is not in our national interest."

What kind of nation are we if stopping the continuation of genocide is not in our national interest? "National interest" has become an argument to prove or disprove involvement anywhere. Under that awkwardly defined phrase it could be "proven" that Burkina Faso is in our national interest and Colombia is not.

"Military action could impair the 'peace process'."

That was true. The United States wanted to achieve peace, and not liberty anymore.

But as we became a world-neutral, four voices from the U.S. State Department were loud and clear in their recognition of the horror of our new policy. George Kenney, Jon Western, Marshall Harris, and Stephen Walker resigned from the State Department, giving up their foreign service careers because they could no longer support that policy of neutrality.

The officials of the administration shook their heads and smiled in disgust, and said that George Kenney and Jon Western and Marshall Harris and Stephen Walker were very low-level employees. They were, but they had the highest level of morality.

And then, in response to the genocide of Bosnia, came a magnificent voice from Great Britain that could not be defined as low-level by any definition: Lady Margaret Thatcher said, "We cannot let things go on like this. It is evil."

Immediately, Defense Minister Malcolm Rifkind responded, saying that her remarks were "emotional nonsense," and Lord David Owen who was engaged with Cyrus Vance in a "peace process" said, "Sometimes Lady Thatcher makes it appear very simple. It is not, unfortunately." U.S. Secretary of State Warren Christopher said of her statement: "A rather emotional response to an emotional problem."

God created three sexes: men, women, and diplomats. Rifkind, Owen, and Christopher were only diplomats, so what they said was unimportant. Therefore, the most chilling remark came from General Colin Powell who was a man and a soldier and the U.S. Chairman of the Joint Chiefs of Staff, who warned that U.S. military action was not advisable in Bosnia. He based his recommendations, not on the criteria of diplomats but on U.S. military capabilities.

What was happening to U.S. military capabilities that our Chairman of the Joint Chiefs of Staff was shaking his head? Was he saying that we wouldn't win?

In 1992 with the demise of the Soviet Union, President Bush recommended a reduction of 50 billion dollars in the budget for our military over the following five years. That meant that our defenses would be funded at their lowest percentage of the federal budget since before Pearl Harbor. As soon as the words were out of his mouth, Democrat leaders yelled that the reduction should be twice as steep, all the way to one hundred billion dollars of reductions. There was no itemization made in such quick advocacy; it was simply the doubling of the reduction recommended by the President. They argued that "the Cold War is over and the reductions should be made accordingly." (But most had advocated steep reductions during the height of the Cold War.) General

Powell argued back that "greater cuts (than recommended by the President) could threaten U.S. readiness."

It was just months later that President Clinton came into office and requested even greater reductions than other Democrat leaders. He called for a cut of 72 billion dollars more than President Bush for a total reduction of 122 billion dollars.

Where did that leave General Powell's warning that greater cuts beyond those of President Bush, could threaten U.S. readiness?

Those State Department resignations should have brought attention to a valid question: not only *should* we intervene in Bosnia, but did we have the military capability *to* intervene?

The question was not raised, the resignations were accepted and then ignored. The Congress agreed to the defense cuts advocated by President Clinton, with barely a voice of protest from the general public.

Polls conducted of U.S. citizens indicated that most Americans believed that defense was somewhere around 50% of the federal budget and that was too much. Very few knew that defense was only 19% of the budget, with President Clinton lowering it further to 18%.

The public had a false belief because of decades of media indoctrination. The term, "defense-spending" had been an every day and every night expression used by the major media. It was the only budget item that had a hyphen and the word "spending" attached to it. There was never a reference to "homeless-spending" or "health-spending" or "arts-spending" or "welfare-spending" or "Amtrak-spending" or "Corporation for Public Broadcasting-spending." The constant reference to "defense-spending" created the impression that it was the major, if not the only real expenditure of the federal government.

Over the decades of the 60s, 70s, and 80s, the major news-media became a powerful force to influence the public against one defensive system after another. It reached its peak in the campaign against the neutron warhead, which provides a text-book lesson in the gullibility and influence of irresponsible media, since it was a campaign that originated in the Kremlin:

The neutron warhead was designed for the purpose of destroying enemy tanks in friendly territory after an invasion by the enemy force. The reason that such a device was felt to be necessary was that by 1978, the Soviets had a massive force of tanks in Europe. (We had approximately 11,000 tanks and they had approximately 45,000.) The governments of Western Europe were concerned since the Soviets had so often used tanks for invasion purposes. Since NATO had no interest in an invasion of the Soviet Union or its satellites, increasing our number of tanks would not have changed the threat. The only change in threat could come if the Soviet Union would destroy their tanks, which was unlikely, or if the West established a deterrent that would make the Soviet tanks impotent, should they stage another invasion. To accomplish that, a device had to be employed that would be able to destroy the invading tanks and, in their destruction, not destroy the people or structures of the invaded western city the Soviet tanks would be occupying. Therefore it would have to be a device that would have near pin-point accuracy with as little surrounding fall-out as possible. That was the purpose and ability of the neutron warhead.

Moscow wanted it stopped. They could see that such a device in NATO's arsenal could make their tanks purposeless and diminish their advantage into parity. Moscow immediately initiated a brilliant propaganda campaign against the neutron warhead. The campaign (after its success) was referred to by the Chief of the International Department of the Hungarian Communist Party as "the most significant and successful political campaign since World War II." The campaign stopped the neutron warhead from being deployed. Through Soviet front-organizations in Western Europe, demonstrations were organized and the demonstrations attracted people who had no idea from where the campaign was originating, and no idea of the actual purpose of the neutron warhead. The demonstrations with their slogans quickly spread throughout Western Europe and on to the United States, with phrases originated in the Kremlin being unknowingly parroted by those in the west.

The Kremlin campaign included changing the name from the "neutron warhead" to the "neutron bomb." That was more potent-sounding and it was a name that masked its purpose. A slogan was originated within the Kremlin: "the bomb that kills people and leaves property intact." By the time the line came to the United States it was "the bomb that kills people and saves buildings."

In short time the people of Western Europe and the United States became so opposed to the neutron warhead that President Carter surrendered its assembly. After it was shelved, the American Bar Association's "Intelligence Report" revealed that the Soviet Union had spent over one-hundred million dollars on that propaganda campaign.

When the neutron warhead was revived under the Reagan Administration, the ABC Network reminded its audience that the restored plan was for "the bomb that kills people and leaves buildings in the target area intact." They were doing it again.

Throughout the cold war the major media downgraded the importance of our military preparedness and when the cold war was done (due to our military preparedness), they used the demise of the Soviet Union as a new justification for the old advocacy of lowering the defense budget.

It had become a familiar piece of public dialogue that "if we cut other departments of government, then defense must take its fair share of cuts," and that argument continues. It is as though all federal departments are co-equals, and as though their budgets are gifts and the giver must not play favorites between them.

That is the reasoning of fools.

Imagine that you live in a neighborhood that has 200 homes in it. (That is close to the number of countries that exist in the world.) The houses in the neighborhood are all getting run down. Luckily, you live in the best home in the neighborhood, but the upkeep on your home keeps costing you more and more money, and the money you take in doesn't buy as much as it did before. The television set keeps needing repair, the plumbing keeps getting clogged, the lock on the front door is broken, the floors are buckling, the carpet is torn, the furniture is showing its age, and some windows have cracks. But even though such disrepair has fallen on your home, you have to cut back on your spending because you cannot afford to go into any more debt.

Inside your house live the people you love. You want them to be healthy and happy and, in fact, you would give your life for them.

So one night you sit down at home with a pencil and paper and a pocket calculator and figure out what you're going to do to control your budget for the next year. With you is a financial consultant. He has brought along his brief-case sized calculator.

That financial consultant says, "Cut everything 10%. Everything. Repairs, plumbing, gas, electricity, everything. And what are these items on your list? You're buying a new lock for the back door and putting in a burglar-alarm system and replacing every broken window? You have to cut those expenditures proportionate to all the others."

You, quite logically, throw him out of your house, saying that "there's no way that I'll allow the people I love to live in danger, and no matter what I need to give up, I'll provide them with the safety they need; because without that safety they can lose everything. Everything. I have seen it happen to others."

But in an appeal to you as you lead the financial consultant to the door, he says, "But look," and he shows you the figure on the display of his calculator. It is high. And you inspect his calculator and by such inspection you are able to understand his reasoning. The problem is that his calculator can only register digits. No other realities. Nothing other than digits. And it's one of the old models. The ones without a memory.

No reduction in the cost of our government should mandate the departments of government as co-equals. If our common defense should fail, all departments of government fail. In fact, if the Department of Defense fails when it's needed most, the nation will be gone.

Therefore, the defense budget should be autonomous from the rest of the budget process so that we never again equate in importance an MX with Amtrak or the SDI with the SBA. If Social Security can be autonomous, and it is, then surely National Security should be autonomous, and it isn't.

There should be a three-word policy to dictate our defense budgets, tying them to the same three-word policy for foreign affairs: "We don't know." We never know what will happen in the world.

After the dismemberment of the Soviet Union began, did anyone in our government predict on August the 1st of 1990 that the next day the forces of Saddam Hussein would invade and conquer Kuwait in 19 hours? Did anyone in our government predict on August the 17th of 1991 that on the next day there would be an attempted coup in Russia and that their nuclear codes would be missing for more than 24 hours? Did anyone in government predict in the closing hours of 1991 that the genocide of "ethnic cleansing" would dominate the independence of a former constituent republic of Yugoslavia in 1992?

No. No one.

On September 1, 1993, Secretary of Defense Les Aspin announced the trimmed-down military plan of the Clinton Administration, explaining that, "We'll have a force based on tomorrow's requirements." How could anyone reduce our defenses based on "knowing" tomorrow's requirements?

There were, however, some things we did know when the Clinton defense cuts were put into print for Fiscal Year '94:

We knew that by the year 2000 some 15 Third World Nations would have missile capabilities.

We knew that ships with cargoes of advanced SCUD missiles were on the high seas having left North Korea on voyages to Syria and that other North Korean cargoes of longer range missiles were enroute to Iran.

We knew that North Korea had violated its signature on the Non-Proliferation Treaty and would not allow inspections of its nuclear and chemical and biological warfare facilities.

We knew that the People's Republic of China was supplying the Rafsanjani Government of Iran with 90 CSS-8 missiles and the People's Republic of China was building two nuclear reactors for Iran's government.

We knew that the leadership of Boris Yeltsin in Russia was fragile, and that Russia, the Ukraine, Byelorus and Khazikstan still had Intercontinental Ballistic Missiles deployed, and their nuclear warheads were not destroyed.

We knew that the Islamic Fundamentalist Revolution was threatening Egypt and terrorism was becoming a daily event there.

We knew that Hindu-Moslem violence was breaking out in northern India.

We knew that there were wars in Somalia, Sudan, Armenia, Azerbaijan, Liberia, Rwanda, Burundi, Zaire, Sri Lanka, Cambodia, and what was Burma.

And those were things we knew.

Most things we didn't know.

There is no Department of Prophecy.

There is, however, a Department of Memory called the Library of Congress. We know the past and so we know that every time any great power gave the perception of weakness, some other power immediately started to fill the vacuum. Always. Not sometimes, but always. It is both human nature and national nature.

And so when President Bush proposed a reduction of $50 billion in our military, within days the People's Republic of China announced they were increasing their military budget 13.8%. And when President Clinton proposed a further reduction to total $122 billion, the People's Republic of China announced they were increasing their military budget another 15%. They already had the biggest army in the world, and they already had ICBMs, and they already had nuclear warheads.

What power was threatening China? None. It was filling the vacuum we were leaving. Since the communist revolution in China, its leaders had proclaimed that by the end of the century all of China's territories would be returned "to the embrace of the Motherland." And it was already established that the mainland would have Hong Kong on July 1, 1997, and would have Macao on December 20, 1999, and new claims were being made on Mongolia, and eight of the Spratley Islands were taken by the People's Republic of China and used as military bases. That left Taiwan.

Deng Xiaoping made it clear, once again, that the use of force would not be excluded to bring back Taiwan to "the embrace of the Motherland."

What would the United States do if the People's Republic of

China used arms against the Republic of China on Taiwan?

The Clinton Doctrine was, "The United States should not be engaged as a partisan in a war."

The threats of totalitarians can be avoided if we reinstate the defense structure we had in the 1980s of approximately $300 billion a year (in 1982 dollars). Fear is the most potent weapon in the world. During peacetime, defense is largely psychological, and the psychology is based on what other powers think we have and what they think we would use. Unlike any other budget item, our military capabilities are totally successful when we don't need to use anything we have bought: not a shot fired, not a bomb dropped, not a missile used, not one combatant. And that should be our pursuit. It takes strength, funds, readiness, and the understanding of the American people. The objective must be that no tyranny would dare to trample on liberty for fear of the reaction of the United States, knowing that we have the means and the will to defend liberty.

Defense is always a guess; there is no certainty, and our defense budget can be established by guessing high or guessing low. Defense expenditures are like insurance expenditures: health insurance, automobile insurance, fire insurance, theft insurance, life insurance. All those guesses are wisely based on preparing for the worst while hoping for the best. When it comes to the survival of our nation and the survival of liberty, the risk is too great to guess low. If we guess too high we will waste money. If we guess too low we will waste the liberty of millions, and perhaps waste the United States.

President Kennedy not only talked about our dedication to liberty around the world, he said, "There can only be one defense policy for the United States and that is summed up in the word 'first.' I do not mean first 'but,' I do not mean first 'when,' I do not mean first 'if.' I mean first 'period.' Only then can we stop the next war before it starts. Only then can we prevent war by preparing for it."

General MacArthur said, "The history of failure in war can be summed up in two words: Too late. Too late in comprehending the deadly purpose of a potential enemy. Too late in realizing the mortal danger. Too late in preparedness. Too late in uniting all possible forces for resistance. Too late in standing with ones friends."

Put the General and the President together. General MacArthur summed up the failure of defense in two words: "Too late." President Kennedy summed up the success of defense in one word: "First."

But those words were said a long time ago.

A long time ahead, an old man will be sitting on a park bench with two canes resting by the bench as he feeds pigeons. And a young man will come up to him, young enough and bold enough and undiplomatic enough and rude enough to ask, "What did you do during the genocide of Bosnia?"

The old man will look him straight in the eyes and say, "I was a ski instructor."

The young man will know the man on the bench is lying, just as I knew other men were lying years back. And then the young man will ask, "Wasn't the population of the United States around a quarter of a billion people at the time of the genocide in Bosnia? "

"Yes, that's right, about 252,000,000. Why?"

"Why did the United States need 252,000,000 ski instructors?"

The old man will have to think for a while. "Oh, no, there weren't that many. Didn't you ever hear of George Kenney, Jon Western, Marshall Harris, and Stephen Walker? They were four who came down from the snow.

"One good thing about the United States, son, is there are always those, sometimes only a few of prominence, but there are always those who will do what is necessary for the liberty of others; those who will pay any price, bear any burden, meet any hardship, support any friend, oppose any foe, in order to assure the survival and the success of liberty."

CHAPTER THIRTY-ONE

HOW CAN THERE BE A NUMBER OF WORLDS ON ONE PLANET?

If visitors from another planet come to Earth, there are three ideas of Man that will defy explanation by those human beings who greet them and will be questioned by them:

1. The Easter Parade down Fifth Avenue in New York: why do they stop all automobile traffic with blockades and allow people to walk down the middle of the street, and how is it possible to know who is in the parade and who isn't? And what does walking down the middle of Fifth Avenue have to do with this religious observance?

2. Halloween on Santa Monica Boulevard in Los Angeles: why are men wearing dresses on the last night of October? If they like wearing dresses so much why don't they wear them all the time and if they don't like wearing them, why do they want to do it on that particular night?

3. The phrase, "The Third World": what are the first two worlds that called for a numbering system, and is there a fourth or fifth world? How many are there?

With tremendous respect for those visitors from another planet, especially if they don't blink and are huge and make the ground tremble when they walk, it is not that we don't want to explain those things to our guests; it is simply that no one can explain them, so getting angry isn't going to do any good. To show good faith towards such swell visitors, I'm at least going to offer a well-intentioned attempt to explain the use of the term, "The Third World."

It all started back in 1951 when the U.S. State Department wanted to issue statements regarding nations that were economically impoverished. Calling them "economically impoverished" or "poor nations" was impolitic, so the State Department called them "Under-Developed Nations."

That phrase was used for years until some Foreign Service Officer who just returned to Washington from a post in one of those "Under-Developed Nations" said that the phrase was insulting to the Chief of State of the host country in which the Foreign Service Officer had just been posted, and that the phrase was not much better than "economically impoverished" or "poor." What Chief of State, he asked, would be flattered or be given high esteem to be called the leader of an "Under-Developed Nation"? This Foreign Service Officer's idea was to call them "Developing Nations." That sounded much better, with the implication that such nations were in the midst of an uplifting metamorphosis.

But then he left the State Department and an Under-Secretary was appointed who thought that "Developing" had a negative ring to it and by its use, we could be accused of being elitist in our language. Such a term, he said, could suggest that *we* had already developed, but not *them*. So he changed the term to "Agricultural Societies."

Nothing wrong with agricultural societies except that unfortunately, some of those countries were not agricultural societies, and had more mineral wealth than agricultural wealth, and so the phrase was simply inaccurate, so it was changed again; this time to "Non-Industrial Societies."

But did the name imply that those nations *wanted* to be more industrialized? Maybe they didn't want to become industrialized. Maybe they were happy the way they were. Why make "industry" the most important characteristic and categorization of nations?

By then it was 1961 and President Tito of Yugoslavia started a conference of delegates called "The Non-Aligned Nations" with a membership of 24 states.

"The Conference of the Non-Aligned" as it became known, gave a political definition rather than an economic definition to its members. The State Department liked the term and started using it, too. The term meant that those countries were not aligned with either the United States or the Soviet Union.

One difficulty: Many of them were aligned with one or the other.

Then Franz Fanon came along — a man who was a French West-Indian revolutionary who said that those countries that President Tito had categorized were so far removed from the two industrialized blocs of nations, capitalist and communist, that they constituted a veritable third world. He was back to a title of poverty but no one would know it unless they asked for an explanation.

The term "The Third World" caught on because it didn't define itself. Those nations were simply countries of "The Third World," with the assumption made that there were two others. Soon Chiefs of State of many nations started saying that they were members of "The Third World," and although Franz Fanon's term was meant to designate economically impoverished nations, even rich nations like Saudi-Arabia and Kuwait wanted to be included in the group. It sounded so right.

The group of nations kept adding more members without any clear criteria to hold down its expansion. At the United Nations Organization they banned together in 1964 to form a power-bloc and because their membership was composed of 77 countries by that time, they called themselves "The Group of 77."

Not a bad title. It had a nice ring. It didn't mean a thing except how many countries were in the group. Very soon "The Group of 77" had 128 countries as members but it was still called "The Group of 77." You can't change a name every time you get new members.

In the meantime, President Tito's group, with a changing leadership, was continuing its meetings and continued to use the name "The Conference of the Non-Aligned." It had expanded from 24 countries to 101 countries and 4 terrorist groups. In 1975 North Korea was granted membership as one of the non-aligned countries despite its alignment with the communist powers, while South Korea and the Philippines were denied membership because of their alignment with the United States.

Within the 1980s these nations, in an informal sense but with increasing frequency, started calling themselves "The Nations of the

South" and talked about north-south relationships rather than relationships or non-relationships with capitalist and communist societies. Both the United States and the Soviet Union were north of the equator and most of the countries in "The Third World" (and the Non-Aligned and the Group of 77) were south of the equator.

But a lot of them weren't.

That term became too debatable.

"The Third World" seemed to be the most accurate of all the inaccurate terms so it lived on.

But then came the 1990s and the demise of the Soviet Union and the dismemberment of its empire. There were still some communist countries but there certainly wasn't a communist *world* anymore.

So what could be done with the numbering system? Without a communist world, does "The Third World" move up to be "The Second World" or what? You can't have a First World and a Third World without having a Second World. Or is that okay?

Why not call them exactly what they are? They are nations who have had crummy governments that didn't allow their citizens to be free, and now they want money that was earned by the citizens of other countries that had decent governments, and we call it The Third World because they are from the southern and the northern parts of the globe, and have somewhere between 77 and 128 countries with a few terrorist groups thrown in as well, that are rich and poor, with unused resources in some cases, and that are developing agriculturally other than the ones who don't need to because they are rich in mineral wealth or are industrialized, and were politically aligned and non-aligned when there was a large communist sphere of influence, and they complain a lot that other nations don't understand them.

If you think the explanation is unworthy to give to fine visitors from another planet, then see if you do any better in explaining to them the Easter Parade or the men who wear dresses on the last night of October.

CHAPTER THIRTY-TWO

AFTER STALIN DIED, GORBACHEV TOOK OVER

When the red flag bearing the hammer and sickle came down the flagpoles of Moscow, and the Soviet Union was dismembered, anti-communism finally became fashionable among the liberals of the United States.

But in their new-found anti-communism, they would not mention the names of Brezhnev, Andropov, and Chernenko. It was as though they hadn't existed. To describe communists, they used the term, "Stalinists" even though Stalin had been dead for 39 years and even preceded Khrushchev. Had they mentioned the names of Brezhnev, Andropov, and Chernenko they would have caused American voters to be reminded of where those liberals stood in the two most recent decades in which those tyrannies ruled the Soviet Union. The liberal leadership of the United States had winked at them and had smiled at them and had nodded at them during the 1970s and 1980s. And they called the anti-Communists of the United States "McCarthyites" and war-mongers" and "cold-war warriors" and worse. Only when the communist empire was dead did the American liberal leaders find it fashionable to direct criticism at the communist empire.

Before its death, it was the conservatives, not the liberals, who wanted to build U.S. military forces to a position so strong that the Soviet Union would go broke trying to keep up with us. And opposing those efforts were Brezhnev, Andropov, Chernenko, and the leadership of the Democrats.

It was the conservatives, not the liberals, who supported the liberation of Grenada, and brought about free elections in that island-nation. Opposing the liberation were Brezhnev, Andropov, Chernenko, and the leadership of the Democrats.

It was the conservatives, not the liberals, who backed Jonas Savimbi in Angola in his quest to end the communist dictatorship of that nation. Opposing aid to Jonas Savimbi were Brezhnev, Andropov, Chernenko, and the leadership of the Democrats.

It was the conservatives, not the liberals, who wanted to bring down the Sandinistas of Nicaragua under Daniel Ortega who was expanding communism in Central America, and it was the conservatives, not the liberals, who supported aid to the Nicaraguan Resistance so that a Soviet Satellite wouldn't be permanently implanted on the mainland of the Western Hemisphere. Opposition to the Nicaraguan Resistance and embracing Daniel Ortega were Brezhnev, Andropov, Chernenko, and the leadership of the Democrats.

It was the conservatives, not the liberals, who wanted to introduce a Strategic Defense Initiative to guard America and make an enemy's ICBMs worthless. Opposing such a defensive system for the United States were Brezhnev, Andropov, Chernenko, and the leadership of the Democrats.

And it was a conservative President, Ronald Reagan, who accurately called the Soviet Union and its hold of satellite nations an Evil Empire. And taking issue with his statement and ridiculing it were Brezhnev, Andropov, Chernenko, and the leadership of the Democrats.

The names of Brezhnev, Andropov, and Chernenko were erased at the beginning of the 1990s so that the international policy of the liberals throughout the Brezhnev-Andropov-Chernenko years would be forgotten.

And there was another change, this one in terminology: The liberal leaders and the U.S. media suddenly called the hard-line communists of the former Soviet Union, "conservatives," and they called the free-market and democratic reformers of the Soviet Union, "liberals." It was a reverse of the American vocabulary and it made no sense, but nothing needed to make sense to those who busied themselves in the rewriting of history.

They knew they could fool the public, because fooling the public had been their careers.

CHAPTER THIRTY-THREE

THE GREAT MIRAGE IN THE MIDEAST

The worst mistake that Israel made since its re-birth as a nation occurred immediately after its victory of the Six Day War in 1967. Israel had just won the Sinai and Gaza and the Golan Heights and Judea and Samaria, and called these areas "administered territories" which became internationally known as "occupied territories." Israel should have called those places of victory, "Israel."

The worst mistake that the United States made in our mideast policy was identifying those areas, particularly Judea and Samaria, as "the root of the problem in the Mideast," and that "the Palestinian question must be resolved to bring peace to the Mideast." Those sentences of policy painted the geopolitical mirage that has prompted tragedy after tragedy in the succeeding years, with more to come.

It all started in 1947 when the United Nations Organization partitioned Palestine into a number of entities: 78% of Palestine became Jordan, 17.5% became Israel and the remaining 4.5% went to Judea, Samaria, and Gaza, with Jerusalem becoming an international zone. The day after partition, Egypt invaded and seized Gaza, and Jordan invaded and seized Judea and Samaria including eastern Jerusalem. The governments of Egypt and Jordan didn't create Palestinian States in those seized areas, they prevented their existence.

Jordan called the captured Judea and Samaria, including eastern Jerusalem, "The West Bank" meaning the west bank of the Kingdom of Jordan, a name that defined it as Jordanian territory, across the river from "the rest of" Jordan. All Jews who survived were expelled, and their historic sites, including graveyards, were destroyed, with gravestones used as latrines. Christians who remained were mandated to send their children to schools to learn the Islamic Religion.

For 19 years following 1948, Jordan ruled Judea and Samaria, not once allowing even the discussion of an independent Palestinian State. Egypt retained jurisdiction of Gaza during the same 19 years and, like Jordan, did not allow even the discussion of an independent Palestinian State. And so it would have gone on if not for the pursuit of Arab Chiefs of State wanting to own all of Israel as well as the territories they had already seized.

In 1967, President Gamal Nasser of Egypt blockaded the Gulf of Aquaba to isolate Israel, and at the same time he started sending his tanks across the Sinai towards Israel. There were U.N. peace-keepers in the Sinai to prevent such an invasion, but President Nasser told them to leave and Secretary General of the United Nations Organization, U Thant, agreed to their departure.

It was for sure that Syria would join Egypt in a joint attack on Israel and it was probable, but not certain, that Jordan would join the invasion forces as well. The threat of Gamal Nasser was to "throw the Zionists into the sea." The war was not for Sinai, not for Gaza, not for the Golan Heights, and not for Judea and Samaria. Egypt already had Sinai and Gaza, Syria already had the Golan Heights, and Jordan already had Judea and Samaria and had already renamed them the West Bank. The purpose of the coming attack was to take over the land that was Israel.

Since it was known that the Egyptian attack would come from the south-west, with a Second Front of Syria from the north, Israel wanted desperately to avoid a Third Front of war that could come from Jordan in the east. Israel and Jordan did not have diplomatic relations so there could be no direct dialogue between the two nations, therefore the government of Israel requested that a U.S. emissary talk to King Hussein of Jordan to give him a pledge from the government of Israel — a pledge that Israel would leave Jordan alone if Jordan would not join the Egyptians and Syrians in the attacks that were imminent. President Johnson sent Under Secretary of State Eugene Rostow on the mission to Jordan to relay the Israeli message to King Hussein. King Hussein listened to Under Secretary Rostow but made no commitment.

On May 18, the Voice of the Arabs Radio announced, "The sole method we shall apply against Israel is a total war which will result in the extermination of Zionist existence."

On May 27, President Nasser of Egypt said, "Our basic objective will be the destruction of Israel. The Arab people want to fight."

On May 29, Nasser said, "We have reached the stage of serious action and not declarations."

On May 30, Nasser said, "The armies of Egypt, Jordan, Syria and Lebanon are poised on the borders of Israel."

On June 4, Nasser received the commitment of Iraq to join Egypt in the war, with President Aref saying, "Our goal is clear - to wipe Israel off the map."

On June 5, Israel launched a pre-emptive strike against Egypt's airfields and the war started with Israel in control of the timing, rather than Egypt and its allies.

King Hussein of Jordan joined Egypt.

Egypt lost the war. Syria lost the war. Jordan lost the war. All in six days. Sinai and Gaza were lost by Egypt, the Golan Heights were lost by Syria, and Judea and Samaria were lost by Jordan. Israel could easily have gone on to the capital cities of all three countries, but Israel now had secure borders, believing those new borders would prevent war in the future.

Decades later Eugene Rostow said of his earlier mission to Jordan, "I myself transmitted the Israeli message to Hussein in 1967, promising him immunity if he did not join the war. If he had stayed out of the war, he would hold the West Bank and Old Jerusalem today."

After the 1967 War, the governments of Egypt, Syria, Jordan and other Arab governments made the first demand for the creation of an Independent Palestinian State. Suddenly the 19 years of their jurisdiction of those territories were lost in the memories of mideast leaders as easily as the wind covers images in the sand. Had they wanted an Independent Palestinian State during those 19 years, all they had to do was not to have invaded and seized them and kept them during that period of time.

The gullible amnesia-prone foreign policy experts of the West allowed the nineteen-year delayed attempt to create an Independent Palestinian State to gain credibility. And it all stems from a bizarre mind-set of the U.S. Department of State.

When an enemy of the United States wins territory in war, our State Department accepts that. It's the past. It's done. The territory belongs to the victor. But when a friend of the United States wins territory in war our State Department feels differently. "All right," our State Department says, "you've won the war. Now give the territory back." If only the government of Israel had as a leader an Emir Adballah or a King Farouk or a Mao Tse-tung or an Ayatollah Khomeini or a Pol Pot or a Pham Van Dong or a Slobodan Milosevic, the United States would have accepted Israel's 1967 victory and made the best of it. (Our State Department would later try to bring about a partition of Bosnia giving captured territory to Serbia, not as occupied territory, but as "facing the fact that it won those territories in war.")

Five and one-half months after the Six Day War of 1967, the United Nations Organization passed a resolution. (All U.N. Resolutions are numbered and this was U.N. Resolution 242.) It was a piece of absolute genius because it seemed to say almost anything any reader wanted it to say. Its most important statement was the affirmation of "withdrawal of Israeli armed forces from territories of recent conflicts." There was an intentional absence of the word "the" or "all" preceding the words "territories of recent conflicts." It only called for withdrawal "from territories," not stating which, how many, or how much of the territories. It could mean that Israel must give up 1% or 100% of the territories. (Eleven years later, Israel could have claimed that it was acting in full compliance of U.N. Resolution 242, since with the signing of the Camp David Accords, Israel gave up 92% of the territories gained in that war, with the return of Sinai to Egypt.)

Three years after the 1967 War, King Hussein of Jordan fought another war, and this time he was victorious. It was not a war against Israel, but a civil war against the PLO in which 10,000 Arab-Palestinians were killed by King Hussein's forces as the PLO tried to take over the Kingdom of Jordan. As a result of Jordan's victory, the PLO sought refuge in Lebanon. It is purely for public relations reasons that the Jordan-PLO War is no longer talked about by the government of Jordan or the PLO or other Arab leaders. It was felt that it was best to have it forgotten rather than to remind the world that an Arab State, Jordan and, in fact, an Arab State that is 78% of Palestine itself, rejected the PLO to the point of warfare against it. That fleeing of the PLO to Lebanon created a mini-state within the nation of Lebanon, with subsequent terror and destruction brought to that nation.

Arab leaders kept mixing colors to add to the mirage. Their foreign policy announcements began by saying that an Independent Palestinian State must be created on the West Bank, even though none of those leaders wanted an Independent Palestinian State anywhere in the mideast. They didn't trust a Palestinian leader on or near their own borders. The only Arab leader to have broken the mirage was Anwar Sadat, who was abruptly tested one day on the NBC television program, *Meet the Press*. It was September the 9th, 1979 when Bill Monroe asked President Sadat an unexpected question:

"Mister President, President Carter says that when he talks privately with Arab leaders, they tell him they do not want an Independent Palestinian State. Do you agree with that? Is that your experience as well?"

President Sadat was surprised by the question. He hesitated and then answered, "It is a family business and I choose better to abstain."

There was no question about what President Sadat was revealing, not that it needed revelation to policy-makers. It had already been the best-known secret of Washington, D.C., but now the secret would be known throughout the United States if the major media headlined it. They didn't. The State Department breathed a sigh of relief. His statement went by unnoticed by the general public.

The reason the U.S. State Department did not want the truth known was not because they were evil people, it was not because they wanted to subvert anyone, it was not because they were prejudiced against Israel or Jews. It was because of the reality of human nature; they wanted to have a good time:

The State Department is largely composed of Foreign Service Officers who have a succession of two-year foreign posts — sometimes a year or so more than that. With 21 Arab countries and another 20 other Moslem countries, and only one Israel, the odds were that the U.S. Foreign Service Officer would serve in one or more Arab or other Islamic countries during a career, and probably not serve in Israel at all. Life is easier for a U.S. diplomat when in a friendly country whose citizens and government like U.S. policies rather than in an unfriendly country whose citizens and government oppose our policies. It's that simple. Make life easy.

And so the U.S. State Department bent towards the dialogue of Arab Chiefs of State, and regarded what was called by our own State Department as "the Palestinian Question" as the root of the problem in the mideast. They knew, however, that "the Palestinian Question" was not a question but an answer to many Arab Chiefs of State who wanted to exhibit unity when they knew that *they* were the root of the crises of the mideast in that they wanted to expand their borders over neighboring lands.

Even if all of Israel ceased to exist, the government of Syria would still want to annex Lebanon and take over Jordan.

The government of Libya would still want to take over Chad, and Sudan, and Egypt.

The government of Iraq would still want to take over Kuwait and Saudi Arabia and the whole of the Persian Gulf.

The government of Iran would still want to take over Iraq and Jordan and, in fact, every Islamic nation.

The government of South Yemen would still want to take over North Yemen.

The Governments of both Yemens would still want to take over Oman and Saudi Arabia.

The governments of Somalia and Ethiopia would still want to take over each other.

Further away, the Polisario would still want to take over the Western Sahara.

And too, Syria would still want to take over the PLO and the PLO would want to take over Jordan, and the only unifying force is that all those nations and political entities wanted to take over Israel.

The quest of expansion by Arab leaders is the root of the problems of the Mideast.

But the mirage enlarged, and on September 13, 1993, in Washington D.C., a "land for peace" agreement was signed between Israel and the PLO. Gaza and Jericho would be under the jurisdiction of Yasir Arafat. It was a massive step back to the 1967 borders.

Should Israel surrender all of Judea and Samaria to the PLO, there will be a war between the powers of the Hashemite Kingdom of Jordan and the new rulers of Judea and Samaria. The victor of that war would then find itself in another war; not with Israel but with Syria. The victor of that war would attack Israel.

As the Arabs say, "It is written."

One of the most visible tragedies beyond the mirage has been the fate of the Arab Palestinians, a people who have become the innocent victims of Arab leaders who professed to be their friends. They were skewered by them, holding them as refugees within Arab Nations since 1948.

The world is filled with refugees that were victims of crisis. There have been refugees from Southeast Asia and Cuba and what was the Soviet Union and Eastern Europe and Iran and one African country after another and they have been absorbed into other lands. Other than the Arab-Palestinian, being a refugee has not been a career, but has been a background. Friendly governments have most often taken the displaced into their nations and integrated them after brief stays in refugee camps for examination and relocation. But the Arab-Palestinian has become a permanent refugee because "friendly" Arab governments have not been friendly. Instead, those governments created a career-status of Arab Palestinian refugees unintegrated into their societies.

By ignoring the truths of the mideast, we missed golden opportunities. Lebanon would have been at peace in 1982 had our policy been to dismiss the Palestinian question as a lie. We would not have sent U.S. Marines into Lebanon to ensure the safe passage of the PLO; we would instead, have nodded to Israel to continue to rout its enemy and leave Lebanon only after the PLO and Syria were pushed beyond Lebanon's borders.

The mirage should have been known by the 1950s and the 1960s and surely by the 1970s, but the 1980s came, and the 1990s came, and Israel's agreement to a land for peace arrangement with the PLO is destined to bring about a State ruled by the PLO and destined to bring about tragedy to the mideast.

During the preceding years there were other errors that evaded peace rather than encouraged it: President Sadat had three Arab nations as allies in his quest for peace; Somalia, the Sudan, and Oman. With almost unbelievable courage, President Siad Barre of Somalia, Prime Minister Nimeiri of the Sudan and Sultan Qaboos of Oman, backed President Sadat's participation in the Camp David Accords. And when he was assassinated, those three governments were the only Arab entities to send delegations to his entombment. That was the time for our quick embrace of those three Chiefs of State in response to their bravery. We had an opportunity to start a new alliance within the mideast, an alliance of Israel, Egypt, Somalia, the Sudan, and Oman. But we didn't seize the opportunity, and without the United States as a shield; Somalia, the Sudan, and Oman had no choice but to lapse back into the arms of the other Arab governments for safety.

Events soon overtook the prospective allies; Somalia became busy with its own war after we abandoned Siad Barre, and Sudan's government fell in a coup that we encouraged by demanding that new and dangerous economic policies be enacted by Prime Minister Nimeiri. Oman stayed with us and as the Ayatollah Khomeini's Islamic Fundamentalist Revolution became an increasing threat to the countries of the Persian Gulf, Sultan Qaboos of Oman argued among his neighbors for friendlier ties with the United States as a deterrent to the new Iranian Government. He was rebuffed, and finally had no choice but to be silent.

Instead of creating a new alliance, we chose to play the Mideast Card Game where, under the table, we tangled with so many feet that it became difficult to know which shoe belonged to whom.

Most shoes belonged to governments that had no interest in liberty, or peace, or democracy, or friendship with the United States based on ideals.

For all these years, the fear of many Israelis had been that direct Israeli annexation of Judea and Samaria into the rest of Israel would eventually bring about an end of Israel, or an end of Israeli democracy. That was because in time, the population of Arabs in those territories added to the population of Arabs in Israel-proper, would become a majority over Jewish voters, therefore creating a 22nd Arab State with the end of the only Jewish State. Israelis feared they would have to choose between that happening or giving up a democratic form of government.

But neither course would be necessary with Israeli annexation. Instead of making such a choice between creating another Arab State or abolishing democracy, Israel could revise its governmental structure. Its current structure is a unicameral, a one-house legislature, called the Knesset. If it changed its structure to two Houses (as in the United States), the lower House could be based on the population of districts (as in the United States), and the upper House, a Senate, could be based on territory (as in the United States), rather than population. This House could have veto power over the lower house. If there were, as example, 20 senatorial districts in Israel, each with two senators, then Gaza and Judea and Samaria, as three senatorial districts, would only have a total of six senators, whereas the combined amount of senators from the other 17 districts would total 34. That would heavily weigh representation in favor of residents, both Jews and Arabs, living within pre-annexation borders and would permit democracy without turning the only Jewish State into the 22nd Arab State.

But we have no jurisdiction over the structure of the Israeli Government and they have chosen to go a different way. We do, however, have jurisdiction over future U.S. policy in the mideast and we should rise from the table and throw the cards down face-up, revealing the truth.

Or we can continue to stare at the mirage and say that it's always been real, and that our Mideast policies will be dictated by the strongest wind that moves the sand.

CHAPTER THIRTY-FOUR

THE LOGAN-FONDA-
CLARK-JACKSON ACT

The auditorium of the University of Michigan was filled to its 2000 seat capacity. The date was November the 21st of 1970 and the attraction was the movie actress, Jane Fonda. Her words were direct: "If you understood what communism was, you would hope, you would pray on your knees that we would some day become communist."

That's okay. That was simply a revelation of her political belief in favor of communism, and the speech was made in the United States. What was not okay was when, some two years later, she went to North Vietnam, and on Radio Hanoi, proclaimed that "We know what U.S. imperialism has done to our country, so we know what lies in store for any Third World Country that could have the misfortune of falling into the hands of a country such as the United States — and becoming a colony."

And this is why it was not okay:

Shortly after this country was born, France seized a U.S. ship and took its U.S. crew as prisoners. A doctor in Pennsylvania got frustrated with the lack of progress our government was making in getting those men out of prison in France. In time he became certain that he could negotiate their release better than President John Adams. And so, without any governmental authority, Dr. George Logan went to France and talked to the captors of the American prisoners.

He succeeded.

He negotiated the release of those crewmen and obtained the return of the ship as well.

Former President George Washington was not at all pleased about the journey of Dr. Logan. He saw it as a dangerous precedent.

And President Adams was so angry about Dr. Logan's act that he talked to members of the Congress about passing a law to prohibit private, unelected citizens from consulting with foreign governments and attempting to influence them in matters that relate "to any disputes or controversies with the United States."

And it was done. The Congress passed the law and it was known as The Logan Act and the President signed it. Penalties were set at up to $5,000 plus three years imprisonment.

But laws aren't always enforced and that one has never been enforced.

172 years later came Jane Fonda and her propaganda broadcasts for North Vietnam including her broadcasts instructing U.S. servicemen to disobey their orders. After the U.S. prisoners of war returned to the United States, it was revealed by them that a number of them had been severely tortured for not agreeing to visit with her in North Vietnam. One such prisoner of war was confined to a punishment cell for four months for refusing to visit with her. The cell was five by three feet. (Try it for four minutes rather than four months.) Another returned prisoner revealed that "I had a broken arm. It was in a cast. I was hung by that broken arm several times and allowed to drop at the end of a rope from a table which was kicked out from under me."

Those prisoners stated that the greater torture would have been to visit with her, which was why they did not.

There was talk of prosecuting the actress for treason under Section 3, Article 3 of the U.S. Constitution in its giving "aid and comfort" clause regarding the enemies. But since we were engaged in an undeclared war, the term "enemies" was judged to be imprecise. There was then a discussion of her violation of The Logan Act. But it wasn't enforced against her, since it had never been enforced.

Ramsey Clark, the former Attorney General of the United States, also went to Hanoi and made propaganda broadcasts for their government (August 9, 1972). When he came back to the United States he assured Americans that the U.S. servicemen who were prisoners of war were "unquestionably being humanely treated." Later, when they came back home themselves, they told America that, as in the case of

Jane Fonda's visit, American prisoners of war had been tortured in Hanoi because they refused to meet with him.

Eight years later, in 1980, during the Iranian hostage crisis, Ramsey Clark went to Teheran to participate in a conference called by the Ayatollah Khomeini dealing with "U.S. crimes." Ramsey Clark sat there without protest when the Ayatollah Khomeini called President Carter a "wild animal" and Clark praised the Ayatollah's revolution and called the U.S. mission to rescue our imprisoned diplomats "a lawless act."

As a result, the U.S. Senate adopted a resolution deploring any actions by private citizens to engage in negotiations affecting the U.S. hostages in Iran. The measure was proposed by Senate Democrat leader, Robert Byrd. But when it came to The Logan Act in relation to Clark's activities (to say nothing of his disobeying the President's travel ban to Iran), the Congress did nothing.

Shortly afterwards, Ramsey Clark went to Nicaragua to visit and support the Sandinistas against U.S. policy, and speak against Eugene Hassenfus, an American being held by the Sandinistas. When Hassenfus told the Sandinista Government that he was unemployed before working for the Contras, Ramsey Clark said, "If unemployment were a defense to crime, then most people in American prisons would have to be released."

Then came the terrorist acts of Mu'ammar al-Qadhafi against Americans. And there in Qadhafi's Libya was Ramsey Clark threatening, not Qadhafi, but threatening to file a suit against the United States of America for bombing Libya in the anti-terrorist retaliation ordered by President Reagan in April of 1986.

Then Ramsey Clark went off to Panama to condemn our invasion there. He seemed somewhat out of place condemning us as Panamanians hugged and kissed American troops.

On to Iraq to condemn our entry into the Persian Gulf War after Saddam Hussein invaded Kuwait.

In summary, Ramsey Clark was more helpful to Ho Chi Minh, the Ayatollah Khomeini, Mu'ammar al-Qadhafi, Daniel Ortega, Manuel Noriega, and Saddam Hussein than he was to five Presidents of the

United States.

Another foreign negotiator without authority was Jesse Jackson. He went to Syria to successfully negotiate with their government regarding the release of captured U.S. Lieutenant Robert Goodmann. During the same year he went to a number of Central American countries, visiting with their leaders, and to Mexico where he denounced the United States.

All three of the people just named went to a minimum of one foreign nation while the government of that nation was holding U.S. prisoners, and during such a visit they publicly condemned U.S. policy. Such a record gives incentive to a government hostile to the United States to take U.S. captives, and wait for some world-known American who denounces U.S. policy to go to that foreign country, and with the spotlight of world attention, obtain that prisoner's release. Any government hostile to the United States could, in fact, take prisoners for the motive of releasing the prisoners to whomever they consider to be the right person at the right time for their purpose.

A law unenforced is no better than a law never written. And by precedent, it is obvious that we are not going to suddenly start enforcing The Logan Act after ignoring it for two centuries. But in view of the harm its non-enforcement has caused, including the torture of American prisoners of war, and broadcasts espousing the side against which we were fighting, and the propaganda advantage of world-known Americans speaking against the United States on foreign soil, the Congress should initiate new legislation restating the objectives of the Logan Act and calling for its enforcement in any such future entanglements by private citizens.

Further, so that treason is considered to be an act of giving an enemy aid and comfort during both declared wars and undeclared wars, within the re-write of The Logan Act should be the addition, "Enemies as described in Article 3, Section 3 of the Constitution are those governments or groups engaged in armed conflict against the military forces of the United States, or those in armed conflict against a government or group supported by the United States."

If the Congress passes such a law, surely the ACLU or some like-minded organization will claim the law is unconstitutional and it would then go through the courts. The courts would probably judge it to be constitutional since the proposed law doesn't deny or change a constitutional phrase, but simply defines it. If, however, the courts should judge it as unconstitutional, then that paragraph should be forwarded through the Congress and state legislatures as a Constitutional Amendment.

Without enforcing the Logan Act or writing a new similarly worded act, diplomatic anarchy can destroy U.S. foreign policy in a future conflict, by someone who wants the headlines of prominence at the expense of the responsibilities of our elected government.

For the future foreign policy objectives of the United States and for the safety of United States service personnel, the Congress should pass the Logan-Fonda-Clark-Jackson Act.

CHAPTER THIRTY-FIVE

SOME THINGS ARE SIMPLY IMPOSSIBLE AND IT'S TIME TO GET THAT IN OUR HEADS

It would have been the greatest accomplishment in the history of defense — a system to be designed that would do injury to no one — a system that would not kill or harm one human being or any other living creature, but rather a system whose purpose would be only to destroy a warhead already coming toward its target from a missile.

But it was said that it couldn't be done. "It will never work. You can't hit a nose cone of a missile by using another missile. It's like a bullet coming at you, and you can't hit a bullet with a bullet."

There were other prophets throughout United States history who were practical men rather than adventurers:

Dionysys Lardner said: "Rail travel at high speeds is not possible because passengers, unable to breathe, will die of asphyxia."

General John Kerr said: "We must not be misled to our detriment to assume that the untried driving machines can displace the proved and tried horse."

The Royal Society of London, a group of the world's most eminent scientists, released a statement that Thomas Edison's plan to electrify cities "defies scientific principle" and "won't work."

Lord Kelvin, President of the Royal Society said: "Heavier than air flying machines are impossible."

Harry Warner, one of the Warner Bothers, said: "Who the devil wants to hear actors talk?"

Dr. Robert Millikhan, Nobel Prize Winner for Physics in 1923 said: "There is no likelihood that man can ever tap the power of the atom."

Lord Rutherford, Nobel Laureate, after the first experimental splitting of the atom in 1933 said: "The energy produced by the breaking down of the atom is a very poor kind of thing. Anyone who expects a source of power from the transformation of the atom is talking moonshine."

Admiral Leahy told President Truman: "The Atomic Bomb will never go off, and I speak as an expert in explosives."

Lee Deforest said: "While theoretically and technically, television may be feasible, commercially and financially I consider it an impossibility; a development of which we need waste little time dreaming."

Darryl Zanuck said: "TV won't be able to hold on to any market it captures after the first six months. People will soon get tired of staring at a plywood box every night."

Eighteen years before the first launch of an Atlas Intercontinental Ballistic Missile, Dr. Vannevar Bush who directed our World War II science effort said: "We can leave out of our thinking a 3000 mile rocket shot from one continent to another."

Dr. F. B. Moulton, Astronomer at the University of Chicago said: "There is no hope for the fanciful idea of reaching the moon, because of insurmountable barriers to escaping the earth's gravity."

Secretary of Defense Bob MacNamara said: "There is no indication that the Soviets are seeking to develop a strategic force as large as our own."

Kenneth Olsen, president of Digital Equipment Corporation in 1977 said, "There is no reason for any individual to have a computer in their home."

Thomas Watson, Chairman of I.B.M. said: "I think there's a world market for about five computers."

Now go backwards in time, to 1899 when Charles Duell, the Director of the U.S. Patent Office said, "Everything that can be invented has been invented."

And in 1983, eight years before our Patriot Missiles knocked down SCUD Missiles in the Persian Gulf, Senator Ted Kennedy said: "You can't hit a bullet with a bullet."

Some things, we are told, just can't be done.
Nuts.
Too bad.

CHAPTER THIRTY-SIX

RETALIATION GUARANTEED

It will be prime time; exactly 9:00 P.M. in Washington, D.C. when the door of the Chamber will open and the doorkeeper will yell it out, "Mr. Speaker, the President of the United States."

The applause will be immediate as the audience of Senators and Representatives and the Supreme Court and the members of the President's Cabinet and his staff rise and the applause will last through the end of the President's journey to the podium and beyond. And the Speaker of the House will say "Members of the Congress, I have the high privilege and distinct honor of presenting to you, the President of the United States." And again the standing ovation.

There will be greatness, not only in the moment, but in this President, with or without the traditional ovation.

"Mr. Speaker, Mr. Vice-President, Distinguished Members of the Senate and House of Representatives, honored guests and fellow citizens:

"As President of the United States of America, I have requested this Joint Session of the Congress to ask this body for a declaration of war against an enemy of the United States of America — a hostile force that is also an enemy of most of the inhabitants of this planet. That enemy is Terrorism.

"As Franklin Delano Roosevelt once came to this chamber to request a declaration of war because of a surprise attack on Pearl Harbor, I am here for a similar declaration, because of repeated surprise attacks on our citizens that have taken place throughout the world. The victims of those surprise attacks have been powerless, and they have been innocent of any crimes. They have often been murdered because they held a passport issued by the United States of America.

"Those attacks have not been a matter of the past alone; we become much too relaxed in the intermissions between attacks. They will come again, maybe next year, maybe in the next moment, but they will come again. And if we do nothing more than we have done, they will escalate in the future. These surprise attacks can come to any citizen of the United States.

"But what do I mean by a declaration of war? With precision, what is it I'm requesting?

"I am requesting that from your declaration forward, the United States of America will regard Terrorism as a sovereign state — as a nation in itself. The Nation of Terrorism is a chain of bases, training camps, safe houses, and other facilities that dot portions of the map of the world, going into and out of other sovereign states. The non-contiguous configuration that the Nation of Terrorism has enjoyed has been a shield since its citizens-by-choice have assumed that they would always be regarded as part of other sovereign states that surround them. That shield must be a thing of the past.

"Our declaration of war will not mean a declaration of war against Iran or Iraq or Libya or Syria or Cuba or North Korea or Sudan, which are those countries on our State Department list of terrorist nations, but against the bases of terrorism within those countries and other countries, as long as those governments permit such bases to exist there.

"As Commander-in-Chief I will see to it that if any American is terrorized; indeed if one hair on the head of an American is touched in hostility, there will be an immediate retaliation by the Government of the United States of America against Terrorism, with our military directed to strike at an unannounced terrorist target we think appropriate within that archipelago of 'islands' that have been built and inhabited within the existing borders of other sovereign states.

"In short, we will no longer simply search for individuals directly responsible for individual acts of terrorism any more than in other wars we would search selectively for an individual grenade-thrower on a battlefield. This will be a clear edict that we are no longer at war against individual terrorists alone when we can find them, but instead, we are at war against Terrorism and we have found it.

"When President Roosevelt addressed this body in December of 1941 he did not say 'Yesterday we were attacked at Pearl Harbor, and we are going to do everything possible to find out who those individual pilots, navigators, and bombardiers were, and capture those men, and bring them to justice.' That would have been a guarantee that we would have lost the war.

"We must recognize that the Nation of Terrorism has already declared war against the United States and has often captured our most prized property — our citizens. As President of the United States I cannot and will not allow that to continue or re-start.

"If terrorists feel that our retaliatory policy puts them at risk of being targeted for individual acts of terrorism that they did not commit, there is only one option for their future safety: to get out of the terrorism business.

"My fellow Americans, intermittently, terrorism, including hostage-taking, has been a crime without sufficient punishment, and often with reward for the hostage-takers. Our policy of searching is done. A new policy of swift and sure retaliation against the Nation of Terrorism will be in immediate effect after you in the Congress make such a formal declaration. Let that declaration be a warning, the only warning to be given, that the citizens of the United States are to be secure against violence on their person wherever they travel throughout the world."

CHAPTER THIRTY-SEVEN
THE GOVERNMENT
OF NO RETURN

The 20th Century will be known as the Century of America. If it wasn't for the United States, the Twentieth Century would be known as the Century of Nazism or the Century of Communism, which ever would have won the final battle, not that it would have made much difference between the two. If we choose not to be a partisan any more, the 21st Century has no chance of being a Century of America. It will, instead, be ripe for the re-birth of totalitarianisms once thought to be done, or new totalitarianisms that are as yet unknown. Maybe there will be another America established somewhere and it will become the world leader, but the candidates for that lust for world liberty are few, and the possibilities remote. Much more likely is the rise of the Islamic Fundamentalist Revolution, or the People's Republic of China, or a Soviet-Style State, and/or the most likeliest of all, the United Nations Organization. That would be a world-horror.

The Charter of the United Nations has been blatantly and regularly violated without any repercussions against those violating members. The frequency and absurdity of those violations has made the U.N. Charter a meaningless document, having been translated into 107 languages and read by none.

The organization started with 51 members and grew and grew in number and diminished and diminished in honor. In the early 1960s as new States attained independence and membership, they became quickly aware that if they voted against the interests of the United States we would shrug and smile and say we understood. If, in those days, nations voted against the interests of the Soviet Union, the Soviet

Union would not shrug or smile or say they understood. There would be repercussions taken against that State.

As membership continued to grow, a coalition formed between the Soviet Union and its satellites along with nations that comprised what was called "The Group of 77." Most members of the coalition were not enamored with the Soviet Union, but they feared the consequences of opposing that government's interests.

The pinnacle of diplomatic success for the Soviet Union came in 1970 when the United Nations Educational Scientific and Cultural Organization (UNESCO) sponsored a Symposium on Lenin in Tempere, Finland. Attending was the Secretary General of the United Nations, U Thant, who declared, "Lenin was a man with a mind of great clarity and incisiveness, and his ideas have had a profound influence on the course of contemporary history. His ideals of peace and peaceful coexistence among States have won wide-spread international acceptance and they are in line with the aims of the U.N. Charter."

What ever morality the U.N. Charter had on that date was, by his remarks, quickly abandoned to the slums along the East River.

It was in the middle of that decade that Daniel Moynihan entered and exited as the U.S. Representative to the United Nations. Upon his leaving he gave three definitions of that organization: a theater of the absurd, a decomposing corpse, and an insane asylum.

Then, giving his remarks support, he quoted a leading British journalist of the time who said that the U.N. was among "the most corrupt and corrupting creations in the whole history of human institutions."

Even the United Nations Children's Emergency Fund (UNICEF) which was financed in large part by U.S. purchasers of UNICEF's Christmas Cards, had sent millions of dollars in aid to North Vietnam during the last year of its war against South Vietnam. UNICEF's spokesman said, "UNICEF has no way to make sure the supplies got to the children. They were dropped off at the airports and docks and we assume they were used as we intended." But what UNICEF had dropped off at the airports and docks were not crayolas, dolls, and vitamins. They dropped off trucks, bulldozers, and heavy construction material.

At the end of that decade, no threat of expulsion was given to the Ayatollah Khomeni's government of Iran for its seizure of U.S. diplomats as hostages. The terrorism of Mu'ammar al-Qadhafi's Government of Libya was enough to expel that government but it was not even warned of expulsion. The genocide of Pol Pot's Government in Cambodia was enough to send that government home but it was not sent home. Any violation from a litany of violations was enough to expel the Soviet Union but it was not even a consideration.

Those who defended the U.N. and maintained that our membership and our host-function to that organization and our taxpayer's bills were worthwhile, generally stated that the U.N. provided a forum for the people of the world to sit together and talk.

It was never an organization for the people of the world to do anything. Instead, it was an organization of governments, most of them unelected by the people of their nations. It is true that it provided a forum — a forum for primitive dialogue advancing the corruption of human values. Three-fifths of its members believed in and supported what they called Wars of National Liberation.

"Peacekeeping" became a synonym for the support of wars waged to further Soviet expansion.

In the U.S. State Department's analysis of the U.N.'s session for the calendar year of 1981, 84.9% of the major matters that came before the General Assembly were decided in agreement with the Soviet Union. That was a year in which the Soviet Union was waging war in Afghanistan, the year in which martial law was imposed on Poland, a year that Vietnam, under the direction of the Soviet Union, was waging war in Cambodia, and a year in which some 12 other wars were being waged by Soviet proxies.

Former U.S. Ambassador to the United Nations, Jeane Kirkpatrick said, "The U.N. can't, or doesn't do much in the way of promoting international peace." In further relation to its peacekeeping activities she said, "Rather frequently, what goes on in the U.N. actually exasperates conflicts rather than tending to resolve them."

Those were the days when the U.N. debated the threat of peace posed, not by Castro's 40,000 troops on the African Continent, but by

U.S. forces in the U.S. Virgin Islands because 14 U.S. Coast Guardsmen were stationed there.

With the fall of the Soviet Empire and the dismemberment of the Soviet Union, there emerged some new hope for the United Nations Organization. Without the power and intimidation of that State, Third World Governments were no longer intimidated into a voting pattern. The Golden Days of the U.N. came when President Bush was able to put together a coalition of governments to support his efforts against Saddam Hussein of Iraq. (Although surely President Bush would have been able to accomplish the same goal without the U.N., by individual agreements with the cooperating nations.)

But then came Secretary General Boutros Boutros-Ghali, and failed actions in Bosnia and Somalia, and a Human Rights Conference that changed the meaning of human rights of the people into economic demands of dictatorships. The Conference mandated an "inalienable right" to economic development of poorer nations. As for personal liberties, the Human Rights Conference decided that such rights could not be itemized since "cultural differences" meant "different things" for different nations and "western definitions" could not apply.

The U.N. grabbed greater and larger responsibilities as the United States felt obliged to work through that organization rather than take action independently or in bi-lateral or multi-national agreements separate and apart from the U.N. The military expansion of the U.N. enlarged from its 1990 level of 11,550 troops under its command, to 80,000 troops two years later.

Secretary General Boutros Boutros-Ghali warned the United States that under existing Security Council resolutions only he had the power to launch air strikes against the Serbian war machine fighting Bosnians, and the United States would be in violation of the U.N.Charter if it acted on its own.

We didn't.

Should we abandon the role we had in the 20th Century and leave the destiny of the peoples of the world to others, so unproved, and so historically unworthy? Should we abandon our position to an organization composed of so many unrepentant kidnappers, thieves, and murderers?

A world government would establish a power furthest from the people, even further from the people than federal governments, and to finance it, new taxes would be imposed upon the people. But most harmful of all is that once that world government achieves political and military power over sovereign national forces, then short of a miracle, there could be no return back to individual sovereignty.

If the U.N. should sustain at all, it should be transformed into an organization with membership restricted to those governments chosen by the people of their respective countries. This Nations of Liberty Alliance would guard against expansion, aggression, and terrorism by non-democracies, with an attack on one free nation regarded as an attack on all, and an act of terrorism against a citizen of the signatories, regarded as an attack on the entire Nations of Liberty Alliance. Non-compliance would be tantamount to expulsion from that alliance.

To prevent even a misinterpretation of any international organization we join, or document we sign, an amendment to our Constitution should state, "No agreement between the United States of America and any other party, may supersede any provision of the Constitution of the United States of America."

When the U.N. was founded, its first Secretary General, Trigvie Lie, praised that organization as a fire-station ready with a hose on the world-stage.

As the horizon passes from the Century of America to the Century of the Yet-Unknown, that fire station is composed of many arsonists, and the United States more and more guarantees future flames by giving the United Nations Organization new responsibilities and powers and undeserved trust.

The 21st Century must be the Second Century of America so that it can be the First Century of World Liberty.

CHAPTER THIRTY-EIGHT

THE NEXT GENERATION
WILL NEVER KNOW

S ome are motivated by their long-ago cowardice, some are motivated by their long-ago advocacies, some are motivated by their long-ago false prophecies, and that's why they have revised the history of the war in Southeast Asia. It has by this time been established by too many historians, journalists, politicians, and other fools who seek to deceive their children and even deceive themselves, that the involvement of the United States in the Vietnam War was immoral, and it was their personal morality that made them reject the mission of our armed forces, and that the United States military lost that war.

And so a new generation has been born and grown into maturity and it is unlikely that they would come to any other conclusions than the ones they have been taught by the revisionists who have such a mammoth personal objective to keep the new generations blinded, as well as themselves.

"We should have lost. What we did was immoral and that's why I wouldn't be a part of it."

What is immoral about fighting to achieve liberty for strangers? That is the highest morality on earth.

No one should have a continuing problem with the youth of the 60s because they were young then and didn't know enough. But there is reason to have a great problem with so many of those of that generation when they became the adults of the 90s because they chose to avoid the truth. They have an excuse for their conduct of the 60s (youth) and no excuse for their conduct of the 90s, one among them being the President of the United States, Bill Clinton.

Has the new generation been told by books, by professors, by movies, why the war was lost? Or have they been told revised history by schools and by the printed and visual media?

The end of that war, devoid of revisionism, is an entirely different history than the one invented:

The U.S. bombing of all North Vietnam targets was suspended during Christmas, 1972, a bombing pause of 36 hours. The United States media calls that period of history, "The Christmas Bombing."

On January 27, 1973, the Paris Peace Accords regarding the war in Southeast Asia were signed. The war was to be done and the world was celebrating. Chapter Four, Article Nine of those accords stated, "The South Vietnamese people shall decide themselves the political future of South Vietnam through genuinely free and democratic general elections under international supervision."

Article Eleven stipulated the insurance of the "democratic liberties of the people; personal freedom, freedom of speech, freedom of the press, freedom of meeting, freedom of organization, freedom of political activities, freedom of belief, freedom of movement, freedom of residence, freedom of work."

Chapter Seven, Article Twenty stated, "The parties participating in the Paris Conference on Vietnam undertake to refrain from using the territory of Cambodia and Laos to encroach on the sovereignty and security of one another."

To attempt to guarantee those objectives, there was an agreement that the United States would re-supply South Vietnam, and the Soviet Union would re-supply North Vietnam, both on a one-to-one ratio for military loss. (One helicopter for a lost helicopter, one rifle for the loss of a rifle, etc.)

The authors of the Vietnam Peace Accords won the Nobel Peace Prize.

Our military left Southeast Asia in January of 1973.

The Soviet Union and North Vietnam immediately disregarded the entire text of the accords, and within a month the Soviet Union was re-supplying North Vietnam on a four-to-one ratio. We stuck to the agreement of a one-to-one ratio until the beginning of 1975 when the U.S. Congress voted to stop all military and economic aid to Vietnam, Laos, and Cambodia. It was not a vote to end our military involvement — that had already ended two-and-one-quarter years before the vote — the vote was against spending any more money for the people of South Vietnam, Laos, and Cambodia, voiding our Paris agreement. General Dung, who was to become the North Vietnam victor, wrote in his memoirs that as a result of our cut-off of aid that President Thieu, the President of South Vietnam, was "forced to fight a poor man's war."

As 1975 continued into the Spring, the Premier of Cambodia, Long Beret, said, "We have no more material means" to continue the struggle and "we feel completely abandoned."

Senator George McGovern said, "Cambodians would be better off if we stopped all aid to them and let them work things out in their own way."

Senator Majority Leader Mike Mansfield said, "The cut-off of aid is in the best interest of Cambodians."

Congressman (later to become Senator) Chris Dodd said, "The greatest gift our country can give to the Cambodian people is not guns but peace, and the best way to accomplish that goal is by ending military aid now."

We did, and on April 17, 1975, Cambodia fell to the Khmer Rouge and the genocide of one-fourth or more of Cambodians began.

On April the 30th of that year, South Vietnam fell and the phenomenon of over one million Boat People began to flee the conqueror.

By June, Laos became a North Vietnam-puppet.

The war was lost because the United States Congress abrogated our word given in Paris two-and-a-quarter years before the surrender of Southeast Asia. They bent to intense pressure from the young, from the press, from fools whose sense of morality did not include personal risk or, in the end, even the economic risk, for the liberty of others. After the invasion of Saigon and its surrender, Senator William Fulbright said, "I am no more depressed about South Vietnam's defeat than I would be about Arkansas losing a football game to Texas."

What he did not say was that Texas would not commit genocide against the citizens of Arkansas, and over a million citizens of Arkansas would not be imprisoned, and another million would not head for the high seas of escape.

But his words set the stage for the revisionists to come, and a generation has grown up unaware of the truth.

It was not an immoral war. It was an immoral surrender by those not in uniform, but by many of those who sat in the chambers of the United States Capitol Building.

CHAPTER THIRTY-NINE

535 COMMANDERS IN CHIEF

When the suicide mission of the truck driver came smashing into U.S. Marine Headquarters in Beirut with a cargo of explosives destined to kill 241 U.S. Marines, that yellow truck loaded with those explosives rammed through a barbed wire fence and went past two sentry posts. At both sentry posts, the Marines on duty were armed with unloaded weapons and the Marine Guards stated that the truck was going too fast for them to load the bullet clips into their automatic rifles and then fire at the truck.

They didn't have bullet-clips already fastened to their rifles because they were obeying orders.

When it was discovered by the Cable News Network that a U.S. soldier in El Salvador was carrying an automatic rifle while he was helping Salvadoran officers replace a bridge that had been destroyed by guerrillas, orders came from Washington for that soldier to be taken out of El Salvador, and he was reprimanded for having that rifle with him while he helped replace the bridge in dangerous territory.

When our ships at sea fired at Syrian-held positions that were blasting Beirut, our commanders were ordered to stop.

What caused these kind of life-risking orders?

The fear of the imposition of the War Powers Act.

If our military acts beyond self-defense, if there is some evidence that would suggest that U.S. forces are in an area of imminent hostility without a declaration of war, then the President of the United States is in jeopardy of being in violation of the War Powers Act passed by the Congress in 1973.

If the War Powers Act had already been enacted in the early

1960s rather than the early 1970s, the United States would not have been able to have responded as we did to the Berlin crisis of 1961, the Cuban missile crisis of 1962, the Congo rescue operation of 1964, the Jordanian crisis of 1970, and the Yom Kippur war of 1973.

And even with the law in place, there is the quiet knowledge that it went unobserved when President Ford ordered the Mayaguez rescue operation of 1975, and unobserved when President Carter attempted to rescue the hostages in Iran in 1980, and unobserved when President Reagan ordered the invasion of Grenada in 1983 and the forcing down of the Egyptian Airliner with Achile Lauro hijackers aboard in 1985 and the retaliation against Qadhafi's Libya of 1986, and President Bush's 1989 military action in Panama and the Persian Gulf War of 1991-1992, and the U.S. action in Somalia of 1992-94 under Presidents Bush and Clinton.

The War Powers Act was passed into law over the veto of President Nixon and it has been a weight on the shoulder of Presidents since that time, and worse than that, it has cost U.S. lives and has cost U.S. interests.

Its constitutionality has been so questionable that in the cases when Presidents obeyed its language, none of them wanted to set the precedent of having observed it, so they were careful not to say that they were complying with it, but only that they were acting under its terms.

One of its provisions establishes that the President has to consult with the Congress "before introducing United States armed forces into hostilities or into situations where imminent involvement in hostilities is clearly indicated by the circumstances, and after every such intro-duction shall consult regularly with the Congress until United States armed forces are no longer engaged in hostilities or have been removed from such situations." By law, that removes the possibility of surprising an enemy. Our planned actions will be published in the Washington Post by the time of the next edition since no one can consult with the Congress and be assured that the consultation will be kept secret. There is virtually no way to prevent someone on Capitol Hill from leaking sto-ries throughout Washington — and in seconds, throughout the world.

The War Powers Act states that, if in consultation with the Congress, within 48 hours, there is agreement to station the troops wherever they may be deemed, then the President has to withdraw the troops within 60 days unless the Congress extends the 60 day period. And it states that the President may extend the time an additional 30 days, but only if he certifies in writing that those thirty days are necessary to protect U.S. forces during their withdrawal.

The War Powers Act gives the power to the Congress to act as Commander in Chief — not only by action but by inaction. If the Congress does nothing, our troops have to leave an area of imminent hostility in 60 to 90 days. During that 60 to 90 day period, the Act states that if the Congress wants an immediate withdrawal of U.S. forces they need only pass a concurrent resolution to that effect which would not be subject to a Presidential veto. That means that the Congress would have the right to veto a Presidential action, clearly against the Constitutional roll given to the Congress. The President would not be able to veto their decision.

In a court case ten years after the passage of the War Powers Act, and separate and apart from a case involving it, the Supreme Court judged a "legislative veto" to be unconstitutional as a breach of the separation of powers. Therefore, that particular provision of the War Powers Act is clearly unconstitutional, while other provisions of the Act are hanging by untested threads.

The greatest danger of the War Powers Act is not only that it can prevent secret military missions of the United States, but that once the United States is engaged, one of the most important military secrets remaining becomes revealed: how long the United States is going to stand by a particular commitment. As soon as any adversary in a particular engagement knows how long the United States will stay, that adversary can schedule its war accordingly.

Such was the case with Hafiz al-Assad sitting in Syria and watching our troops in Lebanon. President Assad knew that if he would wait long enough he would be the dominant force in Lebanon. His coming victory was ordained because although the Congress had extended the deadline to 18 months under the War Powers Act, there was an announced deadline. And President Assad could wait for that deadline to come, and the Reagan Administration would be unable to fire on Assad's forces or his allies unless it was a direct act of self-protection. It was not President Assad that stopped the United States when the United States bombarded Syrian-held positions; it was the threat of Congress' abridgment of the 18 month timetable. The Administration backed-off.

Although the invocation of the War Powers Act is intended to put the President on notice, it gives the adversary an advantage too good to ignore. And if the War Powers Act is not invoked, that adversary knows that by killing Americans, some members of the Congress may rush to put the Act into effect. Outwaiting the United States can become a game anywhere in the world in which our forces are engaged.

Neither a President nor a Congress should ever announce a date of disengagement before that date arrives.

Our War Powers Act should be repealed, as it is little more and nothing less than an announcement to the world that short of a declaration of war (a declaration having been made only five times in our history, out of an estimated 209 military engagements), no matter what our President says at times of military conflict, he is not the Commander in Chief, and his word will be overridden by a published time-table that assures our departure from the scene.

THE BENEDICT ARNOLD AWARD

With a scowl, the television commentator looked in the eyes of the audience and said, "The government isn't telling you what our military is doing over there, and it's the people's right to know. Surely we all believe in that, don't we?"

No.

It would be different if there was some way to confine all information within our own borders, but there is no way to do that. With advanced communications, the information is out to every hostile power not within weeks or days or even hours or minutes, but seconds. The question is, "does an *enemy* have the right to know?"

"We had just come out of Desert Storm," Peter Jennings of ABC said, "in which to this country's disgrace, and to the government's disgrace, and I would also argue the public's disgrace, which did not get up and yell and cry about it, the media was totally locked out of a military operation. The access for the U.S. press to Desert Storm was so negligible as to be non-existent."

Good.

Not so incidentally, we liberated Kuwait and did it with amazingly few casualties.

Similarly, the British had excluded the press from the Falkland Islands War. And they won.

And there was the U.S. victory that brought the argument of press-access to the surface like a volcano. It was the invasion of Grenada, with the press-corps prohibited from accompanying the U.S. invasion-force until three days had passed.

Network executives and on-camera personalities testified against that prohibition to the House Judiciary Subcommittee on Civil Liberties. And from their testimony, if you knew nothing else, you would think that the network executives and on-camera personalities were pathetic public-servants who volunteered to champion the public's right to know.

No one said what should have been said. No one testified this way: "Look, I get paid for what I do. It's a terrific job, a marvelous job, and the more information I can get, the better I can do my job."

That would have been honest. Instead we were told that the media represented "the people" through "the First Amendment," and their mission was to be "the public's watchdog." But no one should be led to believe that those testifying would have been hitting the beaches of Grenada with crews and with cameras and with notepads and cassette-recorders in hand, for free. The media are not filled with public volunteers who, in the spirit of philanthropy, sacrifice away the benefits of another career for one that is dreaded but needed.

When media contract negotiations are in session, the words "the First Amendment" and "the people's right to know" and "the public's watchdog" do not get mentioned. Those phrases would be greeted with much laughter, and contract negotiation meetings would have to settle down in the restoration of composure.

What does get mentioned in those offices and conference-rooms is how much their salary will be, how long it will be paid, how many raises will be given between the signing of the contract and its expiration date, and what perquisites go with the salary. Usually an agent or a manager enters the picture and gets a cut. Nothing wrong in all that. But there is no reference to the Constitution. Really. The participants are not a rag-tag band of fife, flute, and drum-players saying "Let me serve the public!"

It is totally understandable why the media would want to be let in on information that involves national security. They want to reveal it.

"But we accompanied the invasion force on Normandy," they told the public. "Why not any current conflict?"

Because in 1944 no member of the U.S. press corps wanted Hitler to be victorious.

From our involvement in the Southeast Asian War forward, the political beliefs and the code of ethics of many in the U.S. press corps changed dramatically from years past.

Just before the surrender of Cambodia and Vietnam, Sidney Schanberg, a correspondent in Cambodia for the *New York Times* wrote, "Sometimes certain people are executed by the victors but it would be tendentious to forecast such abnormal behavior as a national policy under a communist government once the war is over. I have seen the Khmer Rouge and they are not killing anyone...It is difficult to imagine how Cambodian lives could be anything but better with Americans gone." He won the Pulitzer Prize for his reporting from Cambodia, and he reached hero-status in the film, "The Killing Fields."

Just before the Khmer Rouge's blood bath and genocide of Cambodia began, columnist Anthony Lewis of the *New York Times* wrote, in relation to those who warned of a blood-bath: "Some will find the whole blood bath debate unreal. What future possibility could be more terrible than the reality of what's happening in Cambodia now?"

A *New York Times* editorial said, "Further (U.S.) aid (to Cambodia) would only extend Cambodia's misery."

Syndicated columnist Joe Kraft wrote in *The Washington Post*, "Does it really matter whether or not Cambodia goes communist?...The price is small."

Syndicated columnist Tom Wicker wrote that there "was not much moral choice" between the then current government of Cambodia and the Khmer Rouge.

When Vietnam surrendered, Peter Kalisher of CBS told the United States audience, "For better or worse, the war is over, and how could it be for worse?"

Beth Nissen, *Newsweek's* correspondent in El Salvador, in a conversation with me at the U.S. Ambassador's residence in San Salvador admitted her support for the Marxist-led guerrillas in that country.

Karen DeYoung, who covered the Sandinista Revolution in Nicaragua lectured that, "Most journalists now, most Western journalists at least, are very eager to seek out guerrilla groups, leftist groups, because you assume they must be the good guys."

An editorial in the *Los Angeles Times* stated, "Reagan must acknowledge that a military victory by U.S.-backed forces in El Salvador is not possible, and probably not even desirable."

Further, many in the media revealed information that jeopardized national security, and broke embargoes, and reporters and other journalists decided for themselves what should and should not be kept secret. Some told stories that endangered U.S. missions and our armed forces. The line between a scoop and treason became blurred.

Howard Simons, the Managing Editor of *The Washington Post* said about the Director of the Central Intelligence Agency, "It's his job to keep secrets. That's his job. My job is to find them."

Dan Rather of CBS said, "My job is to publish and be damned."

Lyle Denniston, a reporter for the *Baltimore Sun* said, "It isn't a question of justification in terms of law. It's a question of justifying it in terms of the commercial sale of information to interested customers. That's my only business. That's the only thing I do in life is to sell information, hopefully for a profit."

It was not only the government versus the press. There was a third side which went undiscussed; the side of those in the armed forces whose mission and lives were at stake. Did they want the press corps to be in charge of what the world would know in an instant; did they want the press corps to decide what could or could not place them in jeopardy, or did they want their own commanders to make those decisions?

The most arrogant statement of all was made by Walter Cronkite, former CBS News anchor and managing editor, who said sadly (some months after the invasion of Grenada, with the press uninvited,) that "now we will never know what happened in those first three days."

Total arrogance. People were there. Grenadians. Grenadians knew how to talk. Did the former network anchor and managing editor feel that only someone with a press card of a news service is capable of witnessing events and talking about them?

Fred Friendly, who was once President of CBS News was asked

"Is there a liberal bias to TV News?" He answered, "No. Only an affinity for righting the things that are wrong with society."

Oh.

Is it possible; is it at all possible that what some decision-maker in the media may believe to be the wrongs of society, are not what others believe to be the wrongs of society? If they want to run for office, itemizing what they believe to be the wrongs of society, that avenue is open to them as it is to everyone else. But some in the media seem to believe that the career-aristocracy to which they belong has wisdom and judgment that should take precedence over running for office. Further, they unjustifiably assume that the First Amendment was meant for their administration rather than the public's protection, and that the First Amendment gives rights to those who choose journalism as a career, over all others.

It was in February of 1977 that President Carter called Ben Bradlee, editor of *The Washington Post*, and reporter Bob Woodward, to the Oval Office of the White House. It was there that he tried to dissuade them from publishing stories of Central Intelligence Agency payments to foreign leaders. He explained that the disclosure of the payments to King Hussein of Jordan just before the Secretary of State was to meet with the King, would be highly damaging.

They printed it anyway.

Shortly after the revelations were printed in *The Washington Post*, President Carter stated, "It can be extremely damaging to our relationship with other nations, to the potential security of our country even in peacetime, for these kinds of operations which are legitimate and proper, to be revealed." Obviously, he was right. *The International Herald-Tribune* reported that "a canvas of five PLO leaders in Beirut indicated that it is the consensus of the Palestine movement's umbrella organization that they can use the revelations to resist pressure to go to the peace table as subjects of Jordan," and an Arab commentator stated, "All Arab leaders are now suspect, especially by their armies, if they call for peace."

From that published revelation forward through the Persian Gulf War 15 years later, King Hussein was no longer a friendly government to the west. He continually tried to prove to other Arab Chiefs of State and to his own Kingdom that he was no pawn of the United States. He proved it.

Across the sands of the Mideast was Mu'ammar al-Qadhafi. On November 2, 1985 *The Washington Post* ran a story that claimed President Reagan had approved a plan of the Central Intelligence Agency to bring about conditions for the fall of Qadhafi's Government of Libya. The fall was to come about by either promoting insurrection in his military or by giving a neighboring nation justification for action against his government.

The U.S. plan was scrubbed.

It had to be scrubbed because Qadhafi was informed — by the revelation in *The Washington Post*. Had he not been informed and had the insurrection been implemented successfully, Natasha Simpson, the eleven-year old girl who was killed in the Rome airport from Qadhafi's terrorist attack, might still be alive, as well as four other Americans and fourteen other foreign nationals murdered in that raid. At this time there is no way to know what would have been. What we do know is that *The Washington Post* was given the information and *The Washington Post* chose to publish that information.

What can be done about all this?

The oversight of our intelligence activities needs to be re-organized to reduce the amount of people who go running to the media with stories that jeopardize national security. Our intelligence oversight may never be leak-proof, but such leaks can be minimized by vastly reducing the hundreds of people on Capitol Hill who are told the most sensitive intelligence information. The Senate and House Select Committees on Intelligence now established, include too many members and far too many staff-people. Our oversight of intelligence should be conducted by the National Security Council and the Majority and Minority Leaders from both Houses of the Congress rather than entire committees within both Houses. The Majority and Minority Leaders would be entitled to have an intelligence staff but the staff for sensitive information should consist of no more than three people for each member. That would still insure congressional oversight, but when a secret would be publicly printed, the list of suspects would be greatly reduced from its present list of hundreds.

But what about the publisher or broadcaster? What should we do to prevent *The Washington Post* or CBS or *The Village Voice* from printing or broadcasting a story that jeopardizes an American mission?

In terms of legislation — nothing. Nothing should be done because we must retain freedom of the press. But there is something that someone in government can do:

Some brave member of the Congress should take a cue from Former Senator William Proxmire (D-WI) who for years gave what he called his Golden Fleece Awards for abuses of government spending. Those "awards" publicly given, were more effective in the reduction of wasteful government-spending than any other single effort to put a halt to waste. The attention they received crossed party lines. Some member of the Congress ought to adopt the same idea in regard to abuses of the media, and publicly give Golden Breach Awards to the information outlet that gives the most destructive inaccuracy, the most misleading bias, the greatest breach of responsibility, and in the case of a breach of national security, the information outlet should be named as the recipient of The Benedict Arnold Award — publicly.

It is a constitutional right for the media to inform the public about the government. But that doesn't take away the right of someone in the government to inform the public about the media.

The idea is not to abuse the First Amendment, but to use it.

The problem with the media is that so many prominently engaged in that profession seem to believe that the nation's founders gathered in Philadelphia to write the First Amendment alone, and then hurriedly dashed off a Preamble, seven articles, and nine other amendments as some bothersome after-thoughts.

CHAPTER FORTY-ONE

DISAPPEARING INK

Never believe that a signature of the untrustworthy is valuable. A signature is only as good as the one who holds the pen.

In the future when the President of the United States sits down at a table with the Chief of State of a tyranny with pens in wait, the President of the United States should remember the life of the Union of Soviet Socialist Republics and the disease that it had throughout its lifetime, a disease called "Deceititis" that is common to all tyrannies.

When the Soviet Union was born it was apparent that it had the disease, but people all over the world, including many in the United States, felt it would be better to pretend there was no sickness; it was rude to bring up a disability, and eyes were closed at every new seizure of the disease no matter its severity.

When the Soviet Union was still an infant, its government signed a treaty recognizing the independence of the Ukrainian Republic, but when the Soviet Union was one-year old it invaded and seized the Ukraine.

When the Soviet Union was 4 years old its government broke its newly-signed treaty recognizing the Republic of Georgia, and conquered it.

When the Soviet Union was 17 years old its government signed the covenant of the League of Nations, and when it was 22 years old the Soviet Union was expelled from the League of Nations for not abiding by its signature.

When the Soviet Union was 23 years old its government broke three treaties that had recognized the independence of Latvia, Lithuania, and Estonia. It invaded and seized those three nations.

When the Soviet Union was 28 years old its government signed the Yalta Agreement promising free elections within the countries of Eastern Europe, but the Soviet Union would not allow the elections to take place.

When the Soviet Union was 38 years old its government signed an agreement in Geneva that "the re-unification of Germany by means of free elections shall be carried out." But when the Soviet Union was 44 years old the Berlin Wall was built.

When the Soviet Union was 51 years old its government signed the Declaration of Bratislava with Czechoslovakia, guaranteeing the independence of Czechoslovakia. Less than three weeks after the signing, the Soviet Union invaded Czechoslovakia.

When the Soviet Union was 55 years old its government signed the Strategic Arms Limitation Treaty and Anti-Ballistic Missile Agreement. There were 29 blatant violations that followed the signing that turned the Strategic Arms Limitation Treaty and Anti-Ballistic Missile Agreement into a one-way build-up for the Soviet Union.

When the Soviet Union was 56 years old its government violated the Paris Peace Accords regarding a just conclusion to the war in Southeast Asia.

When the Soviet Union was 58 years old its government signed the Helsinki Accords guaranteeing observances of human rights, with monitors to assure observance. But within months after the signing, no human rights monitors were left in the Soviet Union, all having been imprisoned or exiled or put into insane asylums.

The Helsinki Accords also guaranteed respect for all existing international borders and to refrain from the use or threat of force against any independent nation. But when the Soviet Union was 62 years old its government invaded Afghanistan.

When the Soviet Union was 74 years old it died.

Its signature could no longer be sought, and all the documents, all the agreements, all the accords of 74 years became the antiques of deceit, left for future generations by a dead tyranny. The antiques can only have future value if there is recognition that a signature of a hostile force should never again be celebrated.

PART SIX

THE DESTINATION

CHAPTER FORTY-TWO
TRUMPETS

Those whose thirst can only be quenched by the taste of personal security provided for them should leave the United States and go to a more secure place. Chains are given with citizenship under many governments of the world. In this country they should be unavailable, except to secure the blessings of liberty.

It is those who pursue chains within this nation who are twisting the grandest dream of the world — the United States of America — into the common stream.

Why not one nation that pursues the fulfillment of the dreams of liberty?

Liberty does not give a government guarantee of personal securities, nor should they be guaranteed. Liberty does not provide those things that can be held in hand. For those who find that to be frightening: leave if you're here, and stay in a foreign land if you're distant. The world deserves at least one nation that pursues such a horizon and that has the good sense to preserve itself, and the moral pursuit of helping to bring liberty to others. The United States of America has had that role, and those in the world who crave freedom, need to be assured that they can have that destiny.

As citizens of this nation, we have inherited a magnificent estate from those who have built the American road upon which we travel each day. Previous generations of Americans, through their strength and courage, made us the beneficiaries of gifts never before passed from one generation to the next. We need to maintain those gifts and add to them for the next generations. We can be the continuing carpenters of our national road so strongly constructed and maintained and re-enforced that those future Americans who travel that road and inherit our estate will be challenged by none and will be joined by all.

And then, with the permanence of the United States exhibited, the rest of the world's peoples will have incentive to shed all the chains on so many foreign roads, and they will lift the thousands of trumpets that dominate the earth's landscape; trumpets capable of playing melodies as yet unheard.

PROCEDURES AND LAWS TO ENACT/REPEAL, AND NEW CONSTITUTIONAL AMENDMENTS

1	Balanced Budget Flat Rate Tax	(Chapter 08)
2	Sell Government Owned Land	(Chapter 09)
3	Privatize Social Security	(Chapter 10)
4	Bureaucracy/Appointees Ratio Changed	(Chapter 11)
5	Cabinet Reorganization	(Chapter 12)
6	National Security Reorganization	(Chapter 12)
7	Vice President as White House Chief of Staff	(Chapter 12)
8	Abridge Congressional Perquisites and Privileges	(Chapter 13)
9	Check-Off on Income Tax Form Abolished	(Chapter 13)
10	Deadline of 9-25 on Congress' Budget Submission	(Chapter 13)
11	Line Item Veto When President Submits a Balanced Budget	(Chapter 13)
12	Lower Congressional Salaries	(Chapter 13)
13	Omnibus Bills Abolished	(Chapter 13)
14	Welfare to Local Control	(Chapter 16)
15	Border Patrol Appropriations Increase	(Chapter 17)
16	Repeal Bilingual Laws	(Chapter 17)
17	Revisions of Refugee Act of 1980	(Chapter 17)
18	Sunset Provisions	(Chapter 18)
19	Abolish Affirmative Action Programs	(Chapter 19)
20	FEMA Reduction of Authority	(Chapter 20)
21	Abolish Department of Education	(Chapter 21)
22	School Vouchers	(Chapter 21)
23	Abortion Policy	(Chapter 22)
24	Right to Work - Codify Beck Decision	(Chapter 24)
25	Abolish National Endowment for the Arts	(Chapter 26)
26	Change "Intent" to "Indifference" to Murder	(Chapter 28)
27	Defense Separate from Rest of Budget	(Chapter 30)
28	Terrorism Policy	(Chapter 36)
29	UN Changed to a Nations of Liberty Alliance	(Chapter 37)
30	Repeal War Powers Act	(Chapter 39)
31	Intelligence Oversight Revamp	(Chapter 40)
32	The Benedict Arnold Award = Media	(Chapter 40)
33	Amendment = Congress Obey its Regulations	(Chapter 13)
34	Amendment = Foreign Birth Citizens	(Chapter 17)
35	Amendment = School Prayer & Religious Observances	(Chapter 27)
36	Amendment = Logan Act re Treason	(Chapter 34)
37	Amendment = Nothing Supersedes Constitution	(Chapter 37)

INDEX